Julius Caesar

ARDEN EARLY MODERN DRAMA GUIDES

Series Editors:
Andrew Hiscock
University of Wales, Bangor, UK and Lisa Hopkins,
Sheffield Hallam University, UK

Arden Early Modern Drama Guides offer practical and accessible introductions to the critical and performative contexts of key Elizabethan and Jacobean plays. Each guide introduces the text's critical and performance history, but also provides students with an invaluable insight into the landscape of current scholarly research, through a keynote essay on the state of the art and newly commissioned essays of fresh research from different critical perspectives.

A Midsummer Night's Dream edited by Regina Buccola

Doctor Faustus edited by Sarah Munson Deats

King Lear edited by Andrew Hiscock and Lisa Hopkins

1 Henry IV edited by Stephen Longstaffe

'Tis Pity She's a Whore edited by Lisa Hopkins

Women Beware Women edited by Andrew Hiscock

Volpone edited by Matthew Steggle

The Duchess of Malfi edited by Christina Luckyj

The Alchemist edited by Erin Julian and Helen Ostovich

The Jew of Malta edited by Robert A Logan

Macbeth edited by John Drakakis and Dale Townshend

Romeo and Juliet: A Critical Reader edited
by Julia Reinhard Lupton

Richard III edited by Annaliese Connolly

Twelfth Night edited by Alison Findlay and
Liz Oakley-Brown

The Tempest edited by Alden T. Vaughan and
Virginia Mason Vaughan

Further titles in preparation

Julius Caesar

A Critical Reader

Andrew James Hartley

Bloomsbury Arden Shakespeare
An imprint of Bloomsbury Publishing Plc

BLOOMSBURY
LONDON • OXFORD • NEW YORK • NEW DELHI • SYDNEY

Bloomsbury Arden Shakespeare
An imprint of Bloomsbury Publishing Plc

Imprint previously known as Arden Shakespeare

50 Bedford Square	1385 Broadway
London	New York
WC1B 3DP	NY 10018
UK	USA

www.bloomsbury.com

BLOOMSBURY, THE ARDEN SHAKESPEARE and the Diana logo are trademarks of Bloomsbury Publishing Plc

First published 2016

Editorial matter and selection © Andrew James Hartley, 2016

Andrew James Hartley has asserted his right under the Copyright, Designs and Patents Act, 1988, to be identified as author of this work.

All rights reserved. No part of this publication may be reproduced or transmitted in any form or by any means, electronic or mechanical, including photocopying, recording, or any information storage or retrieval system, without prior permission in writing from the publishers.

No responsibility for loss caused to any individual or organization acting on or refraining from action as a result of the material in this publication can be accepted by Bloomsbury or the author.

British Library Cataloguing in Publication Data
A catalogue record for this book is available from the British Library.

ISBN: HB: 978-1-4742-2037-8
       PB: 978-1-4742-2038-5
       ePDF: 978-1-4742-2040-8
       ePub: 978-1-4742-2039-2

Library of Congress Cataloging-in-Publication Data
A catalog record for this book is available from the Library of Congress.

Series: Arden Early Modern Drama Guides

Cover image taken from the 1615 title page of *The Spanish Tragedy*, by Thomas Kyd

Typeset by Fakenham Prepress Solutions, Fakenham, Norfolk NR21 8NN
Printed and bound in India

CONTENTS

Series Introduction vii
Notes on Contributors viii
Timeline xi

Introduction   *Andrew James Hartley* 1

1 The Critical Backstory   *Daniel Cadman* 17

2 Performance History   *Andrew James Hartley* 49

3 The State of the Art   *Domenico Lovascio* 81

4 New Directions: *Julius Caesar*, Ovidian Transformation and the Martyred Body on the Early Modern Stage   *Lisa S. Starks-Estes* 103

5 New Directions: Striking Our Debt to Moral Tragedy: Retributive Economics in *Julius Caesar*   *Todd Landon Barnes* 125

6 New Directions: What Should Be in that Caesar: The Question of Julius Caesar's Greatness   *John E. Curran, Jr.* 153

7 New Directions: The Death of the Roman Republic: Julius Caesar and Cicero   *Warren Chernaik*   175

8 Resources for Teaching and Studying *Julius Caesar*   *Jeremy Lopez*   201

Notes 227
Bibliography 261
Index 279

SERIES INTRODUCTION

The drama of Shakespeare and his contemporaries has remained at the very heart of English curricula internationally and the pedagogic needs surrounding this body of literature have grown increasingly complex as more sophisticated resources become available to scholars, tutors and students. This series aims to offer a clear picture of the critical and performative contexts of a range of chosen texts. In addition, each volume furnishes readers with invaluable insights into the landscape of current scholarly research as well as including new pieces of research by leading critics.

This series is designed to respond to the clearly identified needs of scholars, tutors and students for volumes which will bridge the gap between accounts of previous critical developments and performance history and an acquaintance with new research initiatives related to the chosen plays. Thus, our ambition is to offer innovative and challenging guides that will provide practical, accessible and thought-provoking analyses of early modern drama. Each volume is organized according to a progressive reading strategy involving introductory discussion, critical review and cutting-edge scholarly debate. It has been an enormous pleasure to work with so many dedicated scholars of early modern drama and we are sure that this series will encourage you to read 400-year-old play texts with fresh eyes.

Andrew Hiscock and Lisa Hopkins

NOTES ON CONTRIBUTORS

Todd Landon Barnes is an Associate Professor of Literature at Ramapo College of New Jersey, USA. His writing appears in *Shakespeare Bulletin*, *Weyward Macbeth*, *Hamlet Handbook* and *Shakespearean Echoes*. He served as dramaturg for the African-American Shakespeare Company in San Francisco, where he also worked in educational outreach.

Daniel Cadman is an Associate Lecturer at Sheffield Hallam University, UK, and the author of *Sovereigns and Subjects in Early Modern Neo-Senecan Drama: Republicanism, Stoicism and Authority* (2015). He has published articles on William Shakespeare, Samuel Daniel and Fulke Greville, and is the managing editor of the online journal, *Early Modern Literary Studies*. He also writes the section on Shakespeare's Problem Plays for *The Year's Work in English Studies* and has contributed a number of entries for the *Lost Plays Database*.

Warren Chernaik is Emeritus Professor of English, University of London, and Visiting Professor at King's College London. He is the author of *The Myth of Rome in Shakespeare and his Contemporaries* (2011), *The Cambridge Introduction to Shakespeare's History Plays* (2007), a study of *The Merchant of Venice* (2005), *Sexual Freedom in Restoration Literature* (1995), *The Poet's Time: Politics and Religion in the Work of Andrew Marvell* (1983) and essays on such seventeenth-century authors as Marvell, Milton, Jonson, Herbert, Rochester and Behn, as well as co-editing books on topics as diverse as detective fiction, changes in copyright law and Andrew Marvell. He was the founding Director of the Institute of English Studies, University of London, and is now a Senior Research Fellow of IES.

John E. Curran, Jr. is Professor of English at Marquette University, USA, and editor of *Renascence: Essays on Values in Literature*. His most recent book is *Character and the Individual Personality in English Renaissance Drama: Tragedy, History, Tragicomedy* (University of Delaware Press/ Rowman & Littlefield, 2014).

Andrew James Hartley is Robinson Professor of Shakespeare studies, UNC Charlotte, USA, and is the author of *The Shakespearean Dramaturg* (2006), *Julius Caesar* (in Manchester University Press's Shakespeare in Performance series, 2014), *Shakespeare and Political Theatre* (2013), and the editor of *Shakespeare on the University Stage* (2015) as well as numerous journal articles and book chapters. From 2003 to 2013 he was the general editor of *Shakespeare Bulletin* (Johns Hopkins University Press) and is a popular novelist.

Jeremy Lopez is Associate Professor of English at the University of Toronto, Canada. He is the author of *Constructing the Canon of Early Modern Drama* (2014), as well as numerous other books and articles on the drama of Shakespeare and his contemporaries. He is currently preparing a revised second edition of the New Cambridge Shakespeare *Julius Caesar*.

Domenico Lovascio holds a PhD in Comparative Literature from the University of Genoa, Italy. He received the Dissertation Prize 2014 awarded by the Italian Association of English Studies to the best PhD thesis in the field in Italy in 2012–13. He has published a monograph on the reception of the figure of Julius Caesar in early modern English drama (2015) and the first English–Italian edition of Ben Jonson's *Catiline* (2011), as well as articles in *The Ben Jonson Journal*, *Medieval and Renaissance Drama in England*, *Early Modern Literary*

Studies and *Notes and Queries*. He is also a contributor to the *Lost Plays Database* and the projected edition of *The Collected Works of Thomas Kyd* (gen. ed. Sir Brian Vickers).

Lisa S. Starks-Estes is Associate Professor of English at University of South Florida St. Petersburg, USA, where she chairs the Department of Verbal and Visual Arts and directs the MLA in Liberal Studies programme. She has published articles, edited special issues of journals and co-edited book collections on sexuality and violence in Renaissance drama, Shakespeare on screen and other topics, including chapters in *Staging the Blazon in Early Modern English Theater* (2013) and *Violent Masculinities: Male Aggression in Early Modern Texts and Culture* (2013). Most recently, she has published a scholarly monograph entitled *Violence, Trauma, and* Virtus *in Shakespeare's Roman Poems and Plays: Transforming Ovid* (2014).

TIMELINE

13 July 100 BCE: Birth of Gaius Julius Caesar.

January 49 BCE: Caesar crosses the Rubicon, thereby instigating civil war against his former ally, Pompey.

48 BCE: Caesar defeats Pompey at the battle of Pharsalus and Pompey is killed.

15th March 44 BCE: A group of aristocratic Senators led by Marcus Brutus and Caius Cassius assassinate Caesar in the Roman Capitol.

7 December 43 BCE: On Mark Antony's orders, Cicero is executed.

October 42 BCE: Mark Antony and Octavius Caesar defeated Brutus and Cassius at the battle of Philippi.

1558: Queen Elizabeth I becomes Queen.

1564: William Shakespeare born in Stratford-upon-Avon.

1582: Shakespeare marries Anne Hathaway.

1583: Shakespeare's daughter, Susanna, born.

1585: Shakespeare's twins, Hamnet/Hamlet and Judith, born.

1594–5: The anonymous plays *The First and Second Parts* of *Caesar and Pompey*, are staged by the London theatre company, The Admiral's Men.

1596: Death of Shakespeare's son Hamnet/Hamlet.

Late 1598–9: Shakespeare writes *Julius Caesar*.

1599: Globe theatre built in Southwark. *Julius Caesar* may have been the first play staged there.

September 1599: Thomas Platter, a Swiss visitor, attends a production of Shakespeare's *Julius Caesar* at the Globe.

1601: Death of Shakespeare's father, John. Shakespeare probably writes *Hamlet*.

1605–6: Shakespeare writes *Macbeth*.

1613: Globe theatre destroyed by fire. It is rebuilt in 1614.

1616: Death of Shakespeare.

1623: Publication of the first Folio (F).

1700–50: 150 performances of Shakespeare's *Julius Caesar* staged in London. The performance text is edited and amended by Dryden and Davenant.

1812: *Julius Caesar* staged at Covent Garden in the 'Grand Style' by John Philip Kemble and Mrs Siddons. The monumental production is characterized by stately visual spectacle and a slow, deliberate style of delivery. There are thirteen complete set changes and over 100 extras.

1864: Edwin, Junius and John Wilkes Booth perform the lead roles in *Julius Caesar* at the Winter Garden in New York.

John Wilkes Booth assassinates President Abraham Lincoln the following year.

1881: A German production of *Julius Caesar* is brought to London's Drury Lane theatre by the Duke of Saxe-Meiningen. The crowd scenes steal the show and indicate a shift in emphasis from Brutus to Antony as the star.

1937: Orson Welles directs *Julius Caesar, Death of a Dictator* at the Mercury theatre, New York, in modern dress with Fascist trappings, and reintroduces the death of Cinna the Poet.

1944: Claus Von Stauffenberg, having just failed in his attempt to assassinate Adolf Hitler, is arrested with an annotated copy of *Julius Caesar*.

1949: David Bradley, a film student at Northwestern University, Illinois, makes a 16mm film of *Julius Caesar* with his boyhood friend Charlton Heston as Mark Antony.

1953: The release of the MGM film of *Julius Caesar*, directed by Joe Mankiewicz and starring James Mason (Brutus), John Gielgud (Cassius) and Marlon Brando (Mark Antony). The black and white film goes on to win an Oscar and a number of BAFTAs.

1970: Stuart Burge directs a colour film of *Julius Caesar* starring Charlton Heston as Antony, Jason Robards as Brutus, John Gielgud as Caesar, Richard Johnson as Cassius, Diana Rigg as Portia and Christopher Lee as Artemidorus. The film is critically and commercially unsuccessful.

1972: Trevor Nunn directs a spectacular modernist *Julius Caesar* for the Royal Shakespeare Company.

1979: Herbert Wise directs *Julius Caesar* for the BBC's Television Shakespeare project.

1993: David Thacker directs *Julius Caesar* at Stratford's most intimate theatre, The Other Place.

1999: *Julius Caesar* is staged for the first time at the reconstructed Globe theatre in London, in Elizabethan dress and with an all-male cast, starring a black Brutus (Danny Sapani).

2001: Edward Hall directs the play for the Royal Shakespeare Company with Greg Hicks as Brutus.

2001: Yael Farber directs *SeZaR* for the Grahamstown National Festival of the Arts South Africa, and a limited UK tour.

2012: Greg Doran directs the play for the Royal Shakespeare Company with an all black, British cast.

2012: *Caesar Must Die* [*Cesare Deve Morire*] movie, set in an Italian prison, made by Paolo and Vittorio Taviani.

Introduction

Andrew James Hartley

Before 1599, the year he probably wrote *Julius Caesar*, Shakespeare had largely written English history plays and comedies. His forays into tragedy had been experimental, a stylized and bloody revenge tragedy in the tradition of Thomas Kyd, *Titus Andronicus*, and a play with a comic structure that focused on adolescent lovers, *Romeo and Juliet*. *Julius Caesar* marks a turn towards grander tragic scope of massive implications, laying the groundwork for the first decade of the seventeenth century in which he would produce *Hamlet*, *Macbeth*, *Othello* and *King Lear*, as well as another Roman tragedy, *Coriolanus*, and a kind of sequel to *Caesar* which functions as a stand-alone play, *Antony and Cleopatra*. To understand why Shakespeare might have considered Julius Caesar as a suitable figure for his first major tragedy, it helps to recognize the scale of the shadow cast by Gaius Julius Caesar across history. He was one of the most important figures in the ancient world and continued to be a central cultural icon well into Shakespeare's days and beyond, famous as a politician, a general and a writer whose work was actively studied in schools well into the twentieth century. In short, his life, achievements and death were the stuff of legend long before Shakespeare wrote the play named after him.

Caesar was born in 100 BC and died on 15 March 44 BC. During his life he rose from the son of an old, but not especially powerful family (the Julii), to be the closest thing possible to a supreme leader of what was then the republic of

Rome, building political and military alliances, fighting with distinction on the battlefield and – as was not uncommon in the period – performing acts of expedient brutality to serve his purposes or make a point about who he believed himself to be. At various times he was both Rome's chief agent of expansion -- leading invasions into various territories adjoining Roman holdings in Spain, Gaul and elsewhere – and its scourge, famously crossing the Rubicon with an army and marching on Rome in 49 BC after the Roman Senate, led by Pompey, had ordered him to disband his forces. Though he had been an ally of Pompey (forming, with him and the wealthy politician, Crassus, what is referred to as the First Triumvirate), Caesar defeated Pompey's forces, and though he was said to have wept over the decapitated remains of his former friend, he entered Rome in triumph and, driven by popular support, was made Dictator in Perpetuity.

Shakespeare's play (written in late 1598 or early 1599 but not printed until the 1623 Folio) dramatizes only the end of this story, constricting time in the process so that it feels like his defeat of Pompey happened immediately before his own assassination, though in fact four years passed in between the two events.[1] Caesar had many political achievements in this time, but his most lasting legacy was his reform of the calendar along Egyptian lines, adding months (including one named after himself – July) and extending the year to 365.25 days, a reform which was only slightly revised in the Gregorian calendar of 1582.[2] The Senate, which was largely composed of old aristocratic families who resented Caesar's populist threat to their own power as well as having doubts about the increasing monopoly on authority which Caesar controlled, honoured him for his expansion of Roman territory elsewhere, but were horrified by his part in the civil war against Pompey. They conspired to kill him, being careful to keep Mark Antony (Caesar's Master of Horse and the high priest of the new cult of which Caesar was the so-called divine head) away from the site of the assassination. Caesar's death effectively ended the Roman Republic, plunging the state into further civil war which was resolved when Caesar's grandnephew Augustus seized power and, after defeating Mark Antony (as depicted by Shakespeare in *Antony and Cleopatra*), became Rome's first Emperor.

It is difficult to overestimate the importance of the historical person of Julius Caesar in Elizabethan English culture. Latin was still the language of statecraft and education, and anyone with any schooling at all – including the son of a Stratford glove-maker – would have been exposed not only to writings about Caesar, but to writing by Caesar himself, whose *Gallic Wars* were considered models of Latin prose style. Moreover, Caesar's place in the history of Rome itself was enormous, a massive, mythic presence on which the fate of an Empire turned, a matter – to the Elizabethans – of far more consequence than mere history could suggest. Caesar marked a moment of historical greatness which was, in many ways, more familiar to the Elizabethans than was their own history of the same period. Latin texts provided a better and more continuous process by which Roman history was passed on and made culturally central to all of Western Europe. Early British history, by contrast, as presented by chroniclers such as Holinshed in 1577, remained shrouded in mystery and legend and was quite different from the detailed documentation of Rome. Rome left its stamp on England's material landscape too. London itself (including – at least in popular conception – the origins of The Tower) exhibited Roman remains. In 1579 Thomas North published an English translation of Plutarch's *Lives of the Noble Greeks and Romans*, a book whose success led to two further expanded editions, one of which came out only four years before Shakespeare wrote his play and was its primary historical source. Ancient Rome in general and Caesar in particular was a national preoccupation for the Elizabethans, evidenced in all aspects of culture, demonstrating – even in the corrupted forms in which it was invoked by people with no education at all – that Caesar was assumed to have far-reaching cultural significance and weight. And while Caesar's Rome was, perhaps, more knowable to Elizabethans than was ancient Britain (or even the early medieval Britain of the post Roman occupation), Julius Caesar also represented one of the final moments in which those Elizabethans could think of history outside the valences of Christianity, whose origin figure, Jesus, was born under the reign of Augustus, and who would overwrite all subsequent periods.

The rise of Christianity and its subsequent division did not so much cancel the importance of the ancient period as it complicated it, opening it up to new symbolic and nationalistic use. Since Henry VIII's separation from Roman Catholicism – briefly revoked under his eldest daughter Mary's rule, but now firmly re-established under his second daughter Elizabeth – sixteenth-century England had begun to see itself as a new emerging model of all that had once been great about ancient Rome: its discipline, its power, its cultural sophistication and its global reach. The nation – or at least many within it – saw itself reclaiming that imperial mantle from a Rome which was now associated with a discredited and corruptly 'Papist' religion. This was the primary reason Elizabeth (who was queen when Shakespeare wrote *Julius Caesar* in about 1599) held on to the Julian calendar despite the demonstrably more accurate Gregorian system proposed by the Pope. England, armed with a new certainty about its global status that came from its Protestant convictions, and fuelled by swelling wealth based on commerce, on successful military resistance to the Spanish Armadas which had tried to reclaim the country for Catholicism and on the rapid growth of a true metropolitan centre – London – saw itself as the new Rome. There was even a complex (and historically spurious) narrative of English nationalism which tied the founding of Britain to Brutus, the mythic descendant of the Trojan, Aeneas, who had established ancient Rome, and Shakespeare's later play, *Cymbeline*, explores this symbolic alignment in detail. The extent to which Caesar continued to play a central role in notions of national identity, of cultural value and historical significance, is expanded upon in several of the essays in this collection, but for the moment it suffices to say that Julius Caesar was a figure of monumental importance to the Elizabethans, one whose story would have been familiar to many, and who was a natural figure around which to build a play, even though not everyone agreed on the precise nature of his significance.

That associations with Caesar were loaded does not mean that they were univocal. Despite the high esteem in which Caesar was held, he was occasionally painted as that most dreaded of Elizabethan bugbears, the tyrant, a figure who exceeds the natural bounds of his authority and, in pursuit of what suits his own will best, rides roughshod over his people. It was for tyranny that Charles I would be formally and publicly executed in 1649, and the discourse of tyranny saturates the period. Despite the relative calm brought to England by Elizabeth's Settlement of Religion, this was still a time of religious persecution, in which deviance from the Church of England – either towards Catholicism or to the more extreme forms of Protestantism which are sometimes pejoratively lumped together as Puritanism – was considered a matter of national security. Catholics continued to be tortured and executed throughout the period, and for some, the suppression of their religion constituted (as it had for some Protestants under Queen Mary) an act of tyranny. Though Dante's *Inferno* famously confined Brutus and Cassius to the innermost circle of hell for their assassination of Julius Caesar alongside Judas Iscariot, there were those in England who were not so sure that they did not have the right – even the responsibility – to remove a tyrannous ruler by force in special circumstances. Elizabeth had been the target of multiple assassination attempts in the course of her reign, as her successor, King James I, would be, and for all her apparent popular appeal there were many in England who despised her, and not all on religious grounds. She was, like Caesar, a divisive presence in matters of personal politics, partly because she was – again, like Caesar – good at holding on to power and ensuring that those closest to her – particularly those powerful families who, like the ancient Roman Senate, were used to wielding a good deal of influence – were kept firmly in their place. She had maintained, through Francis Walsingham, a spy network. She ruined powerful men who did not toe the line and made others waste their time dancing attendance on her in her lavish court while she dangled the possibility of marriage in front of them. She was also, let us not forget, a woman in the almost exclusively male world of national and international politics, a matter which was, for some, insufferable, despite her attempts to instil a manner of worship in her subjects by adopting, for instance, the iconic associations of that most Catholic of images, the Virgin Mary, in her various self-fashionings as goddess and Virgin Queen. She could be, like Caesar, capricious, dictatorial and ruthless, and the fact that she was good at it did not necessarily make her as popular as the official record would have us believe.

In the light of all of the above, it is easy to see why Shakespeare's play had built-in audience appeal when it first appeared and was, far from being the mouldy piece of ancient history it can sometimes seem today, a play on a subject which was both familiar and exciting, deeply rooted in the culture of the day, but also urgent. It spoke in particularly potent ways to ideas which were already circulating in the period, ideas about the limits of monarchical power and when – if at all – people could rise up and remove a head of state by violence.

However, part of the core paradox of Shakespeare's play is that it does not clearly answer that question. Indeed, the Caesar we see in the play is – even to the conspirators – rather more a potential threat than an actual tyrant, and they seem more outraged by the idea of his rise to power than in the specifics of what he has done thus far. Brutus's soliloquy in his orchard, the night he meets the conspirators to plan the logistics of the assassination (2.1.10–33), is a study in vague aphorisms and proverbial wisdom, not in hard facts or the details of personal injury. Caesar himself is another paradox, a giant who speaks of himself in the third person and towers over the play, while being simultaneously deaf in one ear, epileptic and easily manipulated by flattery. The play seems unsure of the extent to which he is either a present monster or an imminent threat, and that might seem to suggest that the audience's sympathies should be entirely with him and those who stand up for him after his murder. None the less, if the play has a protagonist, a point of sympathy, it seems to be Brutus, whose motives seem neither obviously spiteful nor personally ambitious, and after the assassination the real horrors of the play tend to be laid at the feet of Mark Antony, who incites the crowd to arbitrary murder (the hapless Cinna the Poet in Act 3, Scene 3), and then casually eliminates fellow Romans and family members in a chilling study of political expediency in Act 4, Scene 1. If the play has a clear political message, it is less about the rights and wrongs of tyrannicide and more about the failure of political optimism in the face of hard realities. But then perhaps that is the point. Shakespeare's Caesar is at once a man and an idea, one which looms over the play as it loomed over the Elizabethan period, so that the real paradox concerns what happens when we try to reconcile any great cultural figure with the reality of the person themselves.

In truth, if *Julius Caesar* had a clear message, the play probably would not feel like Shakespeare, whose defining strengths in terms of plot are invariably about balance and complexity rather than the singular point. By the late 1590s he had already written numerous English history plays culminating (perhaps in the same year as *Caesar*) with *Henry V*, another study in political complexity which is open to radically contrary readings about the man at its centre. He had already written complex psychologically driven comedies such as *As You Like It* and *The Merchant of Venice*, which wrestle with troubling darkness both personal and social which adds a distinctive base note to the main plots' elements of romance and love. In such plays it becomes increasingly difficult to say 'The play finally say X' or 'Shakespeare clearly believed Y'. Shakespeare trusts his characters, gives them depth and vigour, so that when they speak they sound compelling, but because he does this for all his characters, regardless of their moral or political position, the result tends to be more of that balance and complexity, and less of a single, unmistakable conviction such as we might see in one of his contemporaries.[3] Shakespeare remains elusive, his plays a dialectical study of multiple positions, and this is, I think, part of why he remains powerful today in both the classroom and the theatre: because his even handedness allows us to explore and emphasize those parts which interest us most, interests which shift as time passes.

However, there are aspects of the play which have been fairly constant from one period to the next. Few scholars or theatre companies have found much to laugh at in *Caesar*, for instance. There's the punning cobbler in the opening scene, but things get pretty sombre thereafter, and though there may be some bleak humour in the camp poet who interrupts Brutus and Cassius during their pre-Philippi squabble (a moment often cut in performance), comic relief, or even comic subversion, is not something with which the play is overly concerned. Productions have found momentary laughter in the first exchanges of the mob with Cinna the Poet, but even when they do not start sinister they rapidly turn nasty. This is fairly unusual in Shakespearean tragedy, where some comic element is frequently allowed to undercut or comment upon the main action. The clearest analogue is probably *Macbeth*, a play which owes so much to *Julius Caesar* that the Roman play starts to look almost like a trial run for the Scottish one, and not only in its sparse use of comedy.[4]

Written about six years later, *Macbeth* picks up themes and dynamics which Shakespeare seems to have begun to explore in *Caesar*, though perhaps he felt too constrained by the subject's cultural weight to stray overmuch from the historical record. Like *Caesar*, *Macbeth* has a thoughtful man turned assassin who confides in his wife the night before the killing. It has strange storms which signify a kind of breach in nature. It has ghosts, augury, battles and internecine political wrangling, and it has the death of the aforementioned spouse relayed to the protagonist on the eve of his own death. These and other similarities suggest an author's preoccupations, ideas he wanted to revisit, effects of story and character that he felt he had perhaps not fulfilled on the first attempt.

Caesar has its share of critics who think the play flawed, messy, pompous and boring, and while some of these things are matters of personal taste (and the difficulty of wresting the play from the overly large classicist shadow which made it, for so many years, a 'safe' play for study in schools), some of them are about formal problems with the play itself. It is, for example, oddly named, at least by the standards of other Shakespearean plays, because the ostensible protagonist is dead by the beginning of the third act. A useful way to think of this is in reference to my earlier remark about there being two Caesars in the play, the man and the myth, the latter of which never completely dies, animating Antony and his troops as clearly as it does the ghost, so that Brutus's fifth-act lines over the bodies of his friends have real power and truth: 'Oh Julius Caesar, thou art mighty yet. / Thy spirit walks abroad and turns our swords / In our own proper entrails' (5.3.94–6).

Even with this broader conception of Caesar as a kind of animating idea which drives the play, it leaves us with the problem of identifying the protagonist. Brutus is clearly the man on whom the conspiracy depends, but he is pushed by Cassius, and finally overshadowed by Antony who has the longest and most scene-stealing speech in the play, when he gives the funeral oration which alters the direction of the story (somewhat contrary to Shakespeare's historical sources).[5] It seems to me interesting that when Shakespeare chose to revisit some of the concerns he had raised in Caesar, he combined the loyal wife, Portia, with the instigating Machiavel, Cassius, in Lady Macbeth, finding a rich vein of domestic and sexual psychological pressure which *Caesar* lacks. Brutus's internal discussions about the rights and wrongs of what he is about to do are, by comparison, cerebral, even abstract, and it is not until the assassination itself and the subsequent battle over the will of the people that the play develops a visceral theatricality. By contrast, Macbeth's murder of Duncan takes place much faster than does Brutus's of Caesar and, as a result, the play is more clearly about Macbeth than his victim.

In *Julius Caesar*, what often feels like the climax of the play – the funeral scene and the forum orations – gets a dry run right at the beginning, as Flavius and Murellus chastise the cobbler and his friends for celebrating Caesar's triumph over Pompey. Murellus's strategy is to berate the crowd, to belittle them for their lack of feeling, and though they go quiet, it is not clear that their minds are changed. This is the first of several set piece moments in which oratory wins the day, and it is one of the reasons that the play found favour in late nineteenth- and early twentieth-century schools, which treated the text as a useful repository of speeches on statecraft and citizenship. However, it would be a mistake to reduce the play to a study in oratory or, worse, elocution. The major public speeches (and we might include those less formal moments such as the first extended debate between Brutus and Cassius, Brutus's [mistaken] advice to leave Antony out of the Capitol bloodbath, and Decius's interpretation of Calphurnia's dream, among others, all of which are potent instances of verbal persuasion) explore a range of strategies to change people's minds, but which also reveal the inherently theatrical nature of politics, a subject which does not significantly figure in *Macbeth*.[6]

Much of the play's political dimension is crucially about performance and the deciphering of other people's performances, conscious or otherwise. Flavius and Murellus 'read' the crowd in the first scene, and are furious that the men – contrary to Elizabethan custom – are not carrying the signs of their professions (the tools and clothing which announce their nature and status to the world). Instead, the crowd are in 'holiday' attire, something which annoys the tribunes because in celebrating Caesar's victory they are turning social convention on its head. Their anger is in spite of the fact that it *is* in fact a holiday, the Lupercal, which is why the statues of the city have been bedecked with garlands. So the tribunes are reading the crowd's intentions, seeing under the licence granted by the Lupercal, a celebration of Caesar whose populism actually gives the crowd political power. In denouncing them as blocks, as 'senseless things', Murellus is denying them not just human sensibilities and the capacity to think, he is trying to deny their political might. He seems to win in this opening scene, but is later 'put to silence' (1.2.285) for disrobing Caesar's statue, and the extent of his failure – like that of the aristocratic conspirators who assume they can easily manipulate the populace – is made manifest by what happens in the forum after Caesar's murder.

Before we get there, however, there is the wonderful scene in which Caska relays to Brutus and Cassius the moment in which Caesar refused the crown Antony offered him at the urging of the multitude. It is a complex, layered study of the reciprocal nature of political theatre in which Caesar, suspecting the crowd does not really want him to be king, refuses the crown, which delights them, three times, each time more reluctantly than the last, ending in a kind of seizure. Caesar is the political actor of the scene, and Antony is his agent, but Caesar is also an audience to the performance of the crowd, and he sees that it is his *rejection* of the crown which pleases them. While he is apparently the principal performer, then, he cannot actually do what he probably wants, because to take the crown would, paradoxically, make the crowd think him less suitable to wear it. He is caught in a double bind, the performance of 'Caesarness' – the myth of the man I mentioned earlier – trumping what the actual man wants. In other words, he is not in control of his own performance, and the more absolute he wants to seem, the more he finds himself playing to someone else's script. This is why he is so easy for Decius to manipulate over the matter of Calphurnia's dream. The Caesar myth must override the man himself, so the man cannot reveal that he is in fact afraid of what the dream and the auguries seem to prophesy. Decius's palpably absurd reading of the dream (that the bleeding statue is a good sign) wins out because Caesar the man has been backed into a corner by his own public identity. Something similar happens immediately before his death when he is pressured to grant the return of Publius Cimber by the conspirators. In embracing that abstract, idealized and absolutist model of 'Caesarness' ('I am constant as the northern star' [3.1.60]) he forces the conspirators' hands – literally – shutting down all debate and performing the very tyranny they had been afraid of. He thinks he is performing according to his will, but he is in fact responding in precisely the way they want, enacting why he has to be killed.

Another suggestive performance is the moment when Brutus apparently receives the news of his wife's death twice in the tent scene (4.3). After his argument with Cassius, ostensibly over some financial misdealing but clearly also about everything which has unravelled since the Ides of March, including their friendship, Brutus reveals that Portia is dead (145), but when Messala enters the scene and probes him for news on the matter, he denies all knowledge (180). Critics have argued that the scene suggests some corruption in the text, and the 'second death of Portia' as it is sometimes called is often cut from performance. However, I think it a telling moment in which Brutus attempts another piece of political theatre, performing his stoicism to his men on the eve of battle, trying to make his handling of his wife's death an example which gives them fortitude. It seems to work that way, but the deliberation of the strategy exposes him to Cassius and to the audience as potentially cynical and unfeeling, or would if we did not treat the former emotional outburst at Cassius as somehow bound up with his grief over Portia. It also suggests that these are men who are more comfortable denying their feelings than expressing them, and while this accords with the play's Roman context and its relentlessly stoical masculine discourse (few of Shakespeare's plays have less time for women than *Caesar*), it also suggests why Antony tends to connect better with audiences and understands better how to sway hearts and minds.[7]

The supreme study in political theatre is, of course, the forum scene, and it begins with a series of grave political errors by Brutus, the most obvious of which is his decision – overruling the savvier Cassius – to let Antony live. He also allows Antony to speak *after* him, to bring Caesar's body into the marketplace, and makes the visually terrible decision to have the conspirators enter with their hands and daggers dripping with Caesar's blood. Brutus thinks this will signify their honesty and the fact that they were 'sacrificers but not butchers' (2.1.165), but this assumes that the right gesture can clearly and reliably communicate the thought behind it into the audience's minds, something all actors know is dangerously risky. Bloody hands can mean a lot of things, and Antony will be able to turn their apparent significance around, so that the conspirators look not like sacrificers who have purged their country, but like killers, monsters.

When Brutus speaks to the crowd in his calm, rational and analytical way, he seems to have won them over, but even there his failure is evident in the very enthusiasm of the crowd whose 'Let him be Caesar!' shows how badly they have misread Brutus's speech (3.2.51). The crowd have been swayed by the appearance of nobility and logic, but they haven't grasped the political nuance which supposedly motivated the conspirators. Antony, by contrast, speaks from an entirely different rhetorical position, presenting himself as an ordinary person dealing with the emotional weight of his friend's death. His dealing with the crowd is less about reason than it is a clever and responsive weighing of their mood and pulling them with theatrical devices. He comes down and speaks to them as one of them, he offers personal reminiscences about Caesar, he uses Caesar's mantle as a nostalgic prop and the corpse itself to induce horror and pity. He uses his own (genuine?) tears because he has already learned from the weeping servant that 'passion ... is catching' (3.1.283), and he uses the crowd's own self-interest – as manifested by Caesar's will – to push them into mutiny. It is an extraordinary study in political gamesmanship, and it is not surprising – in these days of media spin – that it still resonates powerfully in good productions today.

That sense of reading and misreading is, of course, a powerful theme throughout the play and continues to affect its action even outside the obviously political arena. The battles which end the play are a study in tactical error, of leaders considering the evidence of their situation and drawing the wrong conclusion. Most striking, perhaps, are Brutus's decision to go to the oncoming enemy instead of resting his forces, and Cassius's disastrous suicide when he misrecognizes who is actually winning, leading to Titinius's profound and resonant observation that he has 'misconstrued everything' (5.3.84). The whole play is a study in trying to deduce meaning from events and the actions of other people, trying and frequently failing, so that it is no accident that Shakespeare was probably also working on that other study in epistemological crisis, *Hamlet*, around the same time. Such moments echo the core problem of the play: what might Caesar become, what does he finally *mean*?

The essays that follow apply that question not just to the man (or the idea of the man) at the heart of the play but to the play itself. They approach the text from a variety of perspectives, encompassing some of the play's reach in literary critical and theatrical terms. We begin with a chapter which assesses the play's place in recent critical history, move to a study of its long performance history, then consider the current state of *Caesar* scholarship. The chapters which follow approach the play from different directions. Lisa Starks-Estes considers the play's metatheatrical study of acting in the context of the discourse of martyrdom, drawing on that staple of early modern education, Ovid. Todd Landon Barnes then analyses the play's moral economy, using Nietzschean notions of tragedy and the neoliberal history of money to explore issues of vengeance and social justice. John E. Curran, Jr. considers the central ambivalences and binary paradoxes inherent in the play and its titular character through the lens of Renaissance humanism. The last essay in this section is by Warren Chernaik and focuses on the juxtaposition of Caesar and Cicero as manifested both in ancient texts and in early modern drama which enacted their hostility, tracking the role Caesar played in later societies' struggles with republicanism, his status remade according to the differing sympathies and agendas of the ages. The final chapter of the collection is Jeremy Lopez's study of *Caesar*'s particular strengths and difficulties as a classroom text and how educators might navigate teaching the play by wrestling with its peculiarities and cultural legacy. It works by making the opposite argument from the one with which I began this introduction: that the very familiarity of the Caesar story has always rendered the play potentially boring! There is also a complete bibliography at the end which will aid students interested in further research. The book as a whole will, I hope, serve as a document of the play's critical and theatrical dimension to date while also pushing the boundaries of new scholarship, illustrating why *Julius Caesar* remains a compelling and relevant play, even in the twenty-first century.

1

The Critical Backstory

Daniel Cadman

The first recorded critical response to *Julius Caesar* (1599) is a diary entry from the Swiss-born traveller, Thomas Platter, who recalls seeing 'an excellent performance of the tragedy of the first Emperor Julius Caesar … in the house with the thatched roof'.[1] As well as providing a vital source for the dating of the play, Platter's comments are notable for highlighting *Julius Caesar* as a transitional play, in terms of both its themes and its place in Shakespeare's career as a dramatist. The labelling of Caesar as the 'first Emperor' highlights a number of the political themes of the play, dramatizing as it does the processes leading to the collapse of republican rule in Rome and its establishment as an imperial power. Platter's reference to 'the house with the thatched roof' also suggests the important point at which this play appears in Shakespeare's career by associating it with the newly-opened Globe playhouse, the performance space with which Shakespeare would become most associated. As well as being one of the earliest, if not the very earliest, of Shakespeare's plays to be performed in the new theatre, *Julius Caesar* also boasts a number of other significant innovations. It is one of the key works that signals Shakespeare's move away from the chronicle history genre and towards tragedy, thus laying the ground for the development of the great tragedies that would come to define his writing career in the early years of the Jacobean period. It is also the first play in which Shakespeare draws upon material from Thomas North's English translation of Plutarch's *Lives of Noble Grecians and Romans*, a source that would also form the basis for his later Roman tragedies, *Antony and Cleopatra* and *Coriolanus*. As well as representing a political system in transition, *Julius Caesar* signals important transitions in Shakespeare's writing career, professional practices and dramatic style. This chapter considers the critical history of *Julius Caesar* and the ways in which it has continued to figure in the various currents and theoretical movements that have characterized scholarship on Shakespeare up to the end of the twentieth century. The pivotal position of the play in Shakespeare's development as a dramatist, and his choice of subject matter, have ensured that *Julius Caesar* has continued to resonate in critical debates in terms of both themes and genre, with critics focusing upon the play's relationship with the tragic genre, its ambivalent representation of tragic heroism, its engagement with Roman history and its interrogation of Roman values, both ethical and political. Later scholarship on the play is also reflective of a number of the preoccupations that would dominate criticism of the late twentieth century, including the ways in which texts respond to their historical moment and interrogate issues relating to gender. This chapter will show how these key issues continued to emerge in discussions of *Julius Caesar* during the first 400 years of its critical afterlife.

Early responses: the seventeenth century to the Victorian period

In spite of attracting its admirers, many of the early critics responding to *Julius Caesar* were either ambivalent towards the play or wholeheartedly dismissive of what they perceived to be its shortcomings. Some of the earliest critical responses were triggered by the rivalry between Shakespeare and his contemporary, Ben Jonson. Jonson was notoriously equivocal in his view of Shakespeare, and *Julius Caesar*, in particular, came under fire in his *Discoveries*, where he recalls Shakespeare's reputation amongst his players that '(whatsoever he penned) he never blotted out a line. My answer hath beene, Would he had blotted a thousand', singling out Caesar's 'ridiculous' lines, 'Caesar doth not wrong, nor without cause / Will he be satisfied' (3.1.47–8), as a worthy contender for being 'blotted'.[2] Jonson himself admitted that his was often regarded as a 'malevolent' view,[3] a point evidenced in a spirited response from the poet Leonard Digges, who recalls how Shakespeare's work had 'ravish'd' its audience, leaving them to consider it a favourable alternative in comparison with Jonson's 'tedious (though well laboured)' Roman tragedy, *Catiline*.[4]

The comparisons between Jonson and Shakespeare were to persist throughout the Restoration period, with posterity increasingly favouring Shakespeare, even though his dramatic writing was largely at odds with the popular neoclassicism that dominated this era. In the prologue to his adaptation of *Julius Caesar* (1672), John Dryden asserts that Shakespeare was the more original talent: 'In imitation *Jonson's* wit was shown / Heaven made his men; but Shakespeare made his own.'[5] In these senses, Jonson became renowned for his fidelity to his historical sources (or what Dryden regarded as his powers of 'imitation'), whereas Shakespeare is praised for his originality and for the powers of his imagination in his characterizations of figures from Roman history. Such a view of Shakespeare is also evident in the *Sociable Letters* of Margaret Cavendish, Duchess of Newcastle, in which she singles out *Julius Caesar* as an example of Shakespeare's 'Wit and Eloquence', asserting 'that *Antonius* and *Brutus* did not Speak Better to the People, than he Feign'd them.'[6]

What Cavendish regarded as praiseworthy was also a source of rancour for some authorities. Thomas Rymer's

A Short View of Tragedy (1693), for instance, attacked Shakespeare's characterization of Caesar and Brutus who, he claimed, 'were above his conversation. To put them in Fools Coats, and make them Jack-puddens in the *Shakespeare* dress is a *Sacriledge*'.[7] Rymer initially seems to be highlighting these characterizations as an affront to tragic decorum; Shakespeare is incapable of imbuing his classical characters with the dignity and gravitas they should embody. It becomes increasingly clear that classism, rather than classicism, is at the root of Rymer's attack. For Rymer, Shakespeare's depiction of these great figures is influenced more by the need to bear in mind the lowly class origins of the actors and audiences of the London theatres than to emulate the nobility of his historical characters; as a result, the 'Language which *Shakespeare* puts in the Mouth of *Brutus* wou'd not suit, or be convenient, unless from some son of the Shambles, or some natural offspring of the Butchery.'[8] His caustic comments are not merely reserved for the male characters, however; he argues that Portia, as she is represented here, 'is the own Cousin-German, of one piece, the very same impertinent silly flesh and blood with *Desdemona*.'[9]

Although the dramatist and critic John Dennis would take many of Rymer's criticisms to task in his dialogue, *The Impartial Critic* (1693), he would also show that he shared many of Rymer's prejudices, particularly when it came to class. He expressed particular misgivings about the play's sense of poetic justice in his book, *The Advancement and Reformation of Modern Poetry* (1701). The assassination of Caesar could, on the one hand, be considered 'a Lawful Action', in which case 'the killing of *Brutus* and *Cassius* is downright murder'; on the other hand, the assassination is an act of murder, in which case Shakespeare should be 'answerable for introducing so many Noble *Romans* committing in the open face of an Audience a very horrible Murder, and only punishing two of them'.[10] In a particularly quaint moralization, Dennis worries about the effect of the latter premise upon a contemporary audience, fearing they could have revolutionary instincts fired and 'draw a dangerous inference from it', which 'may be Destructive to Government, and to Human Society'.[11] Thus, ultimately, Dennis ends up in the same position as Rymer, with concerns about tragic decorum giving way to conservative class commentary.

In another overview of English drama, Gerard Langbaine provides a more positive, yet still ambivalent, response to Shakespeare's play. In his *Characters of the English Dramatick Poets* (1699), he commends the power of Shakespeare's Brutus and Antony to 'ravish you', but complains that the scenes following Caesar's assassination are 'almost redundant'.[12] Langbaine also counters Rymer's objections by asserting that a reader will 'find his *Brutus*, his *Cassius*, his *Anthony*, and his *Caesar* … just as the Historians of those times describe 'em.'[13] By doing so, Langbaine provides a distinct perspective from that of earlier commentators, such as Dryden, by emphasizing Shakespeare's authenticity rather than the power of his creativity. The apparent redundancy of the scenes following Caesar's assassination left some commentators to pose a question that would continually resurface in criticism of the play. Charles Gildon asserted that the play 'ought rather to be call'd *Marcus Brutus* … If it had been properly call'd *Julius Caesar* it ought to have ended at his Death, and then it had been much more regular, natural and beautiful'.[14] Such concerns about the tragic coherence of the play led to John Sheffield, Duke of Buckingham, adapting the play into two separate parts, *The Tragedy of Julius Caesar* and *The Death of Brutus*, with each of the two principal Shakespearean characters becoming the tragic hero of their own respective plays in order for the plot to avoid violating the unity of action. The scholar John Upton also responded to similar issues by excusing Shakespeare's violation of the Aristotelian unity of time by insisting that the play adhered to the unity of action, resulting in a 'Story [that] hangs together as in a heroic poem'.[15]

It was not until the eighteenth century that commentators became more prepared to indulge Shakespeare's lack of attention to formal rules and to consider him as embodying the qualities of 'natural' genius untrammelled by such principles. One of the key ways in which Shakespeare's works were established into the literary canon was through the culture of editing and its drive to produce authoritative versions of Shakespeare's texts. One of the earliest authorities in this field was Alexander Pope, whose practice was driven by a clear agenda to promote the image of Shakespeare's genius by ironing out any blemishes or textual corruptions and attributing them to the practices of the theatre. As the dominant figure of the so-called Augustan writers, who held ancient Roman culture in particularly high regard, Pope was keen to commend *Julius Caesar* for evoking the 'Spirit' and 'Manners' of the Romans, which are 'exactly drawn.'[16] Pope therefore shares the tendency we have seen for critical judgements about the play's quality to stand or fall based upon assumptions about the authenticity of Shakespeare's depiction of Rome. An influential editor who provided a notable exception to this tendency was Samuel Johnson, who asserted that Shakespeare's 'adherence to the real story, and to *Roman* manners seems to have impeded the natural vigour of his genius.'[17] Instead of a channel for Shakespeare's talent, then, Johnson regards the striving for an authentic portrayal of Rome as a hindrance to the promulgation of his 'natural' genius in this play.

The so-called 'Bardolatry' of Johnson was to find considerable sympathy in the Romantic period. In spite of this, though, Samuel Taylor Coleridge considered the characterization of Brutus as flawed and struggled to 'see into Shakspeare's motive, his *rationale*, or in what view he meant Brutus' character to appear'.[18] In a response that is clearly influenced by the political activism and revolutionary sympathies of the Romantic movement, Coleridge is particularly frustrated by Brutus's inability to find a 'personal cause' for his proposed actions against Caesar before asking, 'Had [Caesar] not passed the Rubicon? Had he not entered Rome as a conqueror? Had he not placed his Gauls in the Senate?'[19] The implication is clear that Caesar's actions, and their resultant marginalization of Brutus's political freedoms, should be enough for him to find a 'personal cause' against Caesar and, for Coleridge, Brutus does not embody sufficient revolutionary vigour, at this point at least, in the face of corrupt rule.

For the influential critic William Hazlitt, it was Caesar rather than Brutus who fell short of expectations. As the title of his study, *Characters of Shakespear's Plays* (1817), suggests, Hazlitt's approach was distinctive for focusing upon the representation of Shakespeare's characters, a focus developed from his experiences as a theatre reviewer. It is this emphasis that leads him to remark that the depiction of Caesar does not square with 'the portrait given of him in his Commentaries' and, other than making 'several vapouring and rather pedantick speeches', he 'does nothing. Indeed, he has nothing to do.'[20] Of far more interest here is the character of Brutus, who, for Hazlitt, is the key to the play's political comment. He argues that the plotters' 'design to liberate their country fails from the generous temper and overweening confidence of Brutus in the goodness of their cause and the assistance of others' and points out that the 'humanity and sincerity which dispose men to resist injustice and tyranny render them unfit to cope with the cunning and power of those who are opposed to them.'[21] Brutus is therefore defined by his idealism and is unprepared for the consequences of the assassination or the realities of political life.

In his *Studies of Shakespere*, the editor and critic Charles Knight also shows how the critical emphasis at this point was moving increasingly away from Caesar, and from the seventeenth-century concerns about his marginalization in the play, in favour of Brutus as the principal object of interest. Like Hazlitt, Knight considers how he embodies idealistic principles, this time in comparison with Cassius's pragmatism, before concluding that 'Brutus is the nobler instructor' and 'Cassius the better politician'.[22] Knight remarks that Brutus is 'a man of speculation; one who is moved to kill the man he loves upon no personal motive, but upon a theory; one who fights his last battle upon somewhat speculative principles', yet goes on to commend him as one 'who, from his gentleness, his constancy, his fortitude, has subdued men of more active minds to the admiration of his temper and to the adoption of his opinions.'[23] Knight is also particularly innovative for regarding the shared protagonist of the three Roman plays as the state of Rome itself, a notion that would underpin numerous twentieth-century studies of Shakespeare's Roman works.[24]

This interest in Shakespeare's characters was steered in a distinctive direction by the late Victorian critic Edward Dowden, whose principal work, *Shakspere: A Critical Study of his Mind and Art* (1875), took the innovative and influential step of carrying out a lengthy and sustained biographical reading of the plays. As well as moving away from the Johnsonian notion of Shakespeare's characters as products of 'natural' and timeless genius rather than historical circumstances, Dowden's study is also indicative of the increasingly elevated cultural status of Shakespeare; it is particularly notable that his life and background, often hitherto a source of embarrassment or derision, should come to be regarded as a worthy object of study and a shaping influence upon the plays. In his chapter on the Roman plays, Dowden sees *Julius Caesar* as a product of Shakespeare's admiration for 'great men of action', rooted in the fact that 'he himself was primarily not a man of action.'[25] Such men are contrasted with idealists, represented by Brutus; for Dowden, Shakespeare is 'stern to all idealists, because he was aware that he might too easily yield himself to the tendencies of an idealist.'[26] Dowden considers various aspects of the play, but one of the key recurring points in his analysis is the motif of reading character, or failure to do so. He highlights Brutus's attitude towards Antony, particularly his misjudged dismissal of him as 'gamesome' (1.2.28). He also remarks upon Caesar's solipsistic absorption in his own legendary status and his blindness to his limitations and human frailties, as a result of which he 'disappears for himself under the greatness of the Caesar myth.'[27] A similar view of Caesar is advanced by Paul Stapfer, who, in spite of being underwhelmed by the 'weak and superstitious' Caesar, goes on to argue that the Roman state is defined by the 'spirit of Caesarism' and that Brutus and his fellow conspirators did not reckon upon a situation in which, 'after the violent death of the feeble body, the spirit of Caesar grew immeasurably, covering the whole tragedy with its shadow.'[28] This sense of the disjunction between the idealized image of Caesar and the frail corporeal reality of the figure would be one of the numerous topics that would continue to be explored in the twentieth century.

The twentieth century (1900–79)

The field of literary studies underwent a host of changes throughout the twentieth century, leading to the emergence of numerous critical currents and the establishment of a variety of different methodologies. Thanks to their prominent canonical status, the plays of Shakespeare became some of the key works that were affected by the directions that the discipline was taking, and the numerous and diverse critical responses to *Julius Caesar* are reflective of this. One of the earliest and most influential studies of the twentieth century was A. C. Bradley's *Shakespearean Tragedy* (1904), a major work in the field of character-based criticism. Bradley's book was developed during his tenure as Professor of Poetry at the University of Oxford between 1901 and 1906 and thus signals an important milestone in the professionalization of the field of Shakespearean criticism and, more broadly, in the establishment and development of literary studies as an academic discipline. As a result of these developments, Shakespeare's works would become securely established as objects worthy of serious study and professional attention. *Julius Caesar* is not one of the principal plays upon which Bradley's study focuses, but he does offer some comparisons between the characters of Brutus and Hamlet, who both represent a kind of 'philosophic' tragic protagonist. According to Bradley, both 'are highly intellectual by nature and reflective by habit' and, 'when placed in critical circumstances', they reveal 'a sensitive and almost painful anxiety to do right' and their failures are 'connected rather with their intellectual nature and reflective habit than with any yielding to passion.'[29] Bradley only comments upon *Julius Caesar* in passing, however, and does not consider it to be part of the 'mature' tragedies upon which he focuses; the play instead represents the 'culmination' of Shakespeare's first period of work, in which he reaches only 'a limited perfection.'[30]

Bradley's emphases upon the inner lives of Shakespeare's characters as stimuli for the tragic action can also be seen in a number of early twentieth-century psychoanalytic studies of *Julius Caesar*, influenced in particular by Sigmund Freud's theories of the Oedipus complex. Otto Rank and Ernest Jones focused their attentions mainly upon *Hamlet* but they also saw a number of similar resonances of Freudian theories in the near-contemporary *Julius Caesar*, particularly a number of links between Brutus and Hamlet. Rank argued that *Julius Caesar* enacts the Oedipal dynamic with Caesar representing the father figure and Brutus the son. Rank also argued that the major characters surrounding Caesar embody different attributes of the son figure, with Brutus representing 'the son's rebelliousness, Cassius his remorsefulness, and Anthony his natural piety'.[31] Jones also goes on to consider Brutus's justification for Caesar's assassination – 'not that I loved Caesar less, but that I loved Rome more' (3.2.21–2) – by arguing that 'cities, just like countries, are unconscious symbols of the mother' resulting in a speech that 'reads as if Brutus, in a moment of intense emotion, had revealed to his audience the unconscious motive from which his action sprang', adding another dimension to the Oedipal resonances in the play.[32]

As its title suggests, John Palmer's *Political Characters of Shakespeare* was influenced by Bradley's approach, particularly the sense that the source of the tragic action was in the behaviours of the individual characters rather than fate. Although his primary focus is Brutus, Palmer offers a number of insights into the representation of Caesar and the play's tragic structure. Responding to received views that Shakespeare's characterization of Caesar is 'as a slight, negligent and impertinent libel upon a great man', Palmer argues that the 'greatness' of Caesar is, in fact, 'assumed throughout the play', a strategy that allows Shakespeare to attribute 'human weaknesses' to him and to explore the premise 'that Caesar's spirit is mightier than his person, a suggestion which is essential to the unity of the play'.[33] Whilst, as we have seen, some earlier critics had been underwhelmed by Shakespeare's realization of Caesar and found the play's second half anti-climactic, Palmer here emphasizes that both of these points are essential elements that inform the political aspects of the tragedy as well as its overall coherence.

A renewed interest in Shakespeare and genre was also developing alongside the character-based studies. Advancing upon earlier considerations of Shakespeare's engagement with the premises of tragedy and history, some early twentieth-century critics began to regard the Roman tragedies as belonging to a coherent subgenre; as a result, book-length studies of Shakespeare's Roman plays were to become one of the key avenues for scholarship on *Julius Caesar*. The earliest example of this is M. W. MacCallum's *Shakespeare's Roman Plays and their Background* (1910). MacCallum considers *Julius Caesar* from various points of view and focuses upon Shakespeare's use and modification of his sources, as well as providing individual chapters on Caesar, Brutus, Portia and the minor characters. One of the key elements MacCallum emphasizes is the play's proximity to Shakespeare's English history plays, as well as addressing claims that the titular hero should in fact be Brutus and that *Julius Caesar* is a misnomer for this play by pointing out that 'the Histories are all named after the sovereign in whose reign the events occurred' and that it 'is not improbable that this was the light in which Shakespeare regarded Caesar.'[34] Thus, according to MacCallum, the play's chronological proximity to the histories reveals much about the ways in which Shakespeare approached this work and the bearings it has upon the play's genre and its representation of tragic heroism. Similar emphasis is placed upon questions about the play's genre in the study, *Shakespearian Tragedy*, in which H. B. Charlton argues that *Julius Caesar* may contain a number of elements that lend themselves to the tragic genre, including 'the assassination of a world ruler' and 'the undoing of a noble-minded statesman broken by the practical exigencies of his political idealism', but insists that 'Shakespeare's dramatic mood when he made this Roman matter into a play was not primarily the tragedian's.'[35] Charlton then goes on to explore the affinities between Shakespeare's approaches to *Julius Caesar* and the histories, attaching similar importance to its liminal position in relation to the trajectory of Shakespeare's writing career.

The influential Shakespearean studies by G. Wilson Knight represented another means of departing from the Bradleyan tradition of character criticism. Knight instead adopted a formalist approach characterized by close reading that tended to marginalize any external social or cultural influences upon the work. This led Knight to consider each of Shakespeare's plays as a 'poem' or 'expanded metaphor' with a particular focus upon imagery.[36] His typically idiosyncratic style of criticism is well demonstrated by a chapter in his second book, *The Imperial Theme*, which considers 'The Eroticism of *Julius Caesar*'. Here Knight argues that the play 'is charged highly with a general eroticism' that affects all of the characters and is 'emotional, fiery, but not exactly sexual, not physically passionate', and that 'even Brutus and Portia love with a gentle companionship rather than any passion.' He argues that the play's dramatization of Caesar's murder and its aftermath forms a sequence that represents 'first the disjointing of "spirit" from "matter" which is evil, fear, anarchy; and then the remating of these two elements into the close fusion which is love, order, peace.'[37] For Knight, the play is not 'erotic' in the expected sense; eroticism instead provides a metaphorical framework for a play whose action requires a 'remating' of 'spirit' and 'matter' in order to counter the tragic and chaotic effects of their disjunction.

As its title suggests, Adrien Bonjour's short study, *The Structure of Julius Caesar*, betrays similar interests in form, along with a number of preoccupations of the New Criticism that dominated the discipline of English studies for much of the first half of the twentieth century. These preoccupations included the attention to such features as imagery, paradox and ambiguity as means of uncovering the thematic or aesthetic unity of the text itself. Bonjour highlights some of the ambiguities of *Julius Caesar*, which are reflected in the play's unusual structure that must accommodate two heroes rather than one; in this way, according to Bonjour, Shakespeare is 'deliberately abandoning the usual single hero structure.'[38] Rather than presenting the audience with a choice 'between a confirmed tyrant and a noble, but unlucky, liberator,' Bonjour argues that the play's structure in fact invites them to choose 'between two heroes, each of whom has his own greatness and his faults, each of whom perplexes us then deeply moves us, each of whom is the other's victim and the other's bane.'[39] In this sense, Bonjour provides a means of negotiating earlier criticisms of the play's apparent failure to adhere to ideas of tragic unity. This idea of the play as a moral choice between the perspectives represented by Brutus and Caesar was also the subject for work by Matthew N. Proser and Gordon Ross Smith.[40] Bonjour also goes on to focus upon structural imagery and that which he labels the 'structural role of motives' in order to highlight the role of structure in developing some key themes of the play.

Ambiguity was also the key topic of Ernest Schanzer's study of the play in his book, *The Problem Plays of Shakespeare*. This is the only occasion on which *Julius Caesar* is considered as a 'problem play', a term which is used most commonly in more recent Shakespeare criticism to group together *Measure for Measure*, *All's Well That Ends Well* and *Troilus and Cressida*, as plays whose resolutions present difficulties in terms of generic classification. The term itself had evolved in the late nineteenth century and had generally been applied in discussions of the theatre of Henrik Ibsen and G. B. Shaw. It is very much in this sense that Schanzer uses the term when he compares the content of *Julius Caesar* with Ibsen's *The Wild Duck*, with both plays presenting 'the tragic mischief created by the actions of a young idealist in fulfilment of the highest principles, partly through his utter blindness to what people really are like.'[41] Schanzer highlights the ambiguities surrounding the depiction of Caesar and suggests that Shakespeare was capitalizing upon the ambivalence towards him that was generated by a variety of ancient and contemporary commentators. Also 'problematic' for Schanzer is Shakespeare's manipulation of the audience's responses to the principal characters, which is marked by a practice he labels 'dramatic coquetry', whereby Shakespeare plays 'fast and loose with our affections for them, engaging and alienating them in turn.'[42] Thus, for Schanzer, such ambiguities have clear bearings upon the play's relation to generic classifications. Such points were also considered in the mid-1970s in E. A. J. Honigmann's study *Shakespeare: Seven Tragedies*, in which he argues that *Julius Caesar* anticipates Shakespeare's mature tragedies in that he 'sought for a more intricately mixed response' from the audience than in earlier tragedies.[43] Using methods associated with reader-response theory, and comparing the drama with its sources, Honigmann highlights how Shakespeare went about 'refashioning' the character of Brutus as he appears in Plutarch and that the play represents another example of how 'Shakespeare was much less interested in history than in audience-response.'[44] In this sense, Honigmann's approach shares the tendency of the New Critical tradition to marginalize political implications and considerations of the historical context in favour of a close reading of the text.

Similar preoccupations of the New Criticism were also at the forefront of two significant monographs on Shakespeare's Roman plays. Maurice Charney's book, *Shakespeare's Roman Plays: The Function of Imagery in the Drama* (1961), shares Knight's sense of the plays as dramatic poems and focuses upon Shakespeare's style as the unifying feature of the individual texts. Charney argued that, in spite of their thematic similarities, Shakespeare's Roman plays each have their own distinctive styles and the section on *Julius Caesar* explores the significance of the recurring images of the storm, blood and fire, along with the ways in which the public and private personae of Caesar are constructed. For Charney, *Julius Caesar* represents an instance of Shakespeare adopting a consciously 'Roman' style which is marked by austere rhetoric and a sparing use of imagery. In this way, Shakespeare is engaging in a 'deliberate limiting of imaginative resources in *Julius Caesar*' as a means of achieving a distinctive style 'that can express the clarity of thought and forthrightness of action in the Roman subject matter.'[45] Derek Traversi's book, *Shakespeare: The Roman Plays* (1963), also includes an analysis of *Julius Caesar* in relation to Shakespeare's other two major Roman tragedies. Traversi approaches the play by dealing with it scene by scene, an approach that suggests the influence of the New Criticism and its emphasis upon close reading. In a similar New Critical vein, one of the key points of interest includes the play's ambiguity as a source of thematic unity, along with its provision of a variety of different viewpoints and the representation of the relationships between different groups of characters. For Traversi, the development of the plot is based upon 'an interplay of personalities in contrast' and he comments upon how no 'motive or claim is accepted at its own valuation' and any particular outlook tends to be presented 'as much through the reactions it arouses in others as in itself.'[46] He also highlights the 'contrast between what men propose and what, as political beings, they in fact achieve' as a principal theme that develops throughout the play.[47]

Another reading of *Julius Caesar* that shared an interest in the relationship between theme and structure was Norman Rabkin's 1964 article, 'Structure, Convention, and Meaning in *Julius Caesar*', in which he argues that there are two key elements that provide thematic and structural coherence in the play. The first of these is shown in a comparison between Act 2, Scene 1 and Act 2, Scene 2, a pairing of scenes that highlights a number of parallels between Brutus and Caesar, including their uses of rhetoric, their apparent selflessness (which, in both cases, is matched by 'a self-destructive vanity and a tendency to play to the galleries'), their egotism and their inabilities to 'relax a self-destructive moral rigidity.'[48] He also goes on to argue that *Julius Caesar* also achieves structural coherence if it is treated as a revenge tragedy with Antony in the role of the avenger, a premise that 'justified the title of a play in which the titular hero is out of the way before the third Act has barely got under way'.[49]

Alongside the various studies focusing upon the genre and the ambiguities provoked in relation to the play's representations of tragic heroism, the political issues in *Julius Caesar* have also figured prominently in critical discussions. Questions relating to tyranny, assassination, systems of government and the role of the populace have provided considerable stimulus for a diverse range of critical responses to the play. In contrast to the political readings of Shakespeare that were common in the closing decades of the century, the dominant trend in discussions of Shakespeare's politics at this time is most famously embodied by E. M. W. Tillyard's study, *The Elizabethan World Picture*, which argued that Shakespeare's plays provided a relatively conservative vision that ultimately championed order and political orthodoxy. In his monograph, *The State in Shakespeare's Greek and Roman Plays* (1940), James Emerson Phillips provided a reading of *Julius Caesar* that pre-empts Tillyard's work by emphasizing Shakespeare's characterization of Caesar as 'a just and benevolent sovereign of the Roman state' and the 'divinely appointed lieutenant of God on earth.'[50] In this reading, it follows that the assassination of Caesar is tantamount to the unjust removal of a legitimate and anointed sovereign. Phillips also objects to the assassination on the more pragmatic grounds that it brings about a damaging power vacuum and a period of political instability in which there is 'a virtual absence of government of any kind as party struggled against party for power'.[51] Phillips argues that the victory of the triumvirate contains a 'bitter commentary on the futility as well as the fallacy of the conspirators' political reasoning and the act to which it led', and that 'at the price of ruinous civil strife they have succeeded only in making way for a tyranny far worse than that which they overthrew.'[52]

Whereas Phillips emphasizes the legitimacy of Caesar's rule and the disastrous political consequences of his assassination, John Dover Wilson took a markedly different view by highlighting the negative aspects of the characterization of Caesar. For Wilson, Caesar is a 'Roman Tamburlaine of illimitable ambition and ruthless irresistible genius; a monstrous tyrant who destroyed his country and ruined "the mightiest and most flourishing commonwealth that the world will ever see" – one feature remained to add before the sixteenth century stage-figure of the great dictator was complete, that of a braggart'.[53] Wilson therefore likens Caesar, in turn, to Marlowe's famously ruthless and unstoppable general with a seemingly infinite appetite for conquest, and to the stage figure of the braggart, both moves which serve to undercut the apparent political legitimacy and tragic dignity of Shakespeare's protagonist.

The play's politics are also considered in Brents Stirling's book, *The Populace in Shakespeare* (1949). Stirling's study argues that Shakespeare presented images of mobilized public groups that were aligned with popular conceptions of such groups as wavering, easily manipulated and potentially dangerous. Stirling sees *Julius Caesar*, in particular, as 'not a pretty example of how to manipulate the electorate' and a dramatization of how 'a Roman mob, fickle and discordant, by asserting its democratic influence makes of the political scene a shambles or a madhouse.'[54] Stirling argues that this particular representation of the populace depends upon Shakespeare performing a 'transmutation of source material', as is the case when 'the citizenry plumps solidly for Brutus, only to change over suddenly at Antony's provocation', a development that runs 'entirely counter' to Plutarch's account.⁵⁵ Stirling's reading thus undercuts the praises bestowed upon Shakespeare by earlier critics for his fidelity to his source material. Stirling returns to *Julius Caesar* in his later book, *Unity in Shakespearian Tragedy* (1956), in which he examines the various 'ritual' elements appropriated by Brutus in preparation for the assassination of Caesar. According to Stirling, *Julius Caesar* represents Brutus resolving 'to exalt not only the mission but the tactics of conspiracy: having already accepted republicanism as an honourable end, he sets out to dignify assassination, the means, by lifting it to a level of rite and ceremony.'⁵⁶

In his article 'Political Issues in *Julius Caesar*', Irving Ribner also intervenes in debates about the play's politics. Ribner sets out to argue against the view of Phillips, that 'the play is a vindication of absolute monarchy, represented by Caesar, against the claims of a constitutional system represented by Brutus, with Rome as the actual hero of the play', and that of Virgil Whitaker, that 'the play is a defense of absolutism, with Brutus as the tragic hero who ... falls into the tragic error of opposing the political principle ordained by God.'⁵⁷ Ribner argues that such views oversimplify the complexity of the political issues in the play, which are further complicated by the fact that Caesar 'is not an actual king or symbol of kingship who is murdered by rebellious citizens', but is, in fact, 'a great general who aspires to be king and who is murdered on the eve of his success.'⁵⁸ Rather than representing Renaissance conceptions of divinely ordained monarchy, Caesar is, for Ribner, a potential tyrant, and instead of regarding Brutus as a villain, Ribner argues that Shakespeare follows Plutarch in characterizing Brutus as 'the would-be saviour of his country', who is censured 'not for his ends, but for the means he uses to attain those ends. There is never any question of the menace to Rome which Caesar represents.'⁵⁹ For Ribner, the dangers of Caesar's tyranny and the potential manipulation of the mob pose far greater threats to the Roman state than the motives of

Brutus. The play's politics are also considered in a chapter of Allan Bloom and Harry V. Jaffa's book, *Shakespeare's Politics*, which focuses, in particular, upon tensions between the principles represented by Brutus and the prudence embodied by Cassius.⁶⁰

At the same time as the political implications of the play were being debated, scholars of the mid-twentieth century took a renewed interest in Shakespeare's engagement with Roman history and his use of sources. One of the most influential readings along these lines was T. J. B. Spencer's essay, 'Shakespeare and the Elizabethan Romans', in which the focal point is the extent to which Shakespeare's engagement with Roman history related to that of his contemporaries and the points at which they diverged. Significantly, Spencer takes issue with recent New Critical emphases upon the play's ambiguity by suggesting that Shakespeare 'is almost precisely in step with sound Renaissance opinion' in his treatment of the historical events by keeping in line with the 'Renaissance admiration for Brutus and detestation of Caesar.'⁶¹ J. Leeds Barroll also considers Shakespeare's use of Roman history in an article published the year after Spencer's essay which provides a detailed account of the sources available to Shakespeare and a useful insight into the historiographical debates with which he was engaging in the period.⁶² The interest in Shakespeare's sources also led to the publication of Geoffrey Bullough's eight-volume *Narrative and Dramatic Sources of Shakespeare*, the fifth volume of which focused upon the Roman plays. Bullough's volumes provided editions of the likely sources available to Shakespeare, as well as notable analogues, accompanied by critical introductions that evaluated the ways in which Shakespeare drew on and departed from the materials.⁶³ Like Spencer, Bullough rejected previous scholarly views upon the play's ambivalence, particularly Schanzer's classification of *Caesar* as a 'problem play', arguing instead that Shakespeare's presentation of the historical figures 'is not intended to confuse or offer alternative interpretations' and that any ambivalence the play provokes is instead evidence of the influence of Plutarch, from whom Shakespeare learned 'to represent more clearly than before the paradoxes of human nature, the mixture of good and evil in the same person.'[64]

Also focusing upon the implications of Shakespeare's representation of ancient Rome was Michael Platt's monograph, *Rome and Romans According to Shakespeare* (1976), a study that is particularly distinctive for establishing an analytical framework in which Shakespeare's Roman works chart the rise and fall of the Roman republic, starting with *The Rape of Lucrece*. A major aspect of Platt's reading of *Julius Caesar* is the play's representation of the political state of Rome, particularly the very limited opportunities it offers to escape the influence of politics. Much of the analysis focuses upon the representation of friendship which is, according to Platt, one of only two things which 'claim some autonomy from politics', along with poetry.[65] In spite of this, as Platt shows, both become embroiled in the turbulent political situation. Platt also argues that the 'failure of Brutus to restore the Republic turns out to be the best argument not to have killed Caesar'.[66] Platt argues that ultimately it is only 'the failure of Brutus and Cassius' that 'turns out to vindicate Caesar'.[67] Caesar's assassination, then, does not result in 'the restoration of liberty and honor to Rome', and Platt concludes that 'to fail to achieve those political goals is to declare the assassination an act of butchery'.[68] For Platt, then, the play ultimately focuses upon the plotters' inability to recover the Republican liberties compromised by Caesar. Platt's study is also distinctive for rooting its objection to the assassination of Caesar on the grounds that his regime 'turns out to be the best that could be hoped for'.[69] Platt's view is, in one sense, a conservative reading of the play, yet it is significant that he bases his conclusions upon political pragmatism rather than the idealistic Tillyardian view of the political orthodoxy of Elizabethan England. As we shall see, the departure from this kind of political idealism anticipates the innovations of the political readings of the late twentieth century which saw

Shakespeare's plays as products of ideological struggle rather than political orthodoxy.

The late twentieth century (1980–99)

In the closing decades of the twentieth century, there was a marked proliferation of both the volume and range of critical responses to *Julius Caesar* and the range of issues provoked by its representation of this crucial episode from Roman history. Such was the importance of the setting that, for Robert S. Miola, the city effectively became the 'central protagonist of the play'.[70] Miola's monograph, *Shakespeare's Rome* (1983), is one of a range of book-length studies that placed *Julius Caesar* firmly within the context of Shakespeare's other Roman works to show how they engaged in sustained interrogation of the implications of Roman values. For Miola, this 'central protagonist' is an oppressive presence that 'shapes the lives of its inhabitants, who struggle to act according to Roman heroic traditions.'[71] Miola contends that Shakespeare's principal aim in this play is to 'give his audience a look at a pivotal moment in Roman history' rather than to make any political statement about tyranny or rebellion, as previous commentators had argued. Miola explores how the play focuses instead upon characters who set out to make their marks on Roman history, but end up forsaking their initial principles as they become caught up in the progress of the history they are seeking to influence. Miola also reveals the significances of various allusions and motifs appropriated from Roman sources, and highlights the characters' misinterpretation, or wilful subversion, of signs and portents as a key theme in the play. In this sense, Miola argues that the 'struggle between Romans and the force of history is embodied in the dramatic ironies that constitute the fabric of the play', suggested most readily by the characters' 'paradoxical effort ... to use history, to imitate the heroic past for the approval of the future.'[72]

Vivian Thomas's book, *Shakespeare's Roman Worlds*, also aimed to highlighted the coherence of this group by emphasizing the sense of continuity running through the Roman plays in their presentation of 'a changing Rome' marked by 'the collision of values or the divergence between personal aspirations and obligations to the society'.[73] In the main chapter on *Julius Caesar*, Thomas performs an extensive analysis of the play based primarily upon Shakespeare's use of his Roman sources, focusing particularly upon the play as an exploration of 'the significance of personal and political images and self-images' related to the principal characters.[74] In Geoffrey Miles's book, *Shakespeare and the Constant Romans* (1996), the intertextual coherence of Shakespeare's Roman works is predicated upon their engagement with stoicism. He begins with Brutus's instructions to his fellow conspirators: 'Let not our looks put on our purposes; / But bear it as our Roman actors do, / With untired spirits and formal constancy' (2.1.224–6). Brutus's evocation of constancy points to a 'quintessential' but 'very problematic' Roman virtue that signals Shakespeare's ambivalence towards stoicism.[75] Miles points out some of the ways in which the play interrogates the complexities and inconsistencies inherent in attempting to uphold the virtue of constancy, focusing upon the vexed relationship between constancy and suicide and the premises that constancy encourages repression of suffering rather than liberation from it, and that it also requires an element of performance that leads to the deception of others or, in some cases, self-deception. Though 'not unsympathetic' towards constancy, the play reveals it to be 'a flawed ideal, not humanly attainable, and therefore liable to involve its adherents in continual pretence and self-deception.'[76]

For Jan Blits, republicanism is the untenable value that runs through Shakespeare's Roman works. In *The End of the Ancient Republic* (1993), Blits considers manliness, friendship and gender in relation to the dwindling of republican values in Rome. In Shakespeare's Rome, 'republican forms remain, but they lack republican life' and are no longer animated by the principles for which they once stood. For Blits, the republic has only survived so long because the populace, 'bound by tradition, cling to established forms ... because of their traditionalism' rather than through any confidence in a republican system.[77] Like Platt, Blits emphasizes how the results of the plotters' actions undermine their initial intentions and, as a result, 'what at first appear dull failures in Caesar's attempt to become a king are in fact disguised successes in his attempt to become a god.'[78] As is the case with earlier studies, Blits also emphasizes the mixed potential responses to Caesar's death, an event which, he argues, 'reflects the problematical relation between the old and the new Rome, and hence the dual character of Caesar's death and divinity.'[79] Ultimately, an act that aimed to protect Rome's republican status becomes associated with its new imperial status in Caesar's elevation to divine power.

Though *Julius Caesar* continued to figure in monographs on Shakespeare's Roman texts, some studies sought to accommodate the play within other broader frameworks. One example is Alexander Leggatt's *Shakespeare's Political Drama* which grouped the Roman plays with the English history plays. The chapter on *Julius Caesar* engages with the vexed question of the systems of government represented in the play. Leggatt argues that 'Caesar seems to be not overturning an established order but moving into a power vacuum' and that the play itself, which 'gives little sense of the republican constitution', interrogates 'an ideal of Romanness, something inherent in the blood, guaranteeing integrity of behaviour.'[80] Leggatt focuses his readings particularly upon the ways in which the identities of both Caesar and Brutus are shaped by others in the Roman state. In the case of Brutus, the 'sense of himself depends on what others think of him', leaving him compelled to 'imitate the Brutus other men expect.'[81] Brutus, for Leggatt, has constructed an 'insidiously artificial world in which he is the custodian and exemplar of Roman values and the function of other men is to agree with him.'[82] Caesar's image is also shaped by others; following the assassination, 'Caesar's spirit lives through others' invocations of it, changing shape to meet their different needs', providing another example of the play's representation of the 'interdependence of its characters, who find not just the meaning of their actions, but their very identities, in the eyes of others.'[83] The Roman plays are also considered in relation to the histories in Paul N. Siegel's book, *Shakespeare's English and Roman History Plays: A Marxist Approach*, in which he performs a critique of how 'the play's language, imagery, and course of action indicate clearly enough how the fall of its title character should be regarded: Caesar is representative of the monarchical principle necessary for the well-being of Rome.'[84] Siegel highlights these premises in order to show how ideas relating to divine providence are harnessed for ideological ends in order to promulgate monarchical authority.

In *The Subject of Tragedy* (1985), a landmark study of Renaissance tragedy and its interrogation of the construction of the early modern subject, Catherine Belsey also considers the play's politics and argues that it departs from typical representations of tyranny in the period by opening space to interrogate alternative systems of government. Engagement with Roman history, particularly at this crucial moment, provides the opportunity to consider the contrasts between 'the liberty of the Republic' and 'Imperial tyranny'.[85] Belsey goes on to argue that '*Julius Caesar* brings into conjunction, and indeed collision, two distinct orders of sovereignty' and, although it avoids choosing 'decisively between them', it still 'offers its audience the opportunity to reflect on the differences.'[86] The play's representation of Caesar's regime also gave rise to a number of critical works, including an article by Robert S. Miola and a chapter in a monograph by Rebecca Bushnell, that highlight the play's potential to interrogate the ethics of assassination and the questions about the nature of tyranny.[87]

Critics working in these decades also took advantage of the rise of critical theory in order to undertake a range of distinctive readings of the play. One of the most influential currents of theory to emerge in the field of Shakespeare studies was New Historicism, which tended to see literary texts as part of a network of discourses which reflect the social, political and ideological structures that produce them. In *James I and the Politics of Literature* (1983), Jonathan Goldberg argues that although *Julius Caesar* pre-dates the accession of James I to the English throne, it can be situated in relation to a tradition of Jacobean Roman tragedies that interrogate the 'Roman style' of government adopted by the new king. This style was predicated upon such elements as 'a strong notion of public life, the continuities of history, the recreation of Rome as England's imperial ideal.'[88] Like Miles, Goldberg takes Brutus's 'formal constancy' speech as his starting point, highlighting it as an example of how political authority depended upon the sovereign engaging in a kind of performance (like a 'Roman actor') and arguing that the Roman plays reflect 'the concerns that shaped James's conception of his role', as well as 'the fact that he conceived of it as a role'.[89] For Goldberg, the play exposes the ways in which the self-consciously performative nature of sovereignty results in the disjunction between the public and private images of Caesar (as shown by Cassius's recollection of Caesar almost drowning, an incident at odds with the dominant political image he aims to convey). He also considers the play's representation of a political scene in which the 'Caesar offstage dominates what occurs onstage', which is similar to 'a form of power we know James favoured, withdrawing from view and into his absolute state.'[90] Wayne Rebhorn also adopts a New Historicist approach but, unlike Goldberg, situates *Julius Caesar* firmly in its historical moment by arguing that the play's representation of Caesar's assassination and its aftermath is reflective of the self-destructive factional tensions at Elizabeth's court towards the end of her reign.[91]

Emerging in dialogue with New Historicism was Cultural Materialism. Whereas New Historicism tended to focus upon the ways in which literary texts were shaped by the contemporary power structures, Cultural Materialists would generally regard texts as the sites of ideological struggle rather than a reflection of the dominant discourses of authority. One of the products of the turn to such theoretical readings is Richard Wilson's much-anthologized essay, 'Shakespeare's Roman Carnival', whose starting point is Thomas Platter's 1599 account of witnessing a performance of Shakespeare's play at the newly-opened Globe theatre. Wilson considers this in relation to Flavius's berating of the apparently idle labourers in the opening scene of the play, a moment which highlights the struggle for authority over festivity between the various classes. Wilson argues that this represents similar cultural tensions provoked by the scene's appearance in the new playhouse: 'If working men were present to hear the beginning of *Julius Caesar* and stayed despite it, the implication is clear that they had no business to be there. Theatre, we infer, is now itself a legitimate business with no room for the "idle".'[92] In this way, the rhetoric of the opening scene becomes part of 'the campaign to legitimize the Shakespearean stage and dissociate it from the subversiveness of artisanal culture.'[93] Wilson situates the play in the context of the social unrest that was affecting England in the 1590s as well as efforts of the gentry to assert authority and control over folk and holiday traditions; such premises are reflected in the struggle for authority over the Lupercalian festivities. In this reading, carnival emerges both in the play itself and in the circumstances of its production as 'a symbolic system over which continuous struggle to wrest its meaning was waged by competing ideologies'.[94] *Julius Caesar* therefore appears in Wilson's reading as a site of struggle for authority over festive practices that has clear social and political bearings; whilst the play may represent and, indeed, participate in the containment of these practices, Wilson concludes that it also offers a critique of this containment by exposing its fragility and the attendant violence that results in the playhouse becoming 'the bloody site of contestation between social groups.'[95]

Naomi Conn Liebler's innovative study, *Shakespeare's Festive Tragedy* (1995), which offers a counterpoint to the notion of 'festive comedy' articulated by C. L. Barber, also intervenes in debates relating to theatre and popular festivity.[96] Whereas comedy offers a temporary 'breaking out' from social restraints before returning to political stability, tragedy 'performs an uncontrollable breakage at great expense, despite human efforts, either inevitably or accidentally inadequate to contain its repercussions'; in this way, it also '"celebrates," by reconstructing, re-membering, what is lost.'[97] Liebler's reading of *Julius Caesar* focuses upon the Lupercalian festivities as the site of tensions between various social groups. For Liebler, 'the ancient, sacral, mythic center symbolized by the Lupercalia, the root definition of Roman civilization, has collapsed into a redefinition of Rome "founded" by Julius Caesar, whose appropriation is, in turn, challenged by the tribunes and the conspirators.'[98] Liebler relates such 'ceremonial ambiguity' to such contemporary developments as changes to the calendar that reduced the number of holy days as a result of the Reformation, a move that generated tensions between labourers and landowners.[99] *Julius Caesar* presents a situation in which the instances of Misrule become 'instances of traditional festive practice abruptly factionalized, maneuvered first into a political contest and then into a massacre.'[100] Festivity thus becomes the site of a struggle for authority in a way that resonated with contemporary tensions relating to festive practices.

In a similar vein, John Drakakis highlights the Globe as a site of ideological tension in his essay, 'Fashion it thus: *Julius Caesar* and the Politics of Theatrical Representation', which explores the ways in which the play interrogates the inherent ideological agendas associated with theatricality. It concludes that '*Julius Caesar* is not so much a celebration of theatre as an unmasking of the politics of representation per se' and that the play 'does not *express* meaning; rather, in its readings of Roman history, it *produces* meanings'.[101] Drakakis considers how the various characters appropriate different strategies of representation throughout the play in ways that both sustain and oppose the authority of Caesar. In Drakakis's reading,

Julius Caesar is a play in which there 'is very little ... that does not generate alternative readings, whether it be public display, ritual sacrifice, or psychic phenomenon', resulting in a 'hermeneutic instability, the consequence of the existence of two radically opposed forms of authority in Rome, that returns the analysis to the space now occupied by the theatre which can now claim both to produce *and* to interrogate ideologies.'[102] *Julius Caesar* therefore emerges in this reading as a play that scrutinizes the potential for the theatre itself to perform a self-reflexive examination of its potential to both reproduce and resist prevailing ideologies.

Richard Burt also explores the vexed issue of interpretation, particularly in relation to the Renaissance trend for the 'application' of historical events to the contemporary moment. Burt argues that in *Julius Caesar* characters themselves engage in a similar process of 'application' of historical events, but that the play also reveals that these applications are never unproblematic or politically neutral and that the 'characters do not simply fill in the blanks of an indeterminate text; there is always already an interpretation.'[103] The turn to theory, however, was not universal and one book in particular that goes against the grain of criticism of these decades is Harold Bloom's *Shakespeare: The Invention of the Human* (1998). In his chapter on *Julius Caesar*, Bloom shares Johnson's sense that something is lacking from the play and, like the early twentieth century psychoanalysts, speculates upon the subtextual father–son relationship between Caesar and Brutus; Bloom argues that this premise 'would illuminate the ambiguities of Brutus as nothing else does.'[104] Bloom's approach is curiously out of step with the high theory that characterized the late twentieth century and owes much more to the tradition of 'Bardolatry' associated with the likes of Johnson and Hazlitt, as well as the character-based approaches of Bradley.

As well as providing fresh insights into the play's politics and its engagement with the idea of Rome, late twentieth-century critics also addressed a conspicuous gap in the scholarship by approaching questions relating to gender in a number of significant feminist readings. Coppélia Kahn's study, *Roman Shakespeare: Warriors, Wounds, and Women* (1997), opens by addressing the tendency to equate the Renaissance understanding of Romanness with masculine virtue and arguing that 'Shakespeare's Roman works articulate a critique of the ideology of gender on which the Renaissance understanding of Rome was based.'[105] Kahn's reading of *Julius Caesar* focuses upon the play's grounding of Roman '*virtus* in a specific political ideology, one that both constitutes and fractures its male subjects' and is 'itself constituted by its opposition to the feminine.'[106] One of the key focal points for Kahn's reading is the way in which the ideology underpinning Roman republicanism depends upon both alliances and sharp competition between men. As Kahn argues, it is 'relations between men, not between men and women, that inculcate *virtus*, and male friendships are indistinguishable from politics itself, from which women are formally excluded.'[107] Like Miles, Kahn also considers the role of stoicism, especially its overriding virtue of constancy and the attainability of this virtue for Roman women. This is particularly evident in Act 2, Scene 1, in which Portia wounds herself in the thigh, a move that 'imitates a man's constancy' and 'destabilizes the gendered concept of virtue', resulting in a situation in which 'constancy is haunted by its feminine opposites, making Portia's wound ambiguously, undecideably feminine *and* masculine.'[108] Kahn's reading therefore offers illuminating insights into the vexed questions relating to ideologies of gender at play in Shakespeare's representation of 'Romanness'.

Another example of feminist scholarship on the play is Mary Hamer's contribution to the 'Writers and their Work' series on *Julius Caesar* (1998). Hamer's book focuses upon those who are marginalized in the midst of Shakespeare's play, taking as its starting point the premise that the play is a sustained interrogation of the ways in which 'the powerful Romans treated the nameless men inside Rome' and the 'relations between women and men under such a regime.'[109] Hamer's second chapter makes this connection explicit by focusing upon the opening scenes of the play and comparing the Tribunes' hectoring of the public to the way in which 'Calphurnia is isolated and subjected to public disgrace', leaving the attention of the audience 'directed to the figure of a woman, standing silent at the hub of Rome'.[110] For Hamer, the key factor that determines the statuses of the various characters is language and the ways in which it serves to normalize Roman values, a point that can be discerned in the play's representations of such issues as masculinity, ritual and marriage. This is suggested in the links established between Calphurnia and Portia as women 'who bring into the world of the play knowledge that is unwelcome, knowledge that has been acquired by accurate observation on their part.'[111] Brutus's silence when confronted by Portia is, for Hamer, due to the fact that he has been circumscribed by 'the language that Rome with its particular values and traditions made available to him', and Portia's attempts to penetrate this silence represent a 'triumph of her Roman education' which has 'taught her to despise what she feels as a woman and has cut her off from the promptings of her own voice.'[112] Calphurnia's dream, on the other hand, represents insights that go against the masculine values promulgated in Roman discourse and it 'is because Caesar only pays attention to the voices of men that he will defy Calphurnia's common sense and venture outside.'[113] Hamer's reading of the play therefore highlights the dire consequences, for numerous characters, of the city's investment in Roman values and the action of the conspirators 'only confirms Roman order: it is impossible for men whose interior life is disavowed and misnamed by this order to produce change.'[114]

The studies by Kahn and Hamer complement a range of insightful articles taking a feminist approach to *Julius Caesar*. An essay by Gail Kern Paster combines feminist scholarship with the increasing prominence of the body in cultural and critical theory to examine the motif of blood in the play. According to Paster, *Julius Caesar* represents a case in which the 'meaning of blood and bleeding becomes part of an insistent rhetoric of bodily conduct in which the bleeding body signifies as a shameful token of uncontrol, as a failure of physical self-mastery particularly associated with women.'[115] Caesar's infirm physical body is frequently associated with an apparently feminine lack of self-control, a point crystallized by his bleeding corpse becoming allegorized as 'a lactating figure, a statue or fountain lactating blood.'[116] Caesar's body is also the focus for an article by Cynthia Marshall which draws on poststructuralist and psychoanalytical theory as well as feminist criticism. One of the key points upon which Marshall focuses is the situation of Portia's wounding of her own thigh in relation to the cycle of male violence dramatized by the play. This is a moment when, because she is 'both wielder and victim of the knife/phallus, Portia momentarily brings gender opposition into equilibrium – but only at the cost of violence to herself.'[117] For Barbara Parker, Rome is also the site in which contemporary concerns relating to masculinity are interrogated and 'integrally allied' with questions relating to sexuality and religion to 'form the basis for the subtextual theme of the play.'[118] The play is read alongside contemporary sources to suggest that its themes and motifs align it with Protestant propaganda in which Rome's associations with illicit sexuality and the old religion of Catholicism, two premises that are elided in such sources. In her reading of the play, Barbara J. Bono argued that its confrontation with the effects of history reveals deep-rooted anxieties about the source of this history and its relation to the maternal body.[119] Feminist criticism provided fresh insights into the play's representations of patriarchy, history and the corrosive effects of the drive to attain and uphold the values associated with 'Romanness'.

At the beginning of this chapter, we considered *Julius Caesar* as a transitional play. It is therefore fitting that the play has been made to respond to the various transitions that have taken place within the field of Shakespearean criticism. As well as figuring prominently in the contentious debates over the posthumous reputation of Shakespeare, and in his elevation to the status of national and cultural icon, the play has continued to resonate in such twentieth-century critical movements as character study, formalism and source criticism, and in the fields of new historicism, cultural materialism and feminist criticism that were flourishing towards the end of the century. As the chapter on 'The State of the Art' (Chapter 3) will show, contemporary critics continue to find new and exciting ways of approaching the play as well as steering familiar debates, such as those relating to the play's politics and representations of masculinity, in new directions. The play may not enjoy the reputations of the great tragedies, but the rich and eclectic range of critical responses it has generated over the course of the first 400 years of its afterlife are testament to its enduring appeal. *Caesar* may not always have been praised, but it has most certainly not been buried.

2

Performance History

Andrew James Hartley

Julius Caesar is not an easy play to stage for reasons already referenced in the introduction to this volume: it seems to peak too early, loses its title character and several key supporting roles around the mid-point and seems unsure of who really drives the plot. It is also almost devoid of humour (which is unusual for Shakespeare, even for a tragedy), bereft of romance (and has female speaking roles in only three scenes) and ends in a flurry of bitty fights centring on characters few of whom we have seen before. More than any other major Shakespeare play, its profile has traditionally depended on its suitability to the schoolroom rather than the stage. There its absence of bawdiness and its preoccupation with rhetoric, its investment in an ancient past and in civics have been considered assets, though none of them would fare well in the marketing brochure for a stage production.

Simply put, *Julius Caesar* is not a sexy play.

However, it has been, and while much of what drove its appeal in the pre-twentieth-century period may seem alien to us, we have, in recent years, rediscovered the play as a viable and gripping piece of theatre. In this chapter I will explore the major trends in the play's stage history, touching on some of the landmark productions which have best manifested or shaped that history and the tastes and ideas which came with it. To begin with, let me establish a couple of basic assumptions about what I think theatre is. With *Caesar*, as with all Shakespeare, there is no 'straight' production, a reading of the text which somehow becomes three-dimensional on stage. Any production is mediated by the material conditions of production – the nature of the performance space, say, or the appearance and approach of a particular actor – and these are essential components of what theatre is, because theatre (or indeed film) takes place in an equally material (social and historical) reality, one in which ideas based on readings of the play cannot exist by themselves. Those ideas must be embodied, and to embody ideas is to change them, to give them shape in ways which are not, cannot be, dictated by the script which does not say how tall an actor should be, how he should stand or what he should be thinking. Theatre is a constructive as well as an interpretative medium. As a result, every production which responds to a play is necessarily different, and that would be true even if not a single word of the script was altered. All production is adaptation. All performance is new.

The performance history of *Julius Caesar* is unusual in the Shakespeare canon because it has a very particular start date: 21 September 1599. On this day a Swiss traveller called Thomas Platter crossed the river Thanes to the south bank with some friends to see a production of the play at one of the great thatched theatres there: almost certainly the newly built Globe. It is extremely rare to have this kind of specific reference, and the earliest performances of most other Shakespeare plays are largely a matter of conjecture, but Platter is famously short on detail except to say that the show was good, that it had about fifteen actors and that it ended with an elegant dance by four of the company, two dressed as men and two as women. It is not exactly a wealth of information on which to base a sense of what happened on stage, and the one (to our twenty-first century eyes) surprising detail

– the dance – seems to have been a familiar element of theatrical custom rather than something specific to this particular play. It reminds us that the women's parts would have been played by boys, and suggests that the production was well received, but that's about all.

There is other evidence to suggest the play was successful on stage when it was first mounted. It was staged several times for the royal court (at Whitehall in 1612–13 and twice for King Charles I in 1636 and 1638), seems to be referenced several times in the first decade of the seventeenth century, and is praised in expressly theatrical terms in the prefatory verses written by Leonard Digges for the First Folio of Shakespeare's works (1623), and expanded for the 1640 edition:

> So have I seen, when Caesar would appear,
> And on the Stage at half-sword parlay were,
> *Brutus and Cassius*: oh how the Audience,
> Were ravish'd, with what wonder they went thence ...[1]

Again, the emphasis (as one might expect of a preface) is on how well received the play was rather than on what we might call 'theatrical choices', but when the theatres reopened after the civil war and the archival record becomes significantly more comprehensive, the point is reinforced: *Julius Caesar* was a popular play on stage (editions were reprinted at least six times between 1684 and 1691) and remained so till 1751.

The course of the play's early career has, of course, as much to do with larger events in the culture as it does with the content of the play itself, and what is clear from those productions where we have surviving records, reviews or performance scripts, is that that content was perceived to shift significantly over time. The heart of the play is the assassination of an allegedly tyrannical leader, and the bloody aftermath of that killing, but what we are supposed to think of those events is less clear. Who are the heroes? Who are the villains? Which characters pose the greatest threat to the state, and what ideas about statehood are being championed? In short, what is the play's attitude to rebellion, its political 'message'?

While such questions might seem the stuff of familiar literary analysis or classroom discussion, they take on greater urgency in the theatre, where the very means of presentation can stir the emotions in dramatically evocative or manipulative ways. Such a theatre might be a cauldron not unlike the forum in which Mark Antony pushes his audience into murderous fury. Political theatre rouses passion as well as thought, and as well as changing minds, it can raise hands bent on doing something *right now*.

As this collection makes clear, the ideological frame of such an event is complex and emotive, with Caesar frequently seen as representing the very idea of monarchy. For seventeenth-century England there could be fewer more contentious subjects than the reach of royal power and the authority of the people to remove any king or queen believed to have abused their position. As I mentioned in the introduction, ideas of lawful regicide had been percolating for much of the sixteenth century, particularly in the secret discourse of those repressed, banished or executed in the name of religion. Ever since Henry VIII's break from Roman Catholicism, debates about the limits of monarchical authority had been thrown into sharp relief. The religious back and forth enacted by Henry's children on their accessions to the throne (Edward VI, the adamant protestant; Mary, the equally adamant Catholic; and Elizabeth, under whom England became permanently protestant once more) fuelled the fire, so that fifty years after *Julius Caesar* was first staged, the English parliament felt able to try and publically execute King Charles I for tyranny. That the nation was bitterly divided on this subject was manifested not only by the civil war which raged until 1651, but by the restoration of the monarchy in 1660.

When the theatres reopened after the Restoration, they did so changed. Gone were the outdoor playhouses which had flourished on the south bank of the Thames, and since women could now appear on stage, largely gone too were the boy actors who would have played Calphurnia and Portia. One exception was Edward Kynaston, who continued to play women's roles but who also starred (from 1670 onwards) as Mark Antony in the frequent revivals of Shakespeare's *Caesar* at Drury Lane. It is a telling choice, I think, that an actor who was famously feminine on- and off-stage should play this particular role, suggesting as seems true throughout this period that the Caesar–Antony relationship was figured as an especially close one, and that Antony's actions in the second part of the play emerge not from political cynicism or a bid to power, but from passionate outrage at what was done to his friend. This was a markedly royalist period, and though there is little evidence on which to build conjecture, we might expect audience sympathies to have been with Antony's faction, seeing figures like Brutus in the light of the now vilified republican Oliver Cromwell, who had precipitated the death of the last king and whose head was dug up and displayed in Westminster as that of a traitor until 1685.

There is no hard evidence of what the script of these productions looked like, and though printers of the day published the Folio text and claimed it to represent what was then being acted at the Theatre Royal, this is questionable. Speech prefixes were altered to represent the play as it had been cast (with Murellus replaced by Caska, and Cicero by Trebonius), but the printed dialogue doesn't fully accommodate such changes. As such, these printings cannot be used as an argument that the Folio's text was played largely uncut.

The cutting of Murellus and Cicero is interesting, however, particularly since roles which were almost always cut in later stagings (such as Cinna the Poet) were kept. I have argued elsewhere that replacing Murellus with Caska and Cicero with Trebonius may indicate a memory of how the play was originally staged, those roles being doubled.[2] One of the theatrical problems of the play is the way some of the key characters of the first half vanish in the second, creating the oddity of some of the play's most emotive moments (Brutus's and Cassius's suicides, for instance) in which the people on stage around them are almost unknown to the audience. This is, I think, a modern problem, one which comes from the act of reading the play and giving those character names particular weight, or of productions which have the luxury of dozens of actors so that no role has to be doubled. On the early modern stage, it seems likely that several of these roles were doubled and played by the same actors, so that even if the character technically had a different name in the second half, the audience saw the same presence in the actor's face and voice. Caska's appearance in the opening scene might go some way to explaining why he joins the conspiracy, as well as minimizing the play's clutter of speaking roles which is largely a consequence of Shakespeare's following Plutarch's *Lives* a little too literally. On stage, unless there is actual contradiction between the parts, roles can be easily, seamlessly and productively combined in the body of an actor without disrupting the story.

Thomas Betterton took over the role of Brutus in 1682 and played the part into the first decade of the next century, establishing the character as the play's tragic hero and playing him with dignity and an aura of patriotism. Antony was no less patriotic, but was also driven by grief over Caesar's death, and the high point of the play became the tent scene (4.3) in which the stoic Brutus faced down the irascible Cassius in a stately verbal war about the rights and wrongs of their predicament. The dominant model of the play which prevailed well into the nineteenth century (and, in places, much longer) was thus established: noble and heroic Romans debating the public good and making principled (if misguided) choices in the name of right and the city for whom they were prepared to lay down their lives. This nobility of content was matched with a nobility of style and delivery, key speeches being turned into exercises in oratory, so that the play became a study in civics and rhetoric.

Under Queen Anne and King George I, monarchical power in England was curtailed, and in this climate Brutus became still more admirable, not a populist but a Whig, an aristocratic patriot standing up to royal absolutism. The performance text of the day (adapted by John Dryden and William Davenant) clarified this position further, adding heroic lines to Brutus's suicide monologue which (in classic Whig fashion) managed to champion the idea of Rome while demeaning its people as 'slavish'. The early eighteenth century was also the period in which Shakespeare rose to the level of the National Poet, and *Caesar* was both the first Shakespeare play known to have been staged at a school (in 1728), and, ten years later, was the play used to drive the fund-raising for the playwright's lavish monument in Westminster Abbey. In each case the play was offered as a model of Whiggish notions of nationalistic freedom from monarchical servitude. The political climate changed in the latter part of the century, however, with the general domestic popularity of George III and the highly circumscribed royal power he wielded, and with Caesar's anti-royalist associations well established the play was staged less frequently and not at all between 1781 and 1812.

John Philip Kemble's production of that year brought the play to Covent Garden in what came to be known as the Grand Style, a massive, pictorial idealization of Rome with thirteen lavishly decorated scenic locations and a still more noble (and therefore simplified) notion of the play's heroic characters. The murder of Cinna the poet was still cut, as was the proscription scene (4.1) in which Antony and Octavius bicker over who will be executed as connected to the conspiracy and how they will gut Caesar's will of what was promised to the common people. The edit (the play was cut by 450 lines) stripped the principal roles of their ambiguities and allowed a stately form of honour and stoicism which was manifested in the very gait of the actors: grandiose, ponderous and impressive. This was an ideal Rome, a Rome of abstraction, of principles and of glorified antiquity. Costumes were historical (modelled largely on ancient statuary) and the whole became a tableau, a pageant in which hundreds of extras played window dressing to history making speeches from monumental figures.

In the 1830s and 1840s, William Charles Macready (like Kemble, an actor/manager and impresario) maintained a version of Kemble's approach, increasing still further the number of supernumeraries, though his acting style was a little less grand, a little more human, and the countless extras were now allowed to move around, rather than being clustered into statuesque groupings as Kemble had had them. Macready, like Kemble, played Brutus, and any business of the crowd was silenced when it was the star's turn to speak. The forum scene for Kemble had been a 'set piece' exercise in performative oratory, the citizens of Rome not yet being a thinking or aggressive presence who had real power in what was going to happen (a point made doubly clear by the exercising of the Cinna the poet scene): the major speeches of the play were thus performed in a kind of theatrical vacuum for the restrained admiration of the (off-stage) audience. In Macready's version the crowd began to develop some life of its own and this, like the less unified and idealized approach to the major roles, was a step in a new direction in which the Roman citizens played a decisive role rather than being merely a part of the backdrop against which the heroes showed their greatness.

This new direction was given a still more dramatic shape when a German language production, produced by the Duke of Saxe-Meiningen, was performed at Drury Lane in May 1881. This was the first documented production to truly emphasize the crowd, to make them a real character and arbiter of power in Rome, something achieved by the casting of actual actors (not mere supers) who were encouraged (in the then newly emerging realist mode which would be given greatest voice by Constantin Stanislavski) to think of their parts as glimpses of real people with opinions and back stories of their own. For the first time since the Restoration, the forum scene trumped the tent scene as the play's climax, forcing Antony to struggle with a mass of apathetic and self-interested people just to get their attention. While many critics thought the production went too far in knocking the leads off their pedestals (and that the production lost energy after the forum scene as a result), an important shift had taken place, one which would shape future productions.

Tellingly, the next major production, that by Herbert Beerbohm Tree in 1898 which ran for over 100 performances, retained the massive visuals and the large, volatile crowds but was also the first time that an actor manager chose to play not Brutus but Antony. Tree edited the play into three acts, each ending with a monologue from Antony and a curtain call; anything which took stage time away from him was trimmed (including the tent scene), as was anything which might reflect badly on him (such as the proscription scene and the murder of Cinna the poet). Despite the shift away from Brutus and towards a more responsive crowd, this was still a heroic production, and Tree was not interested in an Antony who might be seen as a cynical political manipulator. Nor was he interested in reducing the scale of the pageantry which, if anything, got bigger, now featuring extended street scenes featuring Roman children playing games which had to be cleared by lictors and soldiers (all dressed in the most meticulously authentic costumes current archaeology could furnish). But for all their colourful presence and their belligerence during the forum scene, the crowds were still contained by the oratory of the major characters, and the second act's curtain fell after Tree's Antony spoke the final words of Act 3, Scene 2. Of the murderous violence he had sparked in the crowd, there was still no sign, and while Caesar himself (played by Charles Fulton) had more dignity than had been the case in the recent past, this was a production cut from the same heroic cloth as its immediate predecessors.

One of the shifts of the late Victorian and Edwardian periods was a move away from the rigorous textual cutting and interpolating which had been the rule in the late eighteenth and early nineteenth centuries. Tree's production cut only 150 lines and did away with the augmentations which had been in common use since the Dryden/Davenant adaptation, a move in keeping with the comparatively new veneration of Shakespeare as author. F. R. Benson's productions between 1883 and 1915 drew particular attention at the Memorial theatre in Stratford, where the play foregrounded the play text not just in terms of its cutting (which, for all the rhetoric to the contrary was not significantly different from Tree's), but also in an emphasis on declamatory verse-speaking at the expense of large scale visual elements. This latter was as much a budgetary concern as it was an artistic one, and though the resultant productions moved faster without the numerous time-consuming set changes, critics still complained of being bored. Whatever else Benson claimed to be doing, his sense of the play was not significantly different from that of the London theatres he was trying to challenge. After the First World War, Benson was succeeded at Stratford by William Bridges-Adams, who took his predecessor's ideas further in pursuit of a quasi-Elizabethan approach to staging Shakespeare. In real terms not that much changed (these were not day-lit performances with boy actors playing women, for instance, nor was there any serious attempt at Elizabethan costuming) save the attitude to the playing script itself which was now the unadorned Folio text with only a couple of significant cuts (including Cinna the poet). This was a model of Shakespeare set in opposition not only to the lavish displays in London but also to the newest form of visual entertainment: cinema. While generations of Shakespeareans have celebrated Bridges-Adams's return (so-called) to a form of textual purity, the productions were rearguard actions, conservative throwbacks to a notion of the past which never really existed. While there is no question that the fuller text complicated *Caesar*'s Romans – particularly in reinstating the proscription scene which revealed a more conniving and pointedly unheroic Antony – the productions themselves did not capture the imagination of the general public, and where they were praised it was not in the visceral terms of theatrical experience, but in the language of people for whom something old, something which was once more widely valued, had been enshrined or cased in crystal. In his own way, Bridges-Adams was rehearsing the Elizabethan past (or rather a past) in much the same way that Kemble had rehearsed a Roman past, each viewing the period in question through a kind of cleansing lens. As such, both were enacting a species of heroic fantasy as much as they were presenting history.

However, the 1930s was a period of extraordinary political upheaval in Europe, and while the productions of Bridges-Adams positively avoided any contemporary context, preferring to stay anchored in the past, one very young director decided to do the opposite. The result was a production of such startling originality that it fundamentally altered the way Shakespeare was performed, and transformed what had become an increasingly stiff and dusty play into something urgent and electrifying. The director was Orson Welles who, at the age of twenty-two, directed the first 'modern dress' *Caesar* at the Mercury theatre, New York, in 1937.

For much of its history, American *Caesars* had been pale imitations of their British counterparts. Little performed in the revolutionary years, the play had become a theatrical staple in the nineteenth century, a fact tied both to the rise of Shakespeare's cultural standing, to its allegedly republican sympathies and to the prominence of oratory in American politics and, by extension, education. *Caesar* was studied as a model both of Roman, patriotic virtue and of rhetorical performance. Character tended to be subordinated to abstract principle and elocution, though one popular production is especially worthy of mention. It starred Edwin Booth as Brutus and played in New York at Booth's own (short-lived) theatre in 1871–2. Booth owed much to Macready as an actor, but he was neither tall nor impressively built and had made a name for himself particularly for his performance of Hamlet, which had been very much in the romantic vein. Of course, his name had also been made for him less positively by his brother, John Wilkes Booth, who had assassinated President Abraham Lincoln in 1865 while quoting the historical Brutus: '*Sic Semper Tyrannis*' ('Thus always to tyrants'). By the 1870s, Lincoln was – to many Americans – a martyr, and any production of *Caesar* risked the possibility of all too concrete an association. Edwin Booth had played Brutus with his brothers Junius and John Wilkes (who took the role of Antony) the year before the assassination as part of the fund raiser for the Shakespeare monument in Central Park, but in the light of subsequent events, attention on Edwin's later Brutus was unusually heightened. Drawing on his Hamlet, Booth played Brutus as a private and conflicted man, and while some critics accused him of sentimentalizing the part, he both avoided seeming to glamourize the assassin, and introduced a subtler take on the character, one which was thoughtful and reflective, even tortured, rather than heroic and statuesque.

This notion of Brutus was taken considerably further in Welles's 1937 production (entitled *Caesar: Death of a Dictator*), which acknowledged recent history in ways no production of the play had done before: it embraced the end of the heroic which had been enacted by the First World War and, even more urgently, anticipated the Second World War, which was already looming in Europe in the rise of Fascist regimes under Hitler and Mussolini. Welles was very much a man of his time, and his notion of what he was doing was in some ways in accord with the actor/manager star-vehicles of the previous century even as it made huge strides into modernism in terms of both the production's content and the technology he used to convey it.

The production had several distinctive features. First, and perhaps most strikingly, it was probably the first major production of Shakespeare to be staged in the clothes of the present moment since the original stagings at the Globe. Those clothes took a few different forms: military uniforms reminiscent of those goose-stepping through the newsreel footage from Europe, contemporary trench coats and fedoras for the crowds, and a few black shirts for the government paramilitaries who occupied the space between. The production relied heavily on bold lighting, particularly the so-called Nuremberg effect: large spots angled up from the ground such as were familiar from Hitler's dramatic rallies. Famously, Welles also put the murder of Cinna the poet back in, the first director to do so for over two and a half centuries, and the scene became the highlight of the production.

Apart from the visceral power of the moment itself, one of the reasons for the scene's prominence was because Welles cut the latter half of the play so drastically, reducing the fourth and fifth acts by two thirds), so that Cinna died surprisingly close to the end of the show. After that theatrical coup de grâce, there was only a truncated version of the tent scene, some lines of farewell between Brutus and Cassius before the battle, and Antony's speech over Brutus's corpse. All the fighting was cut, as was the proscription scene which had so recently reappeared in British productions.

The result was that, for all its pointing to what was happening overseas, the production's final focus was oddly domestic. Its familiarly dressed crowds resembled the strikes and protests known all too well by Americans in the Great Depression, and they focused on one of the key words of the day: isolationism. Welles was portraying the rise of Fascism in Germany, Spain and Italy, but Cinna the poet was clearly an American surrounded by Americans poised to turn lethal when given permission by authority. Welles's own Brutus was a fumbling intellectual, out of his depth and incapable of withstanding the sheer brute power and theatrics of Caesar and Antony. With the battles gone (and modern dress productions always struggle to render battles written to be staged with swords instead of machine guns), this was finally a show not about military power but about politics, theatrical rhetoric and the crisis of the individual conscience faced with an expressly modern will to totalizing power.

Critical response was largely enthusiastic, if sometimes unclear on what the production was finally saying. Much of the praise fell on Welles himself who, despite his youth, was already both prodigy and theatrical enfant terrible, and in this too the show proved a kind of watershed moment. While Welles was working in the actor/manager tradition of the previous century, he was also very much a director in the new mode, a man who, extraordinarily, used a double to play Brutus throughout rehearsal so that Welles could focus on the energy and stage pictures of the whole. His aggressive cutting, his intellectual, aesthetic and emotional manipulation of the audience was done not in pursuit of the true or complete play, or the embodying of a venerable past, but in presenting a very particular inflection, a 'take' on the play designed not to be definitive but, on the contrary, to be partial, to shine a very particular light onto parts of the play and offer it up as new and compelling.

And it was. One of the odd consequences of its success, however, was that for much of the rest of the century the representation of Fascism became the play's default theatrical position. Welles's shadow loomed over every subsequent staging, and it was some time before productions managed to step out of that shadow and find other ways to make the play speak with anything like Welles's insistence and urgency.

To further stifle the appeal of the play on stage, the mid-point of the century also produced one of the most successful Shakespeare films ever made, that directed by Joe Mankiewicz for MGM in 1953, starring James Mason as Brutus, John Gielgud as Cassius, and – most surprisingly – Marlon Brando as Antony. Cinematic Shakespeare had largely been the purview of the British film industry, particularly in the person of Laurence Olivier, whose *Hamlet* and *Henry V* had put Hollywood efforts to shame, so its numerous awards[3] and box office success were especially telling. From the vantage of the twenty-first century, the success of the film might be hard to understand, and after Welles's production it feels like a bit of a throwback. Gone is all the contemporary relevance, lost among all those toga-clad Romans speechifying among all that white marble. The film was even shot in black and white, contrary to many Hollywood films of the day, including another Roman epic released two years before, *Quo Vadis*, from which *Caesar* borrowed some of its sets. Its use of British leads as the principal conspirators seems like a deliberate attempt to cash in on a respectable notion of Shakespeare and it is hard now to see much of mid-twentieth-century America in the film at all.

Mankiewicz knew all about Welles's production at the Mercury, because his own producer – John Housemann – had also worked on that show, but his decision not to pursue echoes of Nazis has sometimes been considered politically cowardly. But the Nazi threat was long over by 1953, and if there were new dangerous political entities, they looked a lot more like Welles's trench-coated crowd than his ranting, Fascist Antony.

Making political films in 1950s Hollywood was a perilous business, one which risked getting your name added to the infamous Black List, which could be career ending, or worse. This was a period under the shadow of what came to be called McCarthyism, when fear of Communist activists and sympathisers had portions of the US government and populace on the kind of high alert which routinely strayed into the territory of the witch hunt. Senator Joseph McCarthy was the most prominent voice on the anti-Communist crusade, but much of the actual privacy-invading investigation was handled by J. Edgar Hoover and the FBI, as well as the House Committee on UnAmerican Activities (HUAC). Rumour, guilt by association, groundless accusation: these became the methodologies of HUAC, and they were targeted in plays such as Arthur Miller's *The Crucible*.

In this climate, Mankiewicz's film deserves a second look. What it was praised for at the time tended to be unobjectionable – the undeniable passion and clarity of its stars, in particular – but though its politics went less commented upon, that does not mean they weren't there. A number of things are striking about the film, not least its minimization of the play's supernatural dimension. The storm is just a storm. Calphurnia's dream is just a dream and one the film doesn't actually show us. Even the soothsayer's prophecies seem to have more in common with a whispering political climate than with mystical insight. Caesar's ghost appears briefly before the battle, but only Brutus sees it, as if it might have been only in his mind, and other ominous portents like the eagles which abandon the conspirators' standards before Phillipi are cut. This is very much a real world of real people, and it is in those people that the dangers lie.

A year and a half before filming on *Caesar* started, Mankiewicz was ambushed by the right-wing director of Hollywood epics, Cecil B. DeMille, who attempted to oust him from his position as the president of the Screen Directors Guild on the grounds of 'un-American' leanings and his refusal to force a loyalty oath through the membership. In a remarkable and incendiary 6-hour meeting, DeMille attempted to turn the assembly of Hollywood's most active and famous directors against him, and he did so through a pastiche of Antony's funeral oration. Throughout the speech, DeMille used Antony's disingenuous 'honourable men' tag – here modified to 'honorable, good Americans' – to defame Mankiewicz and those who stood with him. He invoked the deaths of American soldiers overseas and implied that such atrocities were fuelled by those at home whose patriotism was not all it should be.

The speech backfired. The crowd turned on DeMille and he, alongside his other two co-conspirators (they were referred to as 'the triumvirate'), was forced to resign from the board.

Mankiewicz returned to this remarkable evening several times in his films *People Will Talk* and *No Way Out*, but *Caesar* seems to do so as well, albeit in a different way. Brando's Antony resembles DeMille, popular, charismatic and brutally Machiavellian, re-enacting that fateful night, but this time winning, turning the people with his rhetoric and pushing them into vengeful violence for his own ends. Mankiewicz's version of the proscription scene is one of the film's highlights, showing Antony's callousness and his will to power, not least in that chilling moment when he sits down alone and turns the bust of Caesar to face him, smiling that enigmatic smile of his.

The battle is fittingly presented not as a pitched fight between equals on the plains of Phillipi, but as a canyon ambush, more familiar to a cowboys and Indians flick of the same period. Antony here is not the heroic soldier who shows up in productions on stage and screen, but a watchful general, orchestrating the dubious assault on the hapless armies of Brutus and Cassius much like a movie director orchestrating a

Hollywood epic. He waits forever before ordering his archers to open fire, showing the ruthless deliberation we glimpsed earlier beneath his public persona in the forum, when he turns away from the crowd to weep, but is actually just listening to their responses, gauging his next move. If Welles's production had been about the crowd swayed by Fascist appeals to its basest instincts, Mankiewicz's film returned its attention to the manipulators of that crowd (though the murder of Cinna the poet was cut – against Mankiewicz's wishes – by the studio), and the troubling sense that, in the current political climate, they were where the true power lay.

The visibility of the MGM film and its triumph in what was generally seen as traditional terms scared *Caesar* off many a provincial stage over the next couple of decades, and when major companies tackled the play, they did so clearly with the film in mind. For British avant-garde directors (for whom any American contextualizing political content was especially hard to see in the film), the play was something which needed to be reinvented in expressly modernist terms, though the forms of that modernism varied and the results were generally not considered terribly successful. Lindsay Anderson mounted the play in 1964 at the Royal Court in London, a theatre known for its left-leaning domestic realism, and set out to counter not just the elocutionary power of Mankiewicz's film but the brand of verse-speaking emphasized by Peter Hall and the relatively recently established Royal Shakespeare Company and subsequently at the National Theatre. Anderson's actors wore street clothes, performed in an intimate space close to the audience on an abstractly modernist set, and – most importantly – treated the text (cut, but not extensively) as ordinary speech. The result was small, ordinary and actor-driven. Critics hated it.

In fact they more than hated it. Newspaper reviews of the day were loaded with a kind of furious outrage which treated the production as nothing less than an assault on British values as enshrined within what the various writers assumed Shakespeare on stage should be. Anderson responded in kind, writing letters to the papers blasting the critics' phony reverence and asserting the importance of sense over sound in speaking Shakespeare's lines. And a few critics agreed with him, finding in the production a vision of a debased and unheroic present perfectly articulated by the play and this production, a 'picture of a world in sick decline, where the magic power of the *imperium* rests on the shoulders of a nut-like, neurotic old man.'[4] And indeed such a remark indicates why the more common dislike of the production was so tainted with indignation; however much the critical response was couched in terms of the inadequacy of the halting, conversational verse-speaking, the production was reviled because it was taken to be anti-heroic, a belittling of Shakespeare and of the grandeur of a noble past the play presented. In other words, in spite of Welles's production, the British 1960s had fallen back on a version of the play enshrined in the high-school curriculum and manifested on stage a hundred years or more before, a play about high-minded Romans doing elevated things and, more to the point, speaking of them. A case in point is Robert Speaight, who savaged the production in his review for *Shakespeare Quarterly*, and then wrote to *The Times* in response to Anderson's belligerent defense, arguing that Shakespeare knew things about drama 'far above The heads of our clever young men who so conscientiously contemplate the gutter' (31 December 1964). There was no gratuitous violence in the production (the assassination was actually quite stylized), no sex or nudity. It was those street clothes, that small ordinariness of speech and action which was lampooned as contemplating the 'gutter', and as such such criticism says more, I think, about what people persisted in thinking Shakespeare should be than it does about the inadequacy of the production.

Four years later John Barton directed the play for the RSC, using something of Anderson's character-centred approach but marrying it to a more typically metrically-centred notion of verse speaking. Ian Richardson garnered the best reviews as a fiery and dangerous Cassius, but the production as a whole was considered drab and boring. Barton's brand of modernism was to embrace the ambiguities and contradictions of the text in terms of character, rather than ironing them out into a monolithic 'take' on the play, à la Welles. In resisting a single reading of the play, however, he chose to set it unspecifically, clothing the cast in generic leathers that might have been Elizabethan but seemed to some more like modern dress. There was no spectacle to the show, no scale, and while the production did not incite the rage that Anderson's did, most left underwhelmed, concerned that some of the problem might be the play itself for not taking a strong enough stance towards its subject matter.

Trevor Nunn attempted to rediscover some of the play's old glamour and visual power when he directed it for the RSC in 1972. Responding in part to the rise of spectacular musicals (*Jesus Christ Superstar* opened the previous year), Nunn (who was also the RSC's Artistic Director) organized a massive refurbishment of Stratford's Memorial theatre. As part of this work, the stage was equipped with a whole new system of expensive technological improvements which were shown off for the first time in his *Caesar*. They included hydraulic lifts, a rolling stage which could created numerous levels, and revolving periaktoi. These were used to rediscover something of the pageantry of Victorian productions, though they did so in a stylized rather than realist fashion, and the constantly reconfigured stage was more about creating different *spaces* than it was about creating recognizable *places*. The setting was another vaguely timeless blend of the Imperial Roman and the Fascist, and featured lots of banners and chanting black shirts scattered around the largely white playing space, but the sheer scale of the stage effects rather dwarfed the actors. When parts of it malfunctioned, the production proceeded without them, and when the show transferred to the Aldwych in London, a theatre which could not recreate the stage effects, all the spectacle was dropped, to the relief of some of the actors. However impressive the stage effects had been, they were not used by subsequent productions and soon fell into disrepair.

The critics' uncertainty about Nunn's production – wowed by the visuals, but frequently anxious about them, as if they were detracting from the actors and the lines – is typical of mid-twentieth-century productions where audiences did not seem to know what they wanted from the play. It was famous, familiar and respectable, but audiences seemed to want productions which were at once bolder in approach, but somehow did justice to the complexity of the play's characters while also offering the old virtue of stateliness in look and sound. They liked the idea of a Wellesian broad-brush approach, but also wanted the 'real' play – all of it – so as to be sure they were getting their Shakespeare straight and unadulterated. While other plays like *Lear*, *Hamlet* and *A Midsummer Night's Dream* were finding a contemporary voice on stage that many found electrifying, *Caesar* was caught in its own statuesque past, more monument than piece of living art, and consequently dissatisfying.

By the end of the 1970s, Margaret Thatcher was Britain's prime minister and would remain so until late in 1990, pulling the nation sharply to the right and ruling over an increasingly divided country, many of whose citizens loved or loathed her with a power which had not been seen in British politics in living memory. Whichever side people found themselves on, it was difficult to argue with the idea that she was autocratic, militaristic, dictatorial, combative and inflexible. She made war with Argentina over the Falkland Islands, championed the free market (with her transatlantic colleague, Ronald Reagan), privatized or dismantled industry and built a new, London-centred financial elite. In 1984 she was the target of an IRA bomb which left five people dead and many others seriously injured, an event which in no way softened her manner or political leanings.

She was, in other words, a Caesar figure, which goes some way to explaining the rash of RSC productions of the play:

Between the formation of the RSC's permanent company in 1960 and 1979, there had been only four productions of the play (one about every four and a half years). Between 1983 and 1995, however, there were five (one almost every two years), more than there were *Winter's Tales*, *Twelfth Nights*, *Othellos*, *Hamlets*, *Lears*, or *Macbeths*, more than any other history play (English or Roman), more in fact, than any play except *Romeo and Juliet* which also had five major productions.[5]

What is remarkable about these productions, however, is that they were generally not well received, but that the company kept returning to the play anyway. Of course, a couple of problems are immediately apparent. For one, Thatcher's government was fiercely opposed to arts funding and, insisting that art should be fiscally self-supporting, gutted state support of many theatres, forcing them to downsize or close outright. The issue, of course, was not simply about money. It was also about what kinds of theatre were being staged. In 1980, for instance, the National Theatre was threatened with the discontinuation of its public funding and key members threatened with prosecution for indecency over Howard Brenton's thinly veiled commentary on the so-called 'Irish problem' in *The Romans In Britain*. The most aggressively leftist companies had their funding suspended, but others survived or even expanded operations, though they did so with a clear sense that what they staged would have an impact upon their fiscal status, particularly in the case of Arts Council funding. The RSC weathered the storm, but there can be little doubt that the climate dulled their more subversive political edge.

A simpler explanation of the paradox of *Caesar*'s appeal, but its lack of success on stage, might be put thus. Thatcher might look like Caesar in many respects, but in one she was clearly different: she was a woman. At this stage in history only minor companies or those which advertised a more radically adaptive agenda would consider regendering the title role in *Julius Caesar*. As a result, multiple RSC productions sought general association with the current British regime, but none actually represented it, and that discrepancy stripped the productions of the immediate relevancy which – judging by their programmes which were stuffed with reference to current political issues and leaders – they were trying to achieve. The consequences were productions which – not for the first time – were vague, unspecific in terms of setting, uncertain in their 'take' and lost in the very familiarity of their speeches.

Of these, three are worthy of special mention. David Daniels in 1983 used live video capture and projection to convey key moments, such as Mark Antony's grief-stricken funeral oration, making the crowd scenes into media events, studies in what would come to be known as 'spin' and the kind of media polish Thatcher had so infamously been given by advertising and marketing companies. Unfortunately, the idea was a little ahead of the technological times, and the device (which some also considered unwieldy and distracting) was eventually dropped from the later run of the production.

Steven Pimlott's 1991 production put Robert Stephens in the title role and played him as a giant: haughty, aristocratic – if not without kindness – incontrovertible, and generally a force of nature. In the assassination scene there was a distinct sense that the conspirators wouldn't be able to kill him, and the overall impression was of hyenas trying to bring down an elephant. Stephens's Caesar got hold of Caska's dagger and fought back, spitting in Brutus's face on '*Et tu Brute*' and holding them off for a full two minutes of combat. Mortally wounded, it took him another minute to die. The feeling – for better or worse – resembled the circumstances in which Thatcher had eventually been brought low by her own party, a kind of bureaucratic mugging in which lesser men had ganged up to get rid of her.

Two years later, David Thacker staged the play in Stratford's intimate and flexible theatre, The Other Place, escaping Thatcher's legacy and representing a more global political climate, Caesar himself resembling a Ceausescu, a Yeltsin or one of the other Eastern European demagogues to emerge from the collapse of the Soviet Union. The strength of the production, however, was not in grandeur but in intimacy, the tiny, seatless theatre creating a promenade environment in which the audience had to be moved by the actors as they entered. The contemporary setting (the conspirators wore dark, modern suits, while Caesar sported gilded epaulettes in keeping with his brand of swagger) fed a novel currency, and when Brutus and Antony addressed the forum crowd, they were talking to the audience who were, by default, on stage and only a few feet away. Such a gambit requires a special level of investment from the actors, a need to engage their audience in ways that cannot be achieved by relying on stage pictures and famous speeches, and the results were electrifying.

The battle scenes were a chaos of gunfire and helicopter noises in the dark, the whole evoking the horrors of Bosnia. Cinna the poet was torn to pieces by women in Moslem headdresses but speaking, like other members of the cast, not just in British English, but in regional dialects the like of which had rarely been heard at the RSC before (and remain depressingly infrequent to this day). This was a British *Caesar*, but a British *Caesar* whose notion of what Britain was had changed, and the production thus registered a new world order and sense of culture. The personal and the political fused in the actors, reducing and complicating motives and ideologies at the level of psyche rather than statecraft, while the proximity of the audience seemed to render the inner lives of the characters paradoxically difficult to pinpoint, as if everyone was on camera at all times and could give nothing away. All told it was a thrilling production which proved the topicality of the play, and demonstrated that it did not need a clear political 'message' to work.

This has been the strategy of most of the best British productions of the twenty-first century: a savvy engagement with contemporary politics which makes the play feel specific and topical, while not flattening out its inherent ambiguities. This approach was apparently accelerated by the terrorist attacks of 11 September 2001 and the political and military changes the world saw thereafter. Immediately before this change, productions could still explore the play in comparatively abstract terms. There was an Elizabethan dress production at the newly opened Globe theatre in London in 1999, which made good use of the cobbler in the opening scene, playing him as a disruptive audience member who was heckling obnoxiously before the show even started. The female roles were played by men (as per Elizabethan convention) but Brutus was played by a black actor (Danny Sapani), a choice which did not have obvious political implications but did raise questions about the production's supposedly historicist approach. The production (which was solid but not especially insightful or inflected one way or another) ended with a dance, like that observed by Thomas Platter at the theatre's namesake four centuries earlier.

Edward Hall staged the play for the RSC in 2001, revisiting but rethinking the play's now familiar Fascist trappings, representing Rome as a place which had already sunk into totalitarian dictatorship. The opening scene was replaced by a vaguely Soviet anthem sung in the style of something out of *Cabaret* or *Les Misérables*, rousing and chilling at the same time, and the applauding crowds were liberally peppered with truncheon wielding black shirts. These would be the audience of the funeral orations, dotted throughout the house and banging their metal truncheons on pipes for alarming effect, and they would be the killers of Cinna the poet, a citizen army moving with deliberation to deal with someone who had long been on their watch list.

The show hinged on Greg Hicks's Brutus and on Ian Hogg's Caesar, the latter paunchy, ineffectual and childish in private, but swaggering and declamatory in public. Hick's Brutus was reflective but crisp until the murder, at which point he realized how badly he had miscalculated. His oration in the forum stalled when the crowd called for him to be Caesar, the full weight of their misunderstanding hitting him very hard. The tent scene yielded an extraordinary moment when he revealed Portia's death to Tim Piggott-Smith's Cassius, a long, agonized silence as both men wrestled with the enormity of things lost and past expression. It was a bloody, messy production which forced the audience to see the grim reality of all this idealized talk of peace, freedom and liberty, words already built into the propaganda of the state and used as motive or excuse for wholesale butchery.

After the Twin Towers came down and Anglo-American attention returned to the Middle East, productions of *Caesar* rediscovered some of that urgent global context which had characterized Thacker's staging at The Other Place. One such was Deborah Warner's star-studded production at the Barbican in 2005. Costumes were suits and desert combat fatigues, and the Lupercal festivities looked like the rope line at a Hollywood premier. Ralph Fiennes played Antony as a David Beckham-esque celebrity and Anton Lesser's slick but uncertain Brutus was frequently compared to then Prime Minister Tony Blair, king of New Labour media spin. Simon Russell Beale played Cassius as an impetuous academic, out of his depth in the polished world of international politics, but then so was everyone else. Time seemed to collapse so that the production showed various pasts (ancient Roman, of course, but also Victorian in the scale of the show with its 100 extras) in its insistently contemporary present, as if versions of this expressly Middle Eastern struggle had been going on for centuries.

Though audiences and many critics were enthusiastic, no one was entirely sure what it all meant. They felt its analogues to what was happening in the world outside the theatre, but were divided on whether Caesar was George W. Bush or Blair, or someone else entirely. Warner resisted treating the play as allegory, saying, rightly to my mind, that unless you massively reshape it (as Welles did) the text wouldn't support a clear political agenda. The contemporary resonances were there but audiences should make of them what they would.

Another angle on contemporary issues was taken by Falk Richter's 2007 German-language production at the Burgtheater in Vienna. Since the Second World War, Germany and Austria, though frequent producers of Shakespeare on stage, had rarely tackled this particular play, and when they did it tended to be in politically unspecific terms and avoiding the Nazi/Fascist associations which so characterized twentieth-century productions elsewhere.[6] Richter's production did not make direct associations with specific individuals, but rendered the play a study in the power of contemporary news media. The playing style was naturalistic and the dress contemporary, the only toga wearer being the news anchor whose image was projected onto the various screens which surrounded the playing space, broadcasting FOX-style news trailers. Brutus was another misguided liberal, thinking he could return his nation to its people through a single murderous act, only to discover that the engine of the nation was the media empire which dominated it, something the death of one man had no power to change.

A similar approach was taken by the Dutch Toneelgroep which toured a version of the show in 2009 and 2010 as part of a longer continual cycle of the three later Roman plays (with *Antony and Cleopatra* and *Coriolanus*, but not *Titus Andronicus*), a comparatively rare approach compared to the frequent combination of the English history plays. Toneelgroep treated the entire sequence as an interactive media event in which the audience were encouraged to browse on the show while sitting, eating and drinking, and otherwise behaving as if the production was a news cycle which was going on around them, both live and on video screens. The result was not so much a staging of the play as a different form of theatre which brought the audience inside what was going on, made them complicit consumers of history-as-news, intertwining the fiction of the play with the real life trappings of everyday life and social media.

In South Africa, few plays loomed larger than *Caesar*, a frequently studied high-school text, and a study in revolution for Nelson Mandela and the ANC from the late 1940s onwards. In 1993, a few months before the first post-apartheid elections, a production of the play was staged with a multiracial cast directed by Karoly Pinter in Johannesburg. Caesar was white, as were some of the conspirators, but others were 'coloured' and Octavius – and the crowds – were black. Cinna the poet was killed by 'necklacing', a familiar horror of the apartheid years in which a traitor or collaborator was torched with a petrol-filled tyre around his or her neck. The whole was similarly dotted with distinctly local imagery, and felt like a warning about the dangers of black rebellion fermented by white agitators who had agendas of their own.

In 2001, Yael Farber's produced *SeZaR*, for South Africa's Grahamstown National Festival of the Arts, and the production toured the UK the following year. The show used a hybrid script, half Shakespeare's, the rest a mixture of the languages of the all-black cast: Tswana, Pedi and Zulu. The result was singularly African, and every element of the show was domestically inflected, from its tribal witchdoctor soothsayer to the heap of brown limbs on the stage, recalling recent Rwandan atrocities. Caesar was killed after he refused to wage war on a killer virus (TV screens were also broadcasting coverage of AIDS victims), and the title character might have been equated with any number of regional despots from the previous thirty years. This was a *Caesar* made in Africa's image, one which claimed productive ownership of the play in ways shaking off its potentially colonial associations, and as such it spoke of the agony and anxiety over that continent's recent past and what was yet to come.

Similar images were utilized in Gregory Doran's 2012 production of Shakespeare's script for the RSC, another African setting featuring British actors, the first all-black production mounted by that company. The set incorporated a colossal statue of Caesar, a familiar element of stage productions but one which drew on recent memories of the statue of Saddam Hussein pulled down during the Iraq war, though other components were more clearly African. Reviewers particularly liked the clarity and musicality of the actors' dialects which seemed to suit the play's verse, giving it a stateliness in no way at odds with its plausibility as speech, and the show was widely considered to have given the play not just a new (to most people) contextual moment, but a refreshing urgency and relevance.

Mankiewicz's 1953 film is the best extant movie of the play, but there are others which all have interesting features. In 1949, David Bradley, a film student at Illinois's Northwestern University, made a very low budget 16mm film of the play starring his boyhood friend Charlton Heston as Mark Antony, and utilizing the oversized classical buildings of Chicago as their set. This was not a modern-dress film, however, and the attempt at classicism is literal. Though the film received some festival attention, even an award or two, and it has at times a certain inventive freshness, much of the film looks amateurish, its vaguely existential style laboured, finding in its high-contrast black and white a gravitas that doesn't feel earned by the actual performances or ideas in play. But the film does try to engage the play as film more completely than other more mainstream versions (showing, for instance, the content of Calphurnia's dream rather than relying on the text to explicate it) and soliloquy is performed as voiceover. Heston was the film's only star, and in his confident, aristocratic Antony – passionate and contemptuous in the funeral oration, heroic in single combat at Philippi – we see the backbone of another film version shot two decades later.

Having achieved real stardom in *Ben Hur* and *The Ten Commandments*, Heston took a significant pay cut to play Antony again, directed by Stuart Burge in 1970, and surrounded by British Shakespeareans including John Gielgud (Cassius in the Mankiewicz film) as Caesar. The film was unsuccessful commercially and critically, hobbled by a minimal budget (by Hollywood standards) and a paradoxical impulse to take an epic approach, such as its main box office draw was famous for, but which this film could simply not afford. More damaging still was a lifeless, unengaging Brutus (Jason Robards) who clearly does not understand what he is saying. It is finally not certain what this film is actually about, there being no emotional core, and no intellectual or political point being made. The murder of Cinna the poet was cut, and while that was understandable in the final print of the Mankiewicz film twenty years before, these were less squeamish times and the most successful films of the years to come would push the boundaries of screen violence, sexuality and counter-cultural edginess in ways which combine to make Burge's film feel curiously out of time.

What does seem a matter of the film's cultural moment is Heston's Antony, a rugged, hedonistic individualist who moves from reflective contemplation to passionate outburst and back, an Antony who – more than any other on film – shows the truth of the conspirators' first sense of him as play-goer, drinker and libertine. Compared to the rest of the largely inflexible cast, he seems relaxed, spontaneous and attractive, an Antony who acts on impulse rather than deliberation, and meets his rise to power with a sense not of calculation but of an abandon that approaches recklessness. Even so, it is not finally enough to save a film which won't explore, energize or take a position on this tricky play.

Caesar was a frequent television offering in the first part of the twentieth century, and the BBC alone ran twelve productions (some heavily truncated) between 1937 and 1996. Of these, the most major was that directed by Herbert Wise for the BBC's Television Shakespeare Project, much of which was funded by US companies (Morgan Bank, Exxon, the New York City Public Broadcasting Service (PBS) and Time/Life), who wanted to see 'straight' and unobjectionable productions which could be used in American classrooms. Of course, in attempting to evade anything that might be damned as intrusive, gimmicky or overly inflected towards a particular reading, many of the films made are drab and uninteresting. Being one of the earliest films of the project (it aired in 1979), *Caesar* suffered more than most, giving us a tediously familiar Roman look and flat, stagey acting. Charles Gray's portrayal of the title character is a nicely nuanced balance of hauteur and self-conscious frailty, Keith Michell is a subtle Antony cut from the Heston cloth, and the other principals are at least competent, but the whole is hampered by a film which (again) isn't clear on what it is. It oscillates between movie and stage: long takes of long speeches, often filmed with unsettling intimacy; and there is more of that visually deadening treatment of soliloquy as voiceover here, though the logic of when it is used is unclear. The whole feels awkward and, like Burge's film, hesitant or unsure of what it is trying to say, trapped in its mandate to honour both Rome and Shakespeare in ways as universally inoffensive as possible. As a result, the play feels too big for the small screen but also lacks both grandeur and humanity.

The most recent film of the play is the Italian faux-documentary *Caesar Must Die* (*Cesare Deve Morire*), filmed in 2012 by Paolo and Vittorio Taviani, which won the Golden Bear award at the Berlin Film Festival. Rather than staging the play itself, the film purports to represent in monochrome the rehearsal and staging of a production of *Julius Caesar* by inmates of an Italian prison, and used actual prisoners in most of the roles. Its strength is its use of the prison setting itself (especially in the forum scene, where the crowd are fellow prisoners in their cells, watching from high, narrow windows) and its notion of the art of theatre mediating (and sometimes exacerbating) the tensions and hardships of its incarcerated cast. This being an all-male prison, the play's two female roles are cut, but the production's machismo vibe comes from far more than that decision. This is a film about men and manliness, about masculine virtue and honour and a (very Italian) impulse to both male violence and male sentimentality. Parts of it feel like a low budget chapter of the *Godfather* franchise, Brutus and co., less civic minded aristocrats than local mafiosi. The text is massively cut and simplified, so that roles and goals become clearer, starker, but the consequent loss of complexity strips the film of the capacity to say much about the play. That, of course, was never the film's goal, which is finally about trying to get to some sense of how the purposes of art are complicated or even contradicted be the reality of being in prison.

That the Tavianis chose this particular play for the root text of their film speaks to a certain macho quality built into the text itself, albeit one that has more to do with elevated speeches about the nature of honour and its purpose in government. This is not a funny play, nor one with much room for women, and in the current climate it is easy to see how it could have become, as Jeremy Lopez suggests in this volume (Chapter 8), and as critics of several mid-twentieth-century films and productions have opined, the most boring Shakespeare of them all. It wasn't for the eighteenth and nineteenth centuries, because their interest in oratory, antiquity and (male) virtue was more than enough to carry the drama. But we are not those people. Times have changed, and for the play to continue to work on stage – as it can – it needs to find new and urgent incarnations, productions which show us not simply the past (Roman or Elizabethan) but some version of our present or future. It is no accident that many of the best productions of the last twenty years have found contexts which feel uncomfortably familiar, throwing into sharp relief those personal conflicts which can otherwise become fusty and abstract. We have no room for what Twain and his ilk would call highfalutin' Shakespeare anymore, and *Caesar*, if not handled well, can be Shakespeare as his most highfalutin'. It need not be. *Caesar* remains a gripping and violent study of power and the will to wield it. To come alive on stage – or screen – it needs only an eye for what makes it compellingly present and relevant to where we are today.

3

The State of the Art

Domenico Lovascio

An eerie mixture of despair and Titanism is likely to seize anyone embarking in the equally daunting and alluring enterprise to survey all that has been written about William Shakespeare's *Julius Caesar* over the past fifteen years, as a simple query to the *World Shakespeare Bibliography* returns almost as many as 500 separate entries, *excluding* pieces of work on adaptations. Painful selections had to be made in the writing of this chapter, and it goes without saying that many interesting contributions could not make the final cut. Editions and adaptations were left out, as they would deserve a full stand-alone chapter. Moreover, as they are likely to prove to be the most influential and the ones circulating most widely, I decided to consider only contributions written in English, which I have organized into the following categories according to their primary focus:

- Structure and features
- Hermeneutics
- Machiavelli, agency and ethics
- Masculinity

- Politics
- The People
- Philosophy, Rhetoric and Language
- Religion

A quick glance at this list should make readers instantly alert to how contemporary scholarship on the play differs from how it used to be before 2000. Character criticism has disappeared, forays into psychological aspects have become rarer and rarer, and the interest in the metatheatrical has gradually faded. Likewise, discussions about genre, style, imagery, structural coherence and the transitional role of *Julius Caesar* in Shakespeare's repertory now tend to look outdated. *Quellenstudien* are a thing of the past, and enquiries into Shakespeare's deviations from his source material and their significance have also increasingly diminished.

Critical efforts have concentrated principally – though by no means exclusively – on the analysis of a sweeping array of wide-ranging issues related to the realm of politics, no longer primarily focusing on the question whether Shakespeare leaned more towards monarchy or republic, or whether his Caesar is a tyrant or not. Specifically, a more profound interest has arisen in the relationship between the individual and the masses on the one side, and the broader historical and political processes on the other, accompanied by a deepening sense of the play's grounding within its Elizabethan *milieu*.

Structure and features

As they focus on structural aspects and on Shakespeare's compositional choices respectively, the essays by Joseph Candido and Julia Griffin appear as an appropriate starting point. Candido divides *Julius Caesar* into 'five discrete "movements" …, each with its own character and center of interest, yet each connected to the others by a network of allusions that helps draw separate segments into a unified whole.'[1] Candido names the five movements according to their unifying focus: 'Prelude' (1.1–1.2, raising all the important issues in the play); 'Storm' (1.3–2.4, giving concreteness to the civil turmoil in Rome); 'Exterior Space(s)' (3.1–3.3, with scenes occurring 'in full view of the citizens of Rome'); 'Interior Space(s)' (4.1–4.3, where 'the wide lens of the previous section ... narrows to smaller, more private episodes') and 'Philippi' (5.1–5.5, 'a single, uninterrupted arch of action that builds forcefully toward conclusion').[2]

Fascinating insights into some distinctive features of the play are yielded by Griffin's reading of Shakespeare's tragedy 'as one of many' within the European Caesarean dramatic tradition (1545–c. 1762), a comparative discussion that enables her to assess – especially against Shakespeare's predecessors – the possible meanings of some of his original choices in dramatizing that specific segment of Roman history.[3] First, Shakespeare's *Julius Caesar* emerges as the only Caesar play beginning 'with a crowd scene ..., setting out the political situation not by describing but by showing it'; second, it is almost unique in showing the assassination on stage; third, its Brutus proves to be 'a more complex creation than either his robust forebears or his squeamish successors'; finally, and more importantly, Shakespeare is significantly alone in not giving Caesar any soliloquy.[4] This decision precludes any sense of intimacy between Caesar and the audience, thereby decisively contributing to 'a powerful presence with a blank behind it.'[5]

Hermeneutics

Another distinctive feature of the play is the extent to which it seems preoccupied with meaning, interpretation and judgement. For Ian Donaldson, the play is specifically concerned 'with how one interprets the past, and the present, and their relationship to one another'.⁶ Almost all the major characters die either because they have 'misconstrued' 'the political needs of the time' (Brutus and Cassius) or because they have carelessly relied on the interpretations of others, like Caesar, who dies after accepting Decius's devious interpretation of Calphurnia's dream. Filled as it is with 'hermeneutic puzzles', 'interpretative riddles, mysteries, and misunderstandings', the play proves resistant to any attempt to pinpoint its internal political logic, thereby reminding us how difficult it can be correctly to interpret past and present events at junctures of such momentous historical change.⁷ Robin Headlam Wells similarly contends that in the play 'misjudgment ... determines the course of events' and that '[b]y returning repeatedly to the question of evidence and interpretation, *Julius Caesar* invites us to consider the problem that any historian must deal with in reconstructing the past. How reliable is our knowledge of the facts, and is our interpretation of them justified?'⁸

The issue of ambivalence is central to *Julius Caesar* not only as regards the interpretation of events, but especially when it comes 'to the construing of self', as David Willbern compellingly illustrates in his psychoanalytical reading of the play.⁹ Brutus exhibits an 'intrapsychic split' persuading himself to kill a Caesar that is in fact a deeply ambivalent construction rather than a real man: he 'is both a ruthless political aspirant and a simple creature that merely follows its "mischievous" nature'; in other words, he 'is both culpable and innocent, as a fitting reciprocal to the deep ambivalence that motivates [Brutus's] construction' itself.¹⁰ Brutus's decision is prodded by Cassius during the seduction scene (1.2.25–176), which can ultimately be seen as 'an early-modern adumbration of a psychoanalytical session, in which a patient (Brutus) anxiously assents to self-disclosure or revelation, facilitated by an analyst (Cassius)' who 'works to animate the unacknowledged or repressed side of [Brutus's] ambivalence' towards Caesar.¹¹

The question of misconstruction is linked by Dennis Kezar with the opening of the Globe, which decisively contributed to dissolving 'traditional boundaries ... between actors and audience', thereby inaugurating an era in which any messages conveyed by playwrights 'are challenged and complicated by spectatorial participation'.[12] As a result, all forms of expression in the play 'are subject to politicized readings beyond the author's control', which 'leaves no participant safe from revision and misconstruction.'[13]

Machiavelli, agency and ethics

Several scholars have looked at *Julius Caesar* in the light of Machiavelli. For John Roe, the tragedy is Machiavellian in so far as it meditates 'on the conflict between political imperatives and the individual conscience'.[14] While refraining from imposing a moral perspective on the events, the tragedy uses the republican context to explore 'issues of conscience as they operate in the sphere of the political' and expresses scepticism about the prospect of exercising actual freedom.[15] Roe focuses on Brutus, whose main – paradoxical – fault is his being *not enough* of a Machiavel. His mistaken decision not to kill Antony testifies to his inability to 'behave ruthlessly enough to command *fortuna*': Brutus has too much of a conscience for the 'world without absolutes' depicted in *Julius Caesar*.[16] As it happens, the triumph of 'the man of *virtù*' Antony over 'the man of good' Brutus is ultimately due to the former's Machiavellian awareness 'that rhetoric does not deal in truth but in various and competing versions of events or actions', leading him to rely on emotion instead of logic and rationality – indisputably Brutus's province.[17] By detailing the populace's reaction to this rhetorical competition, the play also seems to cast serious doubts on republicanism by foregrounding 'the malleability of the public, the ease with which they succumb to blatant bribery, and above all their quickness to embrace heedless violence'.[18]

The Machiavellian essence of *Julius Caesar* is also apparent to Robin Headlam Wells, though he specifically identifies it in Shakespeare's choice not to take sides for or against Caesar in order to dramatize 'a pragmatic and sceptical view of politics which recognizes that virtue and utility are not always compatible' and that 'conspiracies seldom achieve their intended effect'.[19] This *Weltanschauung* is evident in the play's central irony 'that an action designed to deflect a feared event hastens that very outcome', namely the death of the republic and the birth of the empire.[20] Unlike Roe, Wells pinpoints 'political naivety' rather than an excess of conscience as Brutus's greatest fault but concurs with Roe's view that his key errors are his decision to let Antony live and his misplaced trust in the people's capacity for rational judgement.[21]

Hugh Grady offers a masterly reading of *Julius Caesar* over two complementary essays that need to be considered as a unity.[22] A prime example of Benjaminesque *Trauerspiel*, the play is Machiavellian in its 'bracketing the issues of moral right and wrong' in order to focus 'on the analysis of actual, non-ideal political behaviour'.[23] This reveals the world of politics 'as empty, a mechanical power struggle destructive in its very essence', and foregrounds how limited the characters' actual possibility is to exercise their moral agency autonomously and to influence 'the large sweep of historical events'.[24] Brutus perfectly epitomizes this predicament, inasmuch as his 'noble intentions are continuously misdirected through the unintended consequences of his moral choices' and as he constantly 'seems considerably less autonomous and in control of events than he thinks he is'.[25]

That in the play 'events have consequences, but not those intended by men and women acting out a script in which they have been assigned parts' is a conviction similarly shared by Warren Chernaik, who believes that '[w]hat encloses and limits characters who think erroneously that they are acting freely is an overarching authorial irony' demonstrating that 'men are at no times masters of their fate, though they think they are.'[26] A different account of the play in terms of personal agency is provided by Adrian Phoon, who reads *Julius Caesar* as 'exposing the institutional structures that circumscribe personal agency and will, by demonstrating how individuals are objects of political ideology and interpellation'.[27] Specifically, the conspirators seem to 'define themselves in terms of their Romanness, and view their public obligations and private interests as inseparable elements of their self-identities', thereby 'inadvertently surrender[ing] their personal freedom to the state.'[28]

Matthew Sims interprets *Julius Caesar* as a tragic meditation on 'the problematic role of ethics in a political system that often requires unethical behavior to achieve success.'[29] Brutus's quest to save liberty and the Republic exemplifies two fundamental political truths: on the one hand, 'that even the noblest of men can be seduced by power when the quest for justice becomes dominated by ideological principles'; on the other, that there exists a 'fragile relationship between personal virtue and the public sphere of politics', as 'often the noblest of intentions can prove to be disastrous in their political consequences', as a result of 'man's limited knowledge' of reality.[30]

Grounding *Julius Caesar* in the early modern rhetoric of sickness, Jennifer Feather likewise pinpoints in the play 'a picture of agency that goes beyond autonomous action.'[31] She argues that despite the characters' efforts 'to separate physical illness and mental struggle' in order to preserve 'the autonomy of the agent, the rhetoric of the play repeatedly conflates the two, unsettling the easy association between corporeal and moral integrity.'[32] Brutus – again – is especially a case in point, in so far as he is portrayed both 'as a rationally deliberating, autonomous subject' and as vulnerable 'to the influence of the social and physical world around him'; more specifically, his 'conflict between the demands of friendship and of autonomy appears as a disruption of corporeal harmony.'[33]

Masculinity

Attention to the treatment of masculinity and its significance has yielded some richly suggestive insights into different aspects of the play. Lloyd Davis argues that in *Julius Caesar* Shakespeare uses 'a series of confrontations between characters over the meanings of the male body as an idea and symbol, as a site where identity is asserted and imposed, and as a means of achieving social goals'.[34] By treating the aristocrats' bodies 'as visual and rhetorical signs whose meanings are judged and fought over', Shakespeare demonstrates that masculinity is not merely an idealized virtue for which all characters compete, but rather a problematic ideological construct that needs negotiating.[35]

Eugene Giddens examines the way *Julius Caesar* reflects upon the tensions of the 1590s emanating from the fact that England had a female monarch.[36] Despite her efforts to fashion a valiant image of herself, many at court saw Elizabeth's femininity and prudence as obstacles in the furthering of a masculine, militaristic image of themselves and the nation, and advocated a more aggressive foreign policy. As the military way to advancement was essentially suppressed, Elizabeth could now more easily distribute honour according to her personal criteria of courtly service, thereby reducing the aristocrats' autonomy, much as it occurs in *Julius Caesar*, where the fact that the dictator rules despite his decrepitude 'causes a crisis of valour and honour' and ultimately brings about his assassination, an act the conspirators need as proof of their own valour.[37] However, like 'those who advocated war in 1590s England, the conspirators completely misread their political climate', because now valour has to be tempered with policy, as Antony and Octavian shrewdly understand.[38]

Politics

Giddens's analysis is overtly political, and discussions of the play's politics, whether in connection with its late Elizabethan background or not, have continued to abound, offering many intriguing interpretative possibilities and proving to be the dominant mode of critical discourse. Barbara L. Parker convincingly shows that when considered as a group in historical order (and not in order of composition) Shakespeare's Roman works can be seen to chronicle a collapse of Rome reflecting the constitutional decline of a State from monarchy to tyranny as illustrated in Plato's *Republic*: *The Rape of Lucrece* (abolition of monarchy), *Coriolanus* (oligarchy), *Julius Caesar* (transition to tyranny), *Antony and Cleopatra* (final stage of tyranny).[39] Admittedly, Michael Platt had already advanced a similar reading of Shakespeare's Roman plays as mapping out the rise and fall of the Roman Republic in 1976.[40] However, Parker's contribution differs from Platt's in her interesting claim that *Julius Caesar* pointedly seems to parallel Plato's *Republic* in dramatizing the process by which the people, grown contemptuous of authority and the law, elect a champion to rule over them; eventually, however, that champion turns into a wolf and the aristocracy starts hating him.

Locating the play more specifically in its political *milieu*, Anthony Miller argues that in *Julius Caesar* 'political interest and ideologies define themselves through conflicting uses of the Roman triumph', the sacred and military ceremony celebrated as the most solemn honour paid to a general of the Roman army who had achieved a resounding military success over the enemy.[41] It is Caesar's odious triumph over fellow Romans that sets the conspiracy in motion, directly prompting the plotters' 'attempt to mount a procession that is an abridged counter-triumph' to celebrate the killing of Caesar.[42] Paradoxically, however, this counter-triumph 'replicates Caesar's opening one for a victory of Roman over Roman' and, in turn, elicits 'the anti-triumph of the plebeians' riot' fomented by Antony's emotional rhetoric.[43] This dynamic mirrors the turmoil of the last decade of the Elizabethan reign. In particular, it seems to allude to the manoeuvres of the subversive faction led by Elizabeth's favourite-turned-rebel The Earl of Essex, not only in Shakespeare's decision to provide 'the conspirators with an Essex-like youthfulness' and Cassius with a choleric disposition, but especially in the fact that the 'new generation of Brutus, Cassius, and Antony struggle to appropriate the triumph' of the old Caesar, just 'as the Essex circle attempted to do' with the ageing Elizabeth.[44]

That Cassius is the character more closely reminiscent of Essex is also underlined by Robin Headlam Wells. He notes that the allusions to the early modern political context are palpable in the conspirators' use of language, as the Roman plotters emphasize the importance of 'honour', heroically conceived of as 'a willingness to use violence in defence of personal or national reputation', and frequently contrast it with 'a cluster of words to do with sleep, dreams, enchantment and idleness', which recalls the writings associated with the Essex faction.[45] In a very different analysis of honour, Suzanne Smith draws attention to how the portrayal of Brutus is instrumental in conveying the idea that honour can actually 'tolerate and even encourage the divorce of moral and political purpose from poetic or dramatic performance of action for its own sake.'[46] Indeed, Brutus's 'concern for the manner in which his action is to be performed and the form of the action itself ultimately overwhelms the purpose to which it was originally attached' – the general good.[47]

In *Shakespeare and Republicanism*, Andrew Hadfield reads the play as 'represent[ing] a necrotic body politic that has abandoned its healthy republican institutions and values', and where 'the public sphere shrinks from the general control of the many to the concern of a few'.[48] Even worse, the notion of liberty appears abruptly 'in the aftermath of a bloody act, [as] something that almost has to be imposed on a reluctant, uncomprehending people who ... have lost sight of what functions their institutions ... actually serve'; and it is precisely the fact that the Roman citizens seem to have 'no stake in their collective destiny' that may have 'struck the English audience at the Globe.'[49]

David Hawkes sees Shakespeare as using Roman history to reflect on Elizabethan class conflict and the progressive impatience of members of the aristocracy and the mercantile class at 'the incremental centralization of power in the hands of the monarch'.[50] In this topical, economics-driven reading of the play, the misunderstandings between Brutus and Cassius about money in Act 4, Scene 3 seem to reflect the early phase of England's transition from feudalism to capitalism.

In a similar vein, *Julius Caesar* is conceived of by Daniela Carpi as dramatizing '[a] gradual passage ... from an uncritical adherence to absolute monarchy, to a more democratic form of government where the people are actually called to participate with their decisions and choices'.[51] This happens especially thanks to Brutus, who has the merit of starting to question the social order, which begins to appear no longer as immutable, but 'as the continuously changing result of functional relations between the various forces at play.'[52] However, Antony, the champion of the institutions, skilfully 'thwart[s] the risk of revolution' by 'immediate[ly] spurring ... a counter-revolution' seeking to strengthen the establishment.[53]

David Colclough focuses on the themes of counsel and flattery, and on how political advice 'is delivered or enacted'; he concludes that the play 'ruthlessly exposes the limits on political advice and action' in 'a world in which having the last word ... is all that really matters.'[54] Not only is counsel depicted in *Julius Caesar* as 'inherently unreliable, untrustworthy and dangerous', but also the 'delivery, reception and interpretation of advice are fatally flawed', thereby highlighting Shakespeare's profound scepticism about the entire sphere of politics.[55]

According to Coppélia Kahn, in *Julius Caesar* 'Shakespeare dramatizes the separation of the inner subjective realm from the distinctively public world of *romanitas* in such a way that it is readable as ideologically produced in that world by the ethos of the Republic.'[56] The most important cornerstones of this ethos are virtue and emulation, and all the main characters and their mutual relationships are shaped by the contradiction 'between republican virtue as sacrifice of self for the common good, and the emulation that inevitably produced one man who stands out as, precisely, supreme exemplar of republican virtue.'[57] The series of suicides that punctuate the last part of the play stand as ultimate testimony to the centrality of emulation, in so far as suicide is not simply a means 'of avoiding defeat, but of defeating one's rival by depriving him of his expected triumph.'[58]

A further take on the depiction of politics in the play is provided by Edward M. Test, who fascinatingly reads Brutus's and Antony's rival interpretations of Caesar's murder in the light of Theodor De Bry's (1590–1624) and Bartolomé de Las Casas's (1552) accounts of the practices of cannibalism and human sacrifice in the Mexica Empire.[59] Although Brutus's killing of Caesar springs from a Mexica-like desire ritualistically to cleanse the community, interrupt the revenge cycle and protect the fabric of society, Antony reframes it as a criminal act, thereby contributing to reinforcing perpetual revenge and disrupting society. Brutus's failure depends on the fact that what he conceives of as sacrifice 'is not communally condoned'; this, in turn, 'points to the inevitable shift ... of nonsacrificial societies toward disorder and vengeance', thereby 'emphasiz[ing] the impossibility of using sacrificial violence in sixteenth-century Protestant England' and reflecting on 'the future of England's commonwealth – a disciplinary order and perpetual violence that is bound to be repeated over and over'.[60]

Test's reading is close to that of Oliver Arnold, who observes that Brutus's attempt to reframe Caesar's murder as communal sacrifice is easily circumvented by Antony, who 'rewrites Caesar's death as a ... failed sacrifice ... that creates community but also produces a Judas', thereby rendering 'the sacredness of Caesar and the necessity of revenge ... continuous rather than opposed'.[61] Analogously, Barbara Joan Baines believes that Antony triumphs over Brutus chiefly because he is able 'to deconstruct Cassius's and Brutus's perception of the assassination' as a 'scene of ritual sacrifice and liberation' by reframing it more literally as a brutal murder.[62]

Reading the play's politics in the light of the early modern proto-geological discourse, Maddalena Pennacchia refreshingly shows how the 'earthquake imagery' permeating *Julius Caesar* seems informed by '[t]he model of the "geological cycle", as a succession of phases of disturbances and quiet, together with the related processes of "solidification" and "liquefaction" that ruled the formation of rocks according to early earth sciences'.[63] In the frame of a socio-political conception of hierarchy that hinged on the theory of the king's two bodies and on the identification of the 'body of Earth' with that of the Ruler, the earthquake in *Julius Caesar* is both physical and metaphorical, in that it mirrors 'the image of the uncontrollable fits that will affect Rome's body politic … when its "head" is overthrown.'[64] In other words, 'the earthquake imagery functions as the "objective correlative" of a radical revolution of the world order' and also impinges on the characterization of the plebs, who are referred to twice as 'stones', first by Marullus and later by Antony, who will eventually manage to move those very same stones to rise and mutiny.[65]

The people

The role of the people in the trajectory of Rome's political evolution is the focus of many competing and sometimes sharply contrasting accounts of the play proceeding in the wake of Brents Stirling's still influential *The Populace in Shakespeare* (1949).[66] Jerald W. Spotswood is convinced that 'Shakespeare allows no authoritative voice to emerge from the masses'.[67] By denying the people any measure of individuality, the play foregrounds the exclusive association of individuality with the elite in order to 'denigrate collective action by associating it with a rabble that by definition holds no interest in the social order'.[68] The real concern of *Julius Caesar* is therefore not with 'the struggle of plebeians' but with the 'intra-elite conflict and power struggle' primarily brought about by the noble Romans' difficulty in coming to terms with 'the turbulent shift from a warrior to a "civilized" society'.[69] The clear distinction drawn by Shakespeare between the elite and the rabble in Rome mirrors the situation of early modern England, where individual achievements were a distinctive mark of the aristocracy as opposed to the indistinguishable mass of the commoners, and where the gentry lived in constant fear of popular uprising.[70]

Lack of individuation in the portrayal of the Roman people is also underscored by Christine E. Hutchins, who draws attention to differences rather than similarities between ancient Rome and Elizabethan England as a way to demonstrate how the Roman leaders' typically patrician disregard or abuse of the commoners contrasts with early modern English concerns with the defining traits of appropriate rule.[71] Hutchins provides a wealth of evidence from contemporary Elizabethan handbooks on the responsibilities of political leaders and shows that, despite the well-known early modern obsession with hierarchy, 'dignified concern for the common people' was considered among the most important traits of good rule.[72]

Jeffrey Edward Green maintains that the play devalues the voice of the people, who have 'little *decisional* power to determine laws'.[73] They have no real will, in so far as they merely respond to the rhetorical suggestions of those in power, and even the notion that the people may exert a sort of regulative function on Caesar's rise to power by means of their denying him the crown 'remains much more of a latent hypothesis than a practical reality'.[74]

A completely opposite view is held by Oliver Arnold, who believes that the people do retain real power, as a consequence of Caesar's habit of appealing directly to them in order 'to transcend all other constituted authorities'.[75] The Caesarism outlined in the play must therefore be conceived of as 'the collapse of the particular kind of mediation political representation institutes between the subject and the ruling class'.⁷⁶ Unlike Caesar, Brutus has no direct intercourse with the people and his conviction that he is acting for the general good is plain delusion. The conspirators' action is reconceived by Shakespeare 'as a defense of the republic from popular dictatorship': removing the scarves from the statues and dispersing the crowd can be interpreted as anti-populist actions that respond to the attacks waged against a culture of representational politics.⁷⁷ Arnold is therefore close to Barbara L. Parker's idea that the people are 'the play's real protagonist, for they control not only Caesar and the other characters but virtually the entire course of events.'⁷⁸

The importance of the plebeians in the play is also stressed by Naomi Conn Liebler. Far from constituting a fickle mob, the plebeians 'are the commodities that produce, and the fodder that fuels, the history' represented in the play, as Shakespeare constantly 'reminds us that ... historical events ... had [their] greatest impact not upon the titular figures ... but upon those who lived to experience those alterations.'⁷⁹ Moreover, the plebs can also be seen as 'the surrogates of many of Shakespeare's Globe theatre audience', on whom the playwright's success was dependent.⁸⁰ Through Antony's 'political hucksterism' and his use of 'the rhetoric of the marketplace' *Julius Caesar* develops a view of the theatre as more akin to 'a market than a pulpit or a political podium', where Brutus and Antony vie for the people's allegiance, which has to be purchased with the coin of language, within a 'mechanism of change operat[ing] through the rhetoric of the Exchange.'⁸¹

The conflict between the elite and the popular base 'about who should be the custodians of England's historical and liturgical memory' is central to Alison A. Chapman's conclusion that only the elite has the power 'to shape the calendar and ritual memory'.⁸² Shakespeare contrasts the cobbler's failure to create a new holiday with Caesar's success in transforming history into ritual by incorporating the Ides of March 'into the annual timetable of memory'.⁸³ With the ageing Elizabeth's soon-to-end reign in mind, 'Shakespeare's play seems to suggest that order can be maintained in part through the unified celebration of the monarch's memory', as long as said celebration is orchestrated from the top of the social ladder.[84]

Political manipulation of communal festivities is also central to Christopher Holmes's reading of the play, influenced by Richard Wilson's discussion of the same issue.[85] In response to Caesar's attempt to manipulate Lupercal by turning 'a ritual election of a Carnival-king into a real coronation', Holmes sees Brutus as trying 'to manipulate the Ides of March by transforming political murder into ritual sacrifice.'[86] The fact that the Ides of March 'always came in Lent and it was the earliest possible date of Palm Sunday' stands at the basis of Brutus's desire that the conspirators 'be sacrificers, but not butchers'; more precisely, that they be not Lenten Butchers.[87] Through the ritual dipping in Caesar's blood, Brutus tries symbolically 'to transform the conspirators from Lenten Butchers into the butchers triumphant after the expulsion of Lent', but his attempt is frustrated by Antony.[88] Holmes's view of the people differs considerably from Chapman's: calling into question conventional wisdom that Cinna is torn to pieces by the mob, Holmes argues that the assault should rather be seen as 'a theatrical political gesture' – namely 'a displaced expulsion of Jack-a-Lent', the symbolic scapegoat that in popular tradition was expelled by the community on Palm Sunday.[89] By expressing their need 'to re-establish [their] own ritual understanding of time', the commoners emerge not as 'a mindless, violent mob' but as 'players in their own right in the struggles for temporal order'.[90]

Philosophy, rhetoric and language

A more circumscribed attention to philosophical, rhetorical and linguistic issues is shared by a few other recent analyses of the play. Claudia Corti sees a multidimensional connection between *Julius Caesar* and *Theologia Platonica*, the core work of fifteenth-century priest and humanist Marsilio Ficino. First, the main characters can be divided 'into three classes reminiscent of Ficino's triple division of human nature: mind–soul–body': Caesar stands for the mind in the light of his striving for constancy; Brutus and Cassius embody the soul by dint of their 'depending on the mobility of ideas and fluctuation of sensations and emotions'; Antony, 'in his passionate psychological constitution', represents the body.[91] Second, another 'analogous tripartite Ficinean scheme can be applied to the play's principal characters' regarding 'the inner division of Man's functions among reason, ... anger ... and desire'; specifically, Brutus 'claims to represent reason', anger is apparent in Cassius's choler, and desire is embodied by Antony.[92] Finally, 'the opposition between firmness and change' typical of all the characters is likewise related to 'an overall Ficinean structure', inasmuch as they 'insist that they are stable and motionless' but turn out to be 'subject to changeability', for 'all human creatures', according to Ficino, 'depend on movement' in both a physical and mental sense.[93]

Informed by the Derridean notion of 'democracy to come', that is of democracy as 'an endless promise' never *completely* fulfilled, Nicholas Royle identifies 'the use and abuse of the future' as one of the central concerns of *Julius Caesar*. The play focuses on 'attempts to predict and seize the future' in a context where time is represented 'as constitutively double', especially through the insistence on the 'impossible experience of anachronism' and on 'the deathly machine-like power of repetition'.[94] Time and the future are also crucial to the essay by Mark Robson, who observes that *Julius Caesar* is replete with instances of the adverb 'now', most of which seem 'to remark on the present as in need of attention', as a result of the political predicament of the Roman Republic, where 'the initiative is to be seized moment by moment and in which speed ... is demanded.'[95] Considerable emphasis is especially laid on the tension 'between predictability and unpredictability', with a future that 'refuses to remain safely at a distance, but keeps bleeding into the present moment, casting a shadow over events'.[96]

Maddalena Pennacchia compellingly reads the rhetorical contest between Brutus and Antony as portraying 'a shift in communication practice' that mirrors both the transition from republic to empire and that 'from a medieval to a modern episteme' in the passage from 'an older, authoritative medium appealing mostly to the ear (rhetoric) [to] a newer one seeking authoritativeness, appealing both to the ear and the eye (theatre).'[97] When he descends from the pulpit to the level of the plebeians, Antony 'breaks free from the rules of *ars oratoria*, and enters the realm of theatre', thereby exchanging a place which is 'overtly political', that is the pulpit, with another that is 'covertly so', namely the ring he asks the plebs to form around him, 'whose circular shape would immediately recall to the offstage audience the theatre in which the play was taking place'.[98]

Language 'is *the central concern*' in *Julius Caesar* according to Barbara Joan Baines, 'more so than in any other play of the canon.'[99] Roman politics appears to be 'consistently shaped and reshaped by rhetorical figures', to the point that the play seems to come down to a battle of metaphors between Brutus and Antony; however, 'whereas Brutus is governed by metaphor, Antony is its master.'[100] Indeed, 'Brutus is not seduced so much by Cassius as by his own metaphors', inasmuch as 'they become the content and the container of his thought.'[101] The ambivalent role of language in both representing and fashioning reality by means 'of symbolic elaboration' is the heart of David Lucking's discussion.[102] The play as a whole is pervaded by a conflict between 'different conceptions of the function of language, and of the relation between words and the world'.[103] Caesar's and Brutus's trajectories especially show that language is under the individual's control only to a limited extent.

Religion

Another question some recent critics of the play have taken up is that of religion, especially in terms of providence, sacraments and calling. It is John W. Mahon's conviction that the workings of divine providence in *Julius Caesar* would be apparent to early modern 'English Christians of every shade of theological opinion', especially through Cassius's and Antony's actions.[104] Unbeknown to them, the two shrewd contrivers actually 'advance God's providential design' by paving the way to Augustus's peaceful empire, which would in turn lead 'to the creation of conditions ideal for Jesus' birth'.[105]

Providence is also dealt with by Andreas Mahler, who contends that for the first time in *Julius Caesar* Shakespeare questions an 'ideology of restitution', of 'disorder being restored to order', as a consequence of the fact that Elizabeth's reign was drawing to a close.[106] The play is based on 'two mutually exclusive, yet complementary plots', both hinging on Caesar's pivotal death, which marks restitution and redress for Brutus, while prompting in Antony a desire for redemption and revenge.[107] In the contrast between the two, Shakespeare opposes 'restitutional agent and individual action', thereby negotiating 'the question of agency in the face of an increasing disintegration of providentialist belief'.[108]

A final angle on religion is offered by Robert McCutcheon, for whom *Julius Caesar* depicts 'the quest for calling in a world devoid of vocation', which reveals 'a theological dynamic' connecting the play to religious discourses on vocation, predestination and identity circulating in early modern England.[109] The play 'draws on two related Pauline doctrines. The first is that of the church as a "congregation of callings"', which is apparent in the conspirators' failed attempt 'to agglomerate into one body' in order to match the colossal Caesar.[110] The second is 'that of vocation', which 'plays itself most fully in Brutus' – a liminal figure 'poised between the political and the domestic, a public and inner self, the instant and the receding future' – who in vain tries to discern his true calling (and identity) in 'a city where a call is difficult to hear.'[111]

Conclusion

At the dawn of the twenty-first century, most interpretations of *Julius Caesar* keep grappling with its quintessential tendency to elicit divided and often conflicting responses on virtually every single issue of interest. In other words, the reason for the very popularity of the play still seems to lie precisely in its intrinsic inability to harmonize the views of the critics, in spite of the decline of New Criticism, which was notably interested in ambiguity, regarding it as the summit of literary quality.

Most of the important questions raised by the play have been submitted to considerate, insightful and productive scrutiny over the past fifteen years, and I am of the opinion that the play has probably never been as critically alive as it is now. Predictably, discussions of politics have dominated the scene, providing insights into a plethora of different aspects both in specific connection with the political context of 1590s England and in relation to broader concerns regarding sovereignty, authority and representation. Notions of conflict have been at the forefront, with interpretations of the people's role proving to be especially divisive. The debate on these issues is still very much alive, and active continuation of these lines of enquiry is to be desired as well as expected.

Discussions of the play's instability and potential for misconstruction and misunderstanding have enabled scholars to deal with a series of complex questions regarding the self, external reality and the meaning of history, as has a handful of compelling contributions on philosophy, rhetoric, language and religion. As for Machiavellianism, moral agency and personal freedom, I am inclined to think that the existing contributions have thoroughly explored those research avenues.

Fertile and rich as this critical landscape undoubtedly is, I none the less feel that attention to female characters has been lamentably missing from discussions of the play and I am convinced that the critical debate on *Julius Caesar* would benefit from wider and fresh consideration of femininity and related issues, especially if this was complemented with further analyses of the question of masculinity, which has proven to be a very fruitful line of enquiry in a couple of articles. Scholars should be inspired rather than discouraged by the series of brilliant feminist takes on the play that marked the last two decades of the twentieth century and should try to add to the critical debate.[112] The fact that scholars probably feel that gender and race have now little outlet in this play beyond what has already been said is probably one of the reasons why *Julius Caesar*, though still very popular, tends to attract fewer critical takes than the other major tragedies.

In addition, while a great deal of attention has been devoted to Brutus, I would recommend that more consideration be also given to the examination of the other characters of the play in future scholarly endeavours. Far be it from me to advocate an anachronistic return to character criticism: what I mean is that wider attention should be given to character in discussion of the wider-ranging issues taken up by the play. I would also like to see attempts to reconsider the play within the wider context of the appropriation of the Roman past in early modern English culture at large rather than merely within the narrower one of Shakespeare's other Roman plays. Finally, scrutiny of the possible interplay between Christian and republican notions may also provide new impulse to scholarly discussions, as the two issues have tended to be considered separately rather than as interacting factors.

At all events, one can only wish that Shakespeare's tragedy continues to stimulate such diverse and intriguing attempts at unravelling its complexity by scholars with different cultural backgrounds and critical interests, so that our understanding of the complex relation between *Julius Caesar* and its socio-political, cultural and historical context be increasingly mapped out.

4

New Directions: *Julius Caesar*, Ovidian Transformation and the Martyred Body on the Early Modern Stage

Lisa S. Starks-Estes

Just before the performance of the play-within-the-play in *Hamlet*, Polonius boasts that he, too, has had some experience on the stage. 'I did enact Julius Caesar', he tells Hamlet. 'I was killed i'th' Capitol. Brutus killed me'. Hamlet retorts with the witty line, 'It was a brute part of him to kill so capital a calf there' (3.2.104–7).[1] This exchange provides more than comic relief at Polonius's expense. Besides the possible in-joke that the same actor cast as Polonius also played the titular role in the earlier production of Shakespeare's *Julius Caesar*, this reference brings to mind the link that this Roman play forges between ritual sacrifice and theatricality. It marks the connection between these two tragedies that so fully explore theatrical practices and foreground the power of the stage.

Moreover, both of these plays share a common fascination with the legacy of Ovid – his mythological subjects and poetic method, along with their multifaceted connections to early modern notions of playing and playgoing. In *Julius Caesar*, Shakespeare explores the relationship between Ovid, acting and the audience's affective responses, which he examines through different lenses later in *Hamlet*, as well as in other plays. Importantly, in *Julius Caesar*, Shakespeare saturates his primary source material, Plutarch, with Ovidian myths and foregrounds the metamorphic possibilities of the theatre in mythic/religious terms by staging the transformation of the human into the sacred. Through Antony's speech over Caesar's bleeding corpse, Shakespeare demonstrates how martyrs are created while recreating the ritual itself onstage. In portraying Julius Caesar through the Ovidian concept of metamorphosis, Shakespeare explores the spectral power of stage representation and the role of the player in the act of theatrical transformation.

Ovid and the early modern theatre

Ovid had a spectral, all-pervasive presence for Renaissance visual artists and writers who drew not only from the subject matter of his poetry, but also from the artistic method he used – metamorphosis, or creative transformation. Ovid's influence led to a widespread application of his poetic approach in early modern artistic practices and discourses. Besides providing the themes, subjects and poetic methods that influenced the dramaturgy of the age, Ovid became the means though which practices of playing and the experience of playgoing on the English stage were self-consciously conceived, explored, articulated and debated. Ovid's legacy itself may be seen as emblematic of the theatrical experience, appropriated by both sides of the political divide on theatricality – the enemies *and* the friends of the stage. In fact, a wide range of writers – Stephen Gosson, William Prynne, Thomas Heywood and so on – indirectly and directly refer to, cite or quote Ovid when either attacking or defending the stage in their treatises. In the late sixteenth to early seventeenth centuries, therefore, Ovid became synonymous with the full theatrical experience: plays, playing and playgoing.

As a poet who became the embodiment of sweet, seductive verse and transgressive attitudes towards authority and dominant tradition, Ovid inspired a deep-seated ambivalence in early modern culture, one that is analogous to contradictory ideas about representation in general and theatre in particular in discourses concerning the stage. Ovid's legacy can be seen as a site of contention in attitudes concerning the poetic imagination, the relationship between the ancients and emergent vernacular tradition, the problems of representation and images and the infusion of the pagan with the Christian. Arthur Golding, himself a devoted Calvinist, attempted to reconcile Ovid's work and smooth over some of these conflicts in the Epistle and Preface following his 'Englished' translation of *Metamorphoses* in 1567, but the unresolved tensions in the Ovidian subject matter, perspective and poetic method of transformation remained.

This tension, dramatized in Shakespeare's *Julius Caesar*, carried over into ideas about the actor, who takes on the shape and emotions of another. In his treatise against the stage, Anthony Munday singles out the portrayal of Caesar, which he thought 'pollut[ed]' the 'eyes and ears' of spectators, particularly through the dangerous, fraudulent nature of acting: 'The martial affaires of Casar, and other worthies, they giue them a newe face, and turne them out like counterfeites to show themselves on the stage'.[2] As in Munday's description of the deceptive 'counterfeites' of Julius Caesar on the stage, Puritans regarded acting – 'metamorphosis' – as fiendishly deceptive. Puritans based their argument on Deuteronomy 22.5,[3] which they interpreted as a commandment forbidding the actor's 'metamorphosing' into 'idolatrous ... brutish formes', in Prynne's words.[4] Nevertheless, as William B. Worthen points out, this biblical support was used to cover up primary fears underlying their prohibition against theatre: that the player's art 'unmakes' God's creation, and that self-transformation leads to a dissolution of identity, a breakdown of 'social hierarchies' and a blurred distinction between genders.[5] Conversely, the pro-theatre camp likened the player's transformation to an inspired act or a godlike re-creation of life's forms, couching their arguments in Neoplatonic philosophers who lauded the divine basis of art.

Significantly, both anti- and pro-theatricalists invoke Ovid in their polemics. Prynne uses the term 'metamorphosing' itself when referring to the actor's damnable art, and Gosson, when speaking about the way the theatrical performance ravishes its audience, references the 'sweete numbers of poetry' as the means of seduction, perhaps suggesting an association with Ovid. Notably, when condemning male effeminacy, which he sees as an effect of playgoing, Gosson appropriates Ovid's description of Roman audiences from *Ars Amatoria*:

> In Rome, when Plaies or Pageants are showne: Ovid chargeth his Pilgrims to creep close to the Saintes whom they serve and shew their double diligence to lifte the gentlewomens roabes from the grounde for rolling in the duste.[6]

In this case, Ovid is placed at the centre of issues concerning gender and the theatrical experience, appropriated to prove its dangerous potential to turn men into slaves of love who shamefully exhibit feminine submission and wallow in sinful behaviour. However, those who defend theatre, such as Heywood, also use Ovid and the same basic arguments, but in support of rather than objection to the stage. Both sides harp on the individual actor's metamorphosis and its powerful effects, focusing on whether or not they are morally corrupting or edifying. Not surprisingly, then, Ovidian subject matter and methods infuse the plays of this period, leading up to and culminating in the English Ovidian theatre at the end of the sixteenth century.

Ovidian transformations structure many of John Lyly's court dramas and, of course, many university plays. Ovid is comically linked to the latter in the Cambridge play *The Second Part of the Return from Parnassus*, when the character of Will Kempe complains that 'Few of the vniuersity [men] pen plaies well, they smell too much of that writer *Ouid*, & that writer *Metamorphoses*' (4.3.1767–8).[7] But, despite this satiric jab at Shakespeare's players, the public theatre was immersed in Ovidian models, with Marlowe and Shakespeare fuelling the Ovid movement. Following Marlowe's lead, Shakespeare exploits the potential of Ovid on the stage in various ways, particularly through pivotal metadramatic scenes in his own plays. It is no coincidence that his *most* Ovidian plays, which involve references to iconic Ovidian figures and tales or direct appropriations of Ovid's poetry – often in multi-layered metadramatic scenes (as in *A Midsummer Night's Dream*, *Hamlet*, *The Tempest* and *Julius Caesar*) – stage a heightened focus on the practice of playing and the power of theatricality to move an audience. In *Julius Caesar*, Shakespeare grafts Ovidian myths of Actaeon, Orpheus and Julius Caesar himself onto his source material from Plutarch, thereby exploring connections between theatre, myth and religious rites.

The year 1599, when *Julius Caesar* was most likely first performed, was one of special importance in the history of Ovidian influence on the early modern English stage.[8] That year marked the end of a decade that had been dominated by the legacy of Christopher Marlowe, whose innovative plays were greatly inspired by Ovid's poetry, methods and perspectives. At this turning point, playwrights like Shakespeare reflected on the role that Ovid would play in the future of the theatre. As Heather James has claimed recently, '[i]n 1599, Ovid mattered more than ever' for Shakespeare – not for his own career, but for the English theatre as a whole.[9] And, I would argue, this importance resonates in the play most likely performed in the autumn of that year, perhaps one of the earliest productions staged at the newly constructed Globe theatre – *Julius Caesar*.[10]

Although *Julius Caesar* is not typically referred to as an 'Ovidian play', it is, nevertheless, infused with intertexts from Ovid's poetry that relate directly to ambivalent views of the theatrical experience. The opening scene of *Julius Caesar* encapsulates the debate between pro- and anti-theatricalists, with Ovid as a meaningful subtext. Shakespeare shifts the historical time frame so that the play opens in mid-February, during the feast of Lupercal – the rites of the god Faunus. Naomi Conn Liebler has examined the importance of this change in relation to Plutarch, but not to Ovid's *Fasti*, a poem that explores the customs, myths and legends corresponding to all the holidays of the Roman calendar.[11] Ovid's narrator explains that runners shed their garments on the festival day of Lupercal because the god Faunus himself distrusted apparel, which he saw as deceitful, for he was fooled – and made a fool of – when he attempted to rape the disguised Hercules by mistake.[12] Ovid's comic anecdote about the falsity of costume adds an undertone of mockery to the serious attitudes of Flavius and Murellus, who – similar to the Puritans' iconoclasm and anti-theatricalists' distrust of theatrical representation – order the plebeians to 'Disrobe the images, / If you do find them decked with ceremonies' (*Flav.* 1.1.64–5), for they will '[l]et no images / Be hung with Caesar's trophies' (1.1.69–70).[13] This Puritanical attitude is made explicit by Cassius who, according to Caesar, 'loves no plays' (1.2.202); and Caska, who compares the cheering crowd to a 'tag-rag people' who responded to the show of Caesar thrice refusing the crown with 'clap[s]' and 'hiss[es]', just as 'they use to do the players in the theatre' (1.2.257–9).

Ovid figures as the nexus in the play's treatment of these positions, as well as those concerning Julius Caesar himself. In Book 15 of his *Metamorphoses*, he facetiously praises the Emperor Augustus – Caesar's successor who banished Ovid – by narrating the events occurring before, during and after the assassination of Julius Caesar as a kind of mock-myth.[14]

Through his over-the-top narration, he exposes the ridiculousness of Augustus's claim to godhead while still seemingly praising the emperor and reiterating his claim to divinity. Venus and the other gods cause atmospheric calamities in response to their knowledge of Julius Caesar's impending murder in Ovid's *Metamorphoses*. Since the gods cannot reverse Caesar's fate, they show their anger by engendering omens in the heavens and the earth, including fire and blood in the sky, earthquakes, weeping statues, howling owls and dogs and so on. In Golding's rendition, 'the stares brands oft seemd burning bright' as '[i]t often rayned droppes of blood', and '[t]he Screeche owle sent from hell / Did with her tune unfortunate in every corner yell'. Statues shed tears and 'dogs did howle, and every where appeered gastly spryghts. / And with an earthquake shaken was the towne' (15.884–96).[15] Of course, as Ovid's description is satirical at Augustus's expense, his narrative should be read as almost tongue-in-cheek.

In *Julius Caesar*, Shakespeare layers Ovid over Plutarch's more 'factual' and underplayed description of the 'straunge and wonderfull signes that were sayd to be seene before Caesars death'.[16] Conversely, the omens in Shakespeare's play are delivered in earnest, not with Ovid's ironic edge, rendering them more ambiguous and terrifying, as they are unrelated to an identifiable source in the gods' behaviour, as in Ovid.[17] Before Caesar's murder in Shakespeare's tragedy, the heavens open up to release a torrential downpour of fire (1.3.10), characterizing what Cassius calls a night 'Most bloody, fiery, and most terrible' (1.3.130). These references – along with a plethora of others – associate the extreme phenomena of the heavens to actions of animals, particularly a lioness giving birth in the street and lions (2.2.17, 46; 1.3.20), to Ghosts and spirits (1.3.63, 69), and to living human beings, such as the 'ghastly women' whom Caska describes as '[t]ransformed with their fear' (1.3.23–4). Caska's horrified humans resemble martyrs in miraculous torments: some consumed in flames, staggering through the streets, another with the left hand blazing (1.3.15–32).

These images of martyrdom relate to the play's intense scrutiny of the deification – and deflation – of Caesar himself. In treating this subject, Shakespeare also supplements Plutarch with Ovid. In response to Cassius's appeal for Publius Cimber, Caesar famously claims that he is 'constant as the northern star', unflinching in his resolve that 'Cimber should be banished, / And constant do remain to keep him so' (3.1.60, 72–3). The simile echoes Ovid's hyperbolic, facetious praise of Caesar as deity who has been transformed into a heavenly star, not for all his conquests, but for the legacy of his heir. In Golding's translation, Jove proclaims upon Julius Caesar's death that '[h]e shall to heaven among the starres' (15.942), to be joined later by his descendant, Augustus, after he has lived a long life. Venus, upon hearing Jove's declaration, effects the metamorphosis, transferring Caesar's 'spryght' to 'the skye among the starres that glister bryght' (15.950–2). She then notices that Caesar's spirit has become 'a goodly shining starre', as 'it up aloft did stye / And drew a greate way after it bryght beames like burning heare' (15.955–6). Importantly, however, by grafting Ovid's mock-myth of Julius Caesar onto Plutarch's serious biographies, Shakespeare is able to create a dual effect: he re-enacts the mythos of Julius Caesar and demystifies it at the same time.

Through this dual effect, Shakespeare exposes the pagan roots of Christianity by conflating mythology with the sacred in a much different way than the moralizing Christian or humanist allegorical interpreters of Ovid had done previously. Shakespeare shows the likeness between pagan and religious myth without a clear Christian message or moral attached to it, primarily through the staging of Ovidian myth fused with early modern religious discourses. Two of Ovid's iconic figures – Actaeon and Orpheus – are associated with hagiography, all culminating in Antony's theatrical transfiguration of Caesar's corpse into a saint. James O. Wood first noted the traces of Ovid's myth of Actaeon in *Julius Caesar*, pointing out the imagery of the 'hart' and hounds or 'dogs' throughout the play, especially in Antony's description of Caesar's death:

> Here wast thou bayed, brave hart.
> Here didst thou fall. And here thy hunters stand
> Signed in thy spoil and crimsoned in thy lethe.
> O world, thou wast the forest to this hart,
> And this indeed, O world, the heart of thee.
> How like a deer, strucken by many princes,
> Dost thou here lie? (3.1.204–10)

Antony's speech here is inflected with the myth of Actaeon, who is transformed into a stag for his transgression of viewing Diana bathing naked, and consequently torn limb from limb by his own hounds. Wood notes that the language here echoes that of Golding, who describes Actaeon as a 'hart' dismembered savagely by his own 'dogges' (3.225–303), and the line 'crimsoned in thy lethe' carries with it a 'hint of mythological undertone'.[18] Furthermore, as Wood claims, Shakespeare changes the number of Caesar's wounds from twenty-three in Plutarch to thirty-three in *Julius Caesar*, which may suggest another connection to Ovid's myth, as Actaeon famously has thirty-three hounds, which are named in *Metamorphoses* (3.245–71) and referenced in Conti's *Renaissance Mythology*.[19]

The image of Actaeon's disjointed corpse is coupled with Shakespeare's depiction of the poet Cinna's death in Act 1, Scene 3, which strongly suggests the Ovidian figure of Orpheus, the god of poetry who also is brutally attacked and mutilated at the hands of enraged female worshippers of Bacchus. Like Actaeon, the figure of Orpheus is associated with the martyr. Cinna provides another fascinating tie to Ovid; as Margaret Maurer notes, although very little of Cinna's own writing survived, he is frequently noted in Catullus's well-known elegies, and his poem *Smyrna* is retold by Ovid as the tale of Myrrha in *Metamorphoses*, Book 10.[20] This tale of a young girl's transgressive, incestuous love for her father is narrated as part of Orpheus's song, following the myth of Pygmalion and preceding the story of Venus and Adonis – Myrrha's son from this incestuous union. Significantly, Cinna's poem, as retold by Ovid, ends with the birth of Adonis, the pagan deity of regeneration who was interpreted allegorically as a type for Christ.

These mythological layers comment on the theatrical, ritualistic assassination of Caesar, the sacrificial 'calf' that Hamlet jokingly calls him in his exchange with Polonius.[21] Despite their earlier comments that align them with anti-theatricalists, Brutus and Cassius see themselves as actors playing a part in a script that they themselves have written. The shift from their earlier negative view of acting to this positive one of their own function as 'actors' and 'playwrights' adds a layer of hypocrisy to their actions. In advising his fellow conspirators on how to act – his own 'advice to the players' speech – Brutus tells them to 'look fresh and merrily. / Let not our looks put on our purposes, / But bear it as our Roman actors do, / With untired spirits and formal constancy' (2.1.223–6). As Roman actors wore masks, Brutus seems to be referring to early modern players, who may have energetically performed intense 'passions' with a dignified fixedness – or restraint.[22] As Paul Menzer has argued, early modern actors were often known to employ such restraint when conveying emotion, thereby demonstrating the character's effort to contain overwhelming passion.[23]

Importantly, Brutus fuses the idea of acting on stage with performing a sacred ritual, one which will make their act immortal. Brutus pleads, 'Let's be sacrificers, but not butchers' (2.1.165) who 'carve ... [Caesar] as a dish fit for the gods' (2.1.172). When he imagines their big scene to come – the ritualistic killing of Caesar – Brutus calls for them to 'bathe our hands in Caesar's blood / Up to the elbows and besmear our swords' (3.1.106–7).[24] Both Cassius and Brutus fantasize that their performance will bring them a kind of immortality, as it will be re-enacted over and over again in future generations. In response to Cassius's question, 'How many ages hence / Shall this our lofty scene be acted over / In states unborn and accents yet unknown?' (3.1.111–13), Brutus prophetically announces, '[h]ow many times shall Caesar bleed in sport / That now on Pompey's basis lies along, / No worthier than the dust?' (3.1.114–16). Here, both Cassius and Brutus remind the audience that Shakespeare's play is just such a re-enactment, one that intimates that actors on stage resurrect the dead – a point that relates to the play's emphasis on the transformative power of theatre, myth and religious transfiguration of the human into the sacred body. Through Antony's oratory over the bleeding body of Caesar, Shakespeare documents the making of a martyr, demonstrating how the blood and wounds of the body accrue meaning when transposed into a holy icon, simultaneously unveiling that process and reinvesting it with ritual meaning onstage.[25]

The martyred body

Julius Caesar's sacrificial blood and martyred wounds, in particular, suggest rich meanings inherited from what Caroline Walker Bynum describes as the late medieval 'cult of blood', a phenomenon centred on Christ's wounds that evidenced the 'violent quality of the religiosity itself – what we might call its visual violence, especially the prominence of the motifs of body parts and of blood'.[26] Medieval Christians contemplated depictions of dismembered, bleeding bodies in order to achieve a transcendent, mystic state, with the flow of blood providing a sensual and spiritual outlet, a kind of 'ecstasy'; and to earn indulgence and be sheltered from life's hardships, they adored and prayed to renditions of Christ's wounds.[27] Portrayals of Christ's dismembered body parts, with wounds foregrounded or disconnected from the figure of Jesus, were omnipresent. This cult of wounds appears in verbal as well as visual culture, as in the recurrent figure of the *imago pietatis* or 'man of sorrows', a visual trope of Christ or another saint pictured upright in his grave, exhibiting the bleeding orifices on his hands and feet.[28] Furthermore, Christ's wounds are fashioned into a blazon in devotional literature, illustrated medieval poetry and medieval drama, combining text and image.[29] The blazon of Christ's wounds is staged in the Towneley Cycle's *Last Judgement,* a play that foregrounds the tortured body on display. In the scene of the last judgement, Christ holds out his arms and exhibits his wounds, providing his own 'verbal blazon of his mutilated body', as Owens describes it, pointing out the map of his wounds on his body and explaining their significance to the Christian's salvation.[30] Shakespeare draws from this tradition in *Julius Caesar* by staging Antony's blazon of Caesar's wounds, noted below, in his double-edged theatrical metamorphosis of the corpse of Caesar into a holy icon.

Shakespeare first introduces the subject of holy blood and its meanings in the two versions of Calphurnia's prophetic dream – the former, Caesar's description, is based on Plutarch, with added detail; the latter, Decius's interpretation, which emphasizes holy blood and sacrifice, is Shakespeare's own invention.[31] Caesar depicts a horrific image of 'lusty' Romans bathing and revelling in blood spouting from his statue: 'She dreamt tonight she saw my statue, / Which, like a fountain with an hundred spouts, / Did run pure blood; and many lustful Romans / Came smiling and did bathe their hands in it' (2.2.76–9). In order to pacify Caesar, Decius gives the dream a positive spin, describing it as a 'vision fair and fortunate'. In his version, the 'smiling Romans bathed' in the nurturing, healing blood 'sporting' from 'pipes' in Caesar's statue, for from Caesar 'great Rome shall suck / Reviving blood' (2.2.84–8). Here, Caesar's blood functions as a kind of holy essence. In these two versions of Calphurnia's dream, Shakespeare explores contradictory senses of blood, framing a shift from the depiction of Caesar as Rome's betrayed military hero to that of a sacred image, setting up for Antony's transformation of Caesar's wounded, dead body into a holy icon.[32]

The fountain 'sporting' reviving, internal blood in Decius's version may be considered positive – revitalizing or exhilarating. In this tradition, holy blood becomes an invigorating liquid that carries 'charges' in its flow to cleanse and even 'inebriate' those who drink it or bathe in it.³³ This image is punctuated by Decius's final note that Caesar's blood will become like that of medieval saints, as 'great men shall press / For tinctures, stains, relics, and cognizance' (2.2.88–9). Decius's reading, given to neutralize Calphurnia's warning, nonetheless foreshadows Brutus's portrayal of the killing as a ritual sacrifice and Antony's rhetorical transposition of Caesar as a sacred image. Through his staging of Antony's 'play-within-the-play', Shakespeare reveals how Julius Caesar, a man – in this case, one who is powerful but nonetheless human, exhibiting obvious physical frailty and weakness – may be magically transformed into a holy martyr.

As Caesar's corpse lies bleeding at the foot of Pompey's statue, it is prime material for martyrdom – that is, for inscription with meanings as a sacred icon. For Julia Reinhard Lupton, the emblematic meanings surrounding the saint are developed through hagiography, the textual making of a martyr, which is structured according to three steps based on three moments of the saint's suffering: 1) the first, *Iconicity*, relates to the exhibition of the martyr's body and its initial wounds; 2) the second, *Canonicity*, refers to the enrolment of the martyr in the list of saints, based on the 'cutting short' of the saint's mutilation through 'decapitation'; 3) the final, *Reliquary Function*, revolves around the sacred rituals employed in the saint's burial.³⁴

Beyond the verbal and visual textual inscription of martyrdom, European cultural practices between the Middle Ages and the Renaissance highlighted the display of holy bodies, a stage that I suggest should be added to Lupton's moments as 4) the *Theatrical Function* of martyrdom. Katharine Park notes that the public display of prospective saints' corpses, including those of popes, further supported this cult of martyrdom. Followers were known to undress the sacred body in the open to stress the fervour of public adoration that was stirred by viewing the holy icon, along with the items used in relation to the saint's body, which were considered to have miraculous power.³⁵ In *Julius Caesar*,

Shakespeare stages this *Theatrical Function* to investigate theatre's deeply rooted investment in pagan and Christian mythology, thereby revealing the very thin line between sacred religious rites and dangerous practices of magic or sorcery.

By staging the creation of Julius Caesar as martyr within a play highly inflected with Ovidian intertexts (Actaeon, Orpheus, and the satirical 'apotheosis of Julius Caesar'), Shakespeare not only discloses the process by which bodies are made sacred, but also he underscores the connection between Christianity and its pagan past, via Catholicism. The idea that the iconic saint replaced past gods is a heated point for Reformation Protestants, who see hagiography as the site where Catholicism and paganism meet. Lupton explains: 'The displayed martyr is a proto-icon who both destroys and stands in for the rejected idols; indeed, in the Protestant discourse on the religious image, hagiography will come to mark the structural and historical complicity between pagan idolatry and Catholic iconography'.[36] Rome itself suggests this association in Protestant discourse and beyond, as the notion that the Catholic Church rose from the ashes of Rome was well known in early modern culture.[37] Shakespeare's Rome, with its clearly anachronistic contexts, emphasizes the grafting together of classical and Christian worlds, and his appropriation of Ovid's (albeit ironic) description of Julius Caesar as a god at the end of his *Metamorphoses* (Book 15) into his own depiction of Caesar as a Christian martyr even more strongly highlights this juxtaposition of the two.

While in soliloquy over the corpse, Antony creates an image of Caesar as martyr drawing from the traditions above, employing the *theatrical function* to highlight the *iconicity* of the saint's body, which he extends into the *reliquary function* in his funeral oration. By emphasizing the *theatrical function* of martyrdom, Shakespeare stresses the tension between the Catholic and Protestant views on the morality of images, especially the problem of theatrical representation, harkening back again to the extreme, iconoclastic Protestant position against the stage. Typically, Shakespeare seems simultaneously to support and to undermine both Protestant and Catholic outlooks. He is at once an iconoclast, unveiling the manipulative process by which Antony transposes Caesar into a martyr; and concurrently an icon builder, affirming the theatrical power of the image.

By unveiling the process of making a martyr, Shakespeare demystifies sacred ritual while at the same time reinvesting it with meaning in the display of actor-as-Caesar's body onstage, particularly in his blazon of Caesar's wounds, which draws from the medieval traditions noted above. Antony first addresses Caesar's body for the off-stage audience only and later for the on-stage plebeians as well. In soliloquy, Antony recalls Ovidian and Senecan traditions by cursing the multitude with war and dissension, calling upon 'Caesar's spirit' to return to exact revenge upon the murderers (3.1.259–75). As he does so, Antony appeals to the ground soaking with Caesar's blood, 'thou bleeding piece of earth', begging for its forgiveness in appearing to secure an alliance with the conspirators, whom he disparages as 'these butchers' (3.1.254–5). Although Caesar cannot consciously display his wounds, Antony does it for him, allowing them to speak, '[w]hich like dumb mouths do ope their ruby lips / To beg the voice and utterance of my tongue' (3.1.260–1).

Antony reiterates this trope of kissing wounds in his public funeral oration at the Forum, first in his display of Caesar's covered body, which he describes as 'marred' and 'wounded', dripping 'gracious drops' of blood through its garments; and then in his dramatic reveal of the corpse, which elicits emotional responses from the crowd, who see the body as a 'piteous spectacle!' and a 'most bloody sight!' (3.2.192–8). Countering Brutus's proclamations of honour, Antony famously points to the bleeding body of Caesar, promising to 'Show you sweet Caesar's wounds, poor poor dumb mouths, / And bid them speak for me', for if Brutus and he switched roles, he would 'put a tongue / In every wound of Caesar that should move / The stones of Rome to rise and mutiny' (3.2.218–23).

Antony brings up the trope again when he declares that if the commons knew what Caesar's will included, 'they would go and kiss the dead Caesar's wounds, / And dip their napkins in his sacred blood, / Yea, beg a hair of him for memory' (3.2.133–5). Through Antony, Shakespeare dramatizes the imagery associated with the cult of Christ's wounds – wounds, lips and tongues – and thus characterizes Caesar as a martyr.[38]

Metamorphosis and the metadramatics of personation

Importantly, here Shakespeare stresses the theatricality of this transfiguration by clearly making his Antony an actor in a deliberately staged scenario for the purpose of affecting audiences. Directly following his stellar performance, Antony lets the audience know that his scene has been consciously played to transform his audience: 'Now let it work. Mischief, though art afoot: / Take thou what course thou wilt' (3.3.251–2). Antony's aside to the audience also reminds them that Antony himself is 'personated' by an actor, and that, as off-stage spectators, they are as vulnerable to the actor's portrayal of the character as the onstage plebeians are to Antony's. The term 'personation', which emerged in writing about acting at this time, referred to the actor's art of portraying a character on stage. Moreover, importantly, Ovidian notions of metamorphosis became the framework from which playwrights imagined and players staged the bodily and facial transformations of acting or 'personating' a role that then was thought to transform audiences.

Indeed, throughout his plays, Shakespeare appropriates Ovid's poetic method of metamorphosis to revolutionize early modern theatrical practices by dramatizing a way that his actors might conceptualize the 'personation' of characters onstage that is neither what we might now term 'naturalistic' nor complete artifice, but rather metamorphic illusion

– transformation that begins with the actor but extends throughout the audience and playing space.[39] Rather than attempting to know the unknowable – exactly how the players 'personated' roles – one may explore how theatrical practices and the theatre itself were rendered meaningful through Ovidian subjects and poetics, analysing the ways in which notions of playing, of 'personation', were conceptualized as metamorphosis or the transfiguration of self into another.

The actor's portrayal of emotion lay at the heart of this transformation, which early modern writers on both sides of the theatrical debate agreed wields tremendous power, whether it was thought to result in negative or positive outcomes for actors and audiences. The polemicists, other commentators and the playwrights themselves emphasized the intensity of emotion embodied by the player, which then carried over to the audience through the actor's change into another self. The early modern meaning of the word 'emotion' draws from the Latin *emovēre*, meaning to 'move out', 'remove' or 'displace'. The early modern sense of this word, in the contexts of the passions (from the Latin *patior*, 'to suffer'), connotes a sense of movement, of carrying over, of disturbance or turbulence.

The player's art was the ability to 'personate' or embody emotion that generated affective responses from audiences, a skill that Shakespeare repeatedly explores through metadramatic scenes that, tellingly, revolve around key Ovidian figures, such as Hecuba (*Meta.*, Book 13), the icon of traumatic loss, in the First Player's speech in *Hamlet* (2.2.448–77; 485–98). In Hamlet's response to the First Player, he registers both the impressive power and the 'monstrous' danger of the Player's demonstration of emotion, which he subsequently holds up as a mirror to himself, berating his own lack of action. This scene, in particular, showcases the overwhelming change in the actor's facial expression and colouring, pointing to a notion of, in Worthen's terms, 'a sense of human identity as malleable and self-created'.[40] Joseph R. Roach briefly relates the early modern obsession with metamorphosis in acting to

Ovid, claiming that '[t]he predilection of the age for Ovidian alterations of bodily state further emphasized the actor's capacity to assume the "perfect shape", as Heywood called it, "to which he had fashioned all his active spirits"'.[41]

Moreover, as Roach explains, this scene and other descriptions of acting indicate the emergent belief in the player's ability to change his interior make-up and exterior shape, to undergo an 'instantaneous' psychophysiological transfiguration that was scripted by playwrights, who ordered that actors 'depict the passions and sudden and violent metamorphoses'.[42] Through the transportation of passions via pneuma, which was thought to carry vital spirits throughout the body, the actor could transform himself and extend the transmutations outwards to his external surroundings and to the audience. For, according to Roach, the player's 'passions, irradiating the bodies of spectators through their eyes and ears, could literally transform the contents of his heart to theirs, altering their moral natures'.[43] The awe-inspiring potential for the shaping of self and others and its flipside, the 'monstrous' dangers of unrestrained emotion and its infective display, are signified by the supreme figure of Ovidian metamorphosis, Proteus.

References to Proteus abound in this era, often used in relation to great oratory and acting. The figure of Proteus was often employed in praise of actors, as in Heywood's portrayal of Edward Alleyn as a 'Proteus for shapes, & Roscius for a tongue'; Richard Flecknoe's description of Richard Burbage as a 'delightful Proteus' who '[s]o wholly transform[ed] himself into his Part, & putting off himself with his cloathes'; and Thomas Randolph's account of Thomas Riley as 'a Proteus, that can take / What shape he please, & in an instant make / Himself into anything: be that or this / By voluntary metamorphosis'.[44] Nevertheless, Proteus is a figure that suggests both this liberating power of metamorphosis and its terrifying hazards. For, although it was often thought to unleash invigorating, creative energy, Protean transformation also was thought to have a frightening edge – the vulnerability to emotion and the threat of imagination's penetration and possession of the body, which could lead to severe melancholy or the dissolution of the self. In his *Anatomy of Melancholy*, Robert Burton points to the dangers of becoming another 'Proteus, or a chameleon [who] can take all shapes,' for it has the force to 'work upon others as well as ourselves'.[45] With the imagination unguarded, the self was thought to be open to penetration by harmful agents, both external and internal. Protean transformation was the most threatening for the actor, whose entire sense of self was at risk in taking on a role, as it left him vulnerable to attack.

The idea of the Protean figure looms over the mythos of Julius Caesar and his death. In the multiple discourses surrounding the story of Julius Caesar, Brutus, Cassius and the others are portrayed as 'actors'; for example, Thomas Beard describes the conspirators as 'actors in this tragedy', and William Fulbecke notes that Brutus served as the 'chiefe actor in Cæsars tragedie'.[46] Shakespeare's treatment of the conspirators' own aversion and compulsion to acting suggests a deeply rooted contradiction in the anti-theatricalists' ideology, which figures significantly in this play. Heywood writes that '*Iulius Cesar* himselfe for his pleasure became an Actor, being in shape, state, voyce, iudgement, and all other occurrents, exterior and interior excellent.'[47] Heywood, most likely drawing from a fusion of narratives from Philemon Holland, cites the legend that Caesar, when he acted in *Hercules Furens*, so fully transformed himself into Hercules's rage that he actually killed the servant playing the character Lychas, who had given the shirt to poison the god to his wife, Deinira.[48] Heywood uses this anecdote to legitimate acting, although the anonymous writer of the 'Refutation', I. G., counters that this story actually provides support for his opposing argument on the dangers of acting.[49] Although Caesar appears in these contexts as the consummate player, as do the conspirators in other writings noted above, it is clear that Antony embodies the Protean figure in Shakespeare's play.

The Protean Antony, infamous for allowing himself to revel in his passions, seems the best able to express and manipulate them in himself and in others. When the Servant first sees the bleeding body of Caesar, Antony responds with apparent empathy, noting the 'infectious' nature of emotion: 'Thy heart is big. Get thee apart and weep', he tells the Servant. 'Passion, I see, is catching, for mine eyes, / Seeing those beads of sorrow stand in thine, / Begin to water' (3.1.283–5). In his soliloquy and here Antony seems to express genuine grief, weeping over Caesar's body, which he continues to do in his performance of grief for the crowd. Of course, Antony's design in his funeral oration is to elicit emotional responses from his audience that will escalate into the violence and havoc that he has planned.

The Protean figure also suggests a link with the supernatural, primarily in the idea that the actor – and the theatrical experience itself – has the power to cast a spell on the audience, with the power to uplift or to cast down. Interestingly, Shakespeare's *Julius Caesar* seems to have garnered a formidable reputation as a play that elicited profound effects on its off- and on-stage spectators, who are transformed by Antony's mesmerizing performance. In 1601, John Weever refers to the importance of Antony's persuasion in the play:

> The many-headed multitude were drawne
> By *Brutus* speech, that Cæsar was ambitious,
> When eloquent *Mark Antonie* had showne
> His vertues, who but *Brutus* was vicious?[50]

The leap from the effect of Antony's speech to the idea that Antony's rhetoric essentially 'raped' the spectators in the theatre, transforming them and thereby generating an intense audience response, is echoed by Leonard Digges much later, in 1623, when he writes:

> So have I seene, when Cesar would appeare,
> And on the Stage at halfe-sword parley were,
> *Brutus* and *Cassius*: oh how the Audience,
> Were ravish'd, with what wonder they went thence.[51]

The idea that theatre 'ravish'd' or bewitched an audience forged a link between the theatrical experience and the supernatural, with its demons who spiritually penetrated their victims and its witches who cast spells on their enemies.

Shakespeare's *Julius Caesar* mixes sacred ritual into this cauldron of theatre and devilish practices of 'damned witchcraft'. The staging of Antony's performance of religious 'magic' – the transfiguration of a bleeding corpse into a holy relic, with its ties to Ovidian mythology and notions of metamorphosis – further entwines the 'magic' of religious ritual with the occult. Shakespeare explores the fusion of Ovid, magic and theatre fully later in *The Tempest*, wherein Prospero embodies the figure of Medea, the Ovidian healer/witch/revenger, casting himself as 'good' in contrast to the 'evil' Sycorax (5.1.33–50). This Medea-like power of raising the dead also surfaces in descriptions of theatre's spectral effects: players often referred to themselves as being ghostlike, composed of insubstantial essences or 'shadows'. Actors, through 'personation', became 'the Ghosts of our ancient Heroes' to have 'walk't againe', as Thomas Gainsford (T. G.) commented; or the Ghost of a hero such as Talbot, 'rais[ed] from dead – bones newe embalmed with the teares of 10,000 spectators', as Thomas Nashe described them in reference to the staging of Shakespeare's *Henry VI*.[52]

In Shakespeare's *Julius Caesar*, Shakespeare raises the famous Roman general from his grave to inhabit the actor's body onstage – only to re-enact his own death, transform into a holy relic and return as avenging ghost. Figuratively and literally, Caesar's spirit haunts this play, and thus the Globe at which it was first staged. The Ghost's 'materialization' on the stage emphasizes the spectral nature of acting, for the actor playing the part of Caesar – who already exists as an apparition or a 'shadow' of Caesar – reappears as the Ghost or 'evil spirit' of Caesar. The actor is, thus, a shadow-of-a-shadow. When visited by Caesar's Ghost, Brutus regards it as a 'monstrous apparition' that has been caused by the frailty of his own perception (4.3.274–5), until the Ghost reveals itself to be '[t]hy evil spirit, Brutus' (4.3.280). Antony refers to Caesar's 'spirit' exacting revenge just after the assassination (3.1.270), and Cassius and Brutus are haunted by the Ghost in their last moments – Cassius sees his death as Caesar's revenge (5.3.45); Brutus views his as fate predetermined by Caesar's Ghost (5.3.94–6, 5.5.17–20). In a play that is so infused with questions about acting and theatrical transformation, the Ghost's manifestation makes explicit the interrelationships between theatre, religious rites and occult 'magic'; and it conjures the spectre of Ovid, which also haunts Shakespeare's play, conflating theatrical magic and Caesar's 'spryght'.

Besides providing this link between the theatre and the supernatural, Ovid was appropriated in ruminations on raising the dead through reincarnation or Pythagoras's theory of metempsychosis or the transmigration of souls, which Ovid expounds at length in *Metamorphoses*, also Book 15. During the sixteenth century, Ovid's discourse on Pythagoras was given great weight of importance; Golding thought that it articulated what he saw as a central theme in the poem and forged a strong link between pagan and Christian beliefs about life after death. Notably, the theory is employed by Francis Meres in his famous comment in which he explicitly connects Ovid with Shakespeare. Meres speculates that '[a]s the soule of *Euphorbus* was thought to live in *Pythagoras*: so the sweete wittie soule of Ovid lives in mellifluous & honytongued *Shakespeare*'.[53] Although Meres cites Shakespeare's poems as examples of this association, the similarity between this notion of the transmigration of souls and the ability of theatre to raise the dead and to transport souls from one body to another seems obvious. Besides the compliment of Shakespeare's talent with verse, Meres's remark suggests a spectral chain that, like the descriptions of theatre itself, traces the haunting of Ovid's spirit through Shakespeare, then the actor, who by 'personation' radiates it outwards into the space of the theatre and into the embodied souls of its audiences. In 1599, Ovid was metamorphosed, again, on the Shakespearean stage – this time through Caesar's Ghost.

5

New Directions: Striking Our Debt to Moral Tragedy: Retributive Economics in *Julius Caesar*

Todd Landon Barnes

John Forlines III, an entrepreneur, former investment banker and JPMorgan Chase executive whose family has served for four generations as major patrons of Duke University, NC, recently joined Duke as a Visiting Professor of Economics. Forlines's course, entitled 'Shakespeare and Financial Markets: Why "This Time" Is Never Different', teaches students about how 'human biases in decision-making transcend cultural and historic boundaries'.[1] *Duke Today* reports that the 'bad decision-making leading up to the 2008 crash is one of the reasons Forlines came up with the course.'[2] According to Forlines, 'A lot of these human behaviors Shakespeare examines exist today, and recognizing them in ourselves is important. Human behavior and policy errors leading to bubbles and bursts are, in fact, ones that Shakespeare addressed in most of his plays 400 years ago'.³ However, historians of modern money flatly disagree, arguing that such booms and busts are products of our contemporary market, unnecessary and impossible until shortly after Shakespeare's lifetime.⁴

These historians argue that our time *is* different. Contrary to the tropes of timelessness and natural evolution – tropes which still dominate the neoliberal economic histories rehearsed by business schools and policy makers – economic historians from anthropology, law, sociology and cultural studies have urged economists to recognize historical difference. Many prominent economists *within* the field of economics itself have averred this necessity. The booms and busts with which we're familiar today are the result of how markets and forms of money, credit and debt have been intentionally designed over time.

In press interviews, Forlines was often asked what insight Shakespeare offers contemporary money managers; time and again Forlines turns to Brutus's speech in *Julius Caesar*:

> There is a tide in the affairs of men
> Which, taken at the flood, leads on to fortune:
> Omitted, all the voyage of their life
> Is bound in shallows and in miseries.
> On such a full sea are we now afloat,
> And we must take the current when it serves,
> Or lose our ventures. (4.3.216–22)⁵

This passage, shorn of context, is a favourite among today's Shakespearean money managers. Contemporary men of affairs are repeatedly drawn to the way this passage naturalizes and dehistoricizes capital's flows, all of which, like the tide, ebb and flow without regulation or design by the state. Forlines – and perhaps Brutus, too – ignores the historically variable nature of collectively organized tides and the ventures they are designed to keep afloat (or sink).

In their last conversation, Brutus and Cassius, like broken

Wall Street bankers, discuss suicide and shame. But unlike Wall Street bankers, their role is more political than economic, their loss a public loss, not a private failure. They cannot raise funds because they lack the political authority to do so, not because they lack business acumen. When Cassius faces the possibility that they have misconstrued everything, the austere Brutus continues to rely on the Invisible Hand of a 'providence of some high powers / That govern us below' (5.1.106–7). There may in fact be a lesson here about the global financial crisis, but Forlines misses the opportunity to learn it. When Forlines reads ancient reversals of fortune into contemporary losses of the Fortune 500, he frames history as an eternal repetition of the same, one that eternalizes Brutus's Stoic optimism and his stubborn faith in the nature of the market's tide.

Forlines is just one of many bankers using Shakespeare to 'construe things after their fashion / Clean from the purpose of the things themselves' (1.3.34–5). In an issue of *Time* magazine published just after the financial crisis, New York City mayor Michael Bloomberg described JPMorgan Chase CEO Jamie Dimon as a Shakespearean hero:

> He has certainly experienced as many spectacular reversals of fortune as any Shakespearean hero. Ten years ago, he was expected to be crowned head of his firm, Citigroup, as it merged with the Travelers Group. Instead he was abruptly pushed aside. But he returned in triumph when he sold Chicago's Bank One to JPMorgan Chase and quickly ascended to command of the House of Morgan himself.[6]

Just after the subprime mortgage crisis had become legible in the winter of 2007, the *New York Times* published a similar piece on Shakespeare and finance, focusing on Jamie Dimon's relationship to his mentor, Sandy Weill, who, according to *Business Insider*, 'pushed Jamie Dimon out of Citigroup because he was too ambitious.'[7] We might wonder if he, like Brutus, claimed that it was not that he loved Dimon less but that he loved Citigroup more. In the *Times* piece, Dimon too reduces the financial crisis to a problem of 'character':

> You can go a long time and be fooled by people's behavior, but Shakespeare gives you insights that help you understand the people you are dealing with. I don't relate what's happening so much to the market as to how people behave ... Shakespeare is even better than Freud in showing you the characters you are dealing with.[8]

Character and psychology are, of course, important, but so is understanding their constitution within the markets such characters ostensibly control. Nevertheless, Dimon disavows the power of the market to shape character and avows Shakespeare's value as a guide for 'dealing with' timeless characters.

Forlines, Bloomberg and Dimon are not the first to coin such analogies between Wall Street and Shakespeare. In fact, the comparison is a commonplace of contemporary journalism and a tried and true formula for a bestseller. Many scholars have explored the booming cottage industry built around bringing Shakespeare's 'timeless' characters into the boardroom.[9] The argument I want to make, however, is not that economists and business executives misunderstand the historically variable nature of 'character' as a literary technology; this much is obviously true. Their fatal flaw is more destructive than this. I want to argue that these economists and business executives do not even understand the main character of their own narratives: the character of money itself. So while economists are busy borrowing art and forging history for their own profit, we can work alongside historians of art to recover a new history of money. In tracing the complex character of money in *Caesar*, I hope to offer such a counter-history.

Literary studies, Shakespeare studies in particular, has long worked to historicize the role of money and markets as they have developed alongside language and drama. In his landmark study, *Money, Language, and Thought*, Marc Shell notes the simultaneous emergence, in ancient Greece, of coinage, tyranny and tragedy.[10] By examining Plutarch's *Lives* and Shakespeare's *Julius Caesar*, this essay traces how these three technologies – monetary, political and dramatic – emerged from the ancient world, were radically redefined during the early modern period and again underwent change in the twentieth century. Shakespeare's *Caesar* compounds two significant yet distinct transformational periods: the dawn of the Roman Empire and the emergence of new forms of finance in early modern Britain. During these periods, the basic tenets underpinning classical liberal economics were incubated, revised and carefully crafted; then, over time, they slowly came to be understood as natural and eternal. Although we have since forgotten and naturalized money's character, a careful reading of *Caesar* can help us track how early modern tragedy dramatized the restructuring of ancient and medieval finance. Rather than assume some transhistorical 'tide in the affairs of men', we might instead notice how the very character of money is contested and crafted throughout the play.

Shakespeare's Roman plays have often been read like palimpsests. Henry Peacham's drawing of *Titus Andronicus*, with its polychronic costuming (i.e. drawn from and combining ancient, medieval and Renaissance clothing) and disregard for historical realism, registers the political force of an early modern stage designed to mobilize contemporary concerns thinly habited in ancient drag. The tales of Elizabeth and Caesar spoke to each other, across time, in many registers, and they can speak to us, too. Both sovereigns reigned over a time of rapidly increasing demand for coin; perhaps more importantly, however, both sovereigns reigned during periods immediately prior to massive transformations in how their citizens understood the nature of coin's liquidity value. Unlike credit–debt relations, which were deeply social and durational, coin's liquidity allowed it to transact anonymously, instantly and without a trace.

Jean-Christophe Agnew describes this transformation: 'The desire for liquidity thereby came to mean something more than the thirst for solvency; it suggested simultaneous readiness and reluctance to transact – a threshold moment of indecision in the cycle of exchange, a moment frozen in the money form itself.'[11] Agnew argues that, unlike the theatrical and public nature of the ancient or medieval markets, the intimacy and subtlety of private exchange was beginning to shape affective performance within, and imaginings of, the early modern marketplace.[12] Increased liquidity produced a new speculative posture, one that entered economic discourse through a novel usage of the word 'deal'. No longer simply a *public*, physical distribution of goods' organized by a fiscal plan, 'deal' came to define the bilateral negotiations of parties engaged in negotiating *private* exchange.[13] In *Caesar*, we find traces of this emerging marketplace. When he reports how 'such a *deal* of stinking breath' (1.2.245) was expended in negotiations between Caesar and Antony in the marketplace, Caska uses 'deal' in a way that straddles both definitions. Antony offers a crown. Caesar refuses. Then we hear of Caesar's speculative posture, his begrudging hesitation, his 'putting it by' though 'he fain would have had it', the repeated offer, Caesar's second refusal 'though he was very loth to lay his fingers off it', and finally Caesar's closing offer: he asks Caska to 'ope his doublet', offering his 'throat to cut' (1.2.238–65). Though Plutarch recounts a similar scene, the affective economies and the language of the early modern market do not appear in his tale. In Shakespeare's *Caesar*, the linguistic hallmarks of an emergent market-place ('deal of breath') are layered atop Rome's ancient market, with its emblematic, illiquid currencies (the crown offered Caesar) and its embodied stakes (Caesar's sovereign vitality).

Those living through Rome's transition from republic to empire witnessed a series of civil wars and conquests, events that ushered in radical changes in the assumptions ancients could make about the nature of money. Similarly, but with crucial differences, the basic assumptions about money held in Jacobethan England would not survive the seventeenth century, which – with the introduction of fractional reserve lending, interest bearing loans and depersonalized forms of transferable debt – culminated in a radical redesign of the money form, the inauguration of England's national debt and the founding of the Bank of England.[14] This chapter works to untangle these strands and recover the differences elided by neoliberal notions of an eternal marketplace. Instead, we will see how various 'deals' in *Caesar* dramatize tensions between emerging and contested forms of ancient and early modern finance. In this essay, I hope to show how *Caesar*'s tensions are structured, in part, by its characters' radically different – and historically specific – ways of understanding the character of money. Caesar's ancient economy of generosity, supported by the bounty of his absolute sovereignty, is challenged by Brutus' austere economy, one rooted in the morality of Neostoicism. The play's dramatic and political conflicts produce a series of economic crises, crises that index historically specific debates about the changing character of money. In the wake of these conflicts, Antony will be forced to save Rome by re-inventing finance. Today, we can read *Caesar* with a new ear for these discourses, but in order to do so, we must first review a new body of heterodox economic scholarship.

The deal is 'all amiss interpreted': heterodox histories of money

Fortunately, since the global financial crisis, new scholars have emerged in an effort to historicize that which Bloomberg, Dimon and Forlines would rather explain away as a transhistorical flaw in human character. New work in the history of finance challenges the theoretical assumptions and historical narratives cherished by the disciplinary field of economics. The 2011 walkout of Harvard University's Economics 10 course perhaps best emblematizes these challenges.[15] The walkout, part of a larger Occupy Harvard movement, registered frustration with orthodox economics' inability to account for, or make narrative sense of, the financial crisis. The walkout included teach-ins questioning classical economics' outmoded narratives, such as its narrative of money's origins, which we might summarize thus: a private and decentralized barter economy naturally and spontaneously gives rise to the convenience of a particular commodity, e.g. gold, which serves as money, an ostensibly 'neutral veil' transparently lubricating even more private exchanges. This narrative, like that articulated by Forlines's Brutus, imagines the state as a mere market actor, one occasionally regulating, from its periphery, a nearly autonomous and private market.

Contemporary economics' fantasy of money's natural and private origins – a myth most recently popularized and perpetuated by Carl Menger's 1892 'On the Origin of Money' – has been thoroughly and repeatedly debunked by historians, anthropologists and legal historians.[16] Despite wide-ranging interdisciplinary consensus that no barter economy has ever given rise to money, Menger's origin story still dominates economic textbooks, curricula (as at Harvard and elsewhere), monetary policy and 'common sense'. This story of money's origin in private property persists, in no small part, because it preserves and eternalizes the neoliberal values of unfettered private exchange.[17] How did this happen? Cambridge sociologist Geoffrey Ingham argues that a 'division of intellectual labor', with economics on one side and social and historical sciences on the other, began with the *Methodenstreit*, the methodological dispute at the turn of the twentieth century between the Austrian School (represented by Menger) and the German Historical School (the school of Max Weber and G. F. Knapp). Since then, Ingham argues, the social sciences have 'abnegated their responsibility for the study of money, by either simply ignoring it or uncritically accepting orthodox economic analysis.'[18] The consequences of this acquiescence have been massive.

A number of recent studies, such as anthropologist David Graeber's *Debt: The First 5000 Years*, legal scholar Christine

Desan's *Making Money: Coin, Currency and the Coming of Capitalism* and sociologist Nigel Dodd's *The Social Life of Money*, are now crossing this disciplinary divide. Graeber's study returns to the premises of the German Historical School to illustrate how '[w]e did not begin with barter, discover money, and then eventually develop credit systems. It happened precisely the other way around. What we now call virtual credit money came first. Coins came much later, and their use spread only unevenly, never completely replacing credit systems.'[19] As we will see, *Caesar* dramatizes economies in such monetary transition. In her talk at the Occupy Harvard teach-ins, Christine Desan warned against thinking of money's origin in private, bilateral barter. Instead, she provided an alternative narrative in which modern money was constituted and designed as a legal technology of the state. Desan concluded that 'Money, it turns out, is an enormously effective mode of governance.'[20] Moving from the thirteenth to the eighteenth centuries, Desan's book tells a riveting chronicle of the changes in England's monetary design. She discovers that money's shape, far from being the spontaneous and natural result of barter, comes instead as a consequence of legal and political will. She writes, '[T]he moneys that result are highly engineered projects, not the happy by-product of spontaneous and decentralized decision[s].'[21] These new histories, which give the lie to the commodity form of money, have renewed interest in 'state theories' of money, theories that show money's origins in tokens, promises, credits and/or debts engineered by the state (both Caesar's and Elizabeth's). Rather than projecting the origins of money into a mythical past of private barter, these scholars have found money's origins in the sovereign's demand for tax/tribute and the law's prerogative to adjudicate debt and determine recompense. As a consequence, scholarship has moved away from largely Marxian interrogations of private commodity exchange and the *capital–labour relation* (e.g. the primitive accumulation of capital via enclosure laws, exports of wool, grain hoarding, etc.) towards new studies of how money's legal and political design negotiates promises and tokens within the *creditor–debtor relation*.

Forgiving ambition's debt: historicizing moral economies

In order to reckon with this history, to understand, for example, the economic and moral calculus of Brutus's claim that, in Caesar's death, 'ambition's debt is paid' (3.1.83), we must examine the emergence, within law, of moralized debt relations. In the wake of neoliberal financialization, the increased prominence of the creditor–debtor relation has returned heterodox economists to Nietzsche's writings on debt, punishment and revenge. The touchstone for these scholars is the second essay of *On the Genealogy of Morality*, where Nietzsche traces the history of legal and moral 'guilt' (*Schuld*) back to its roots in early Judeo-Christian interpretations of 'debt' (*Schulden*). Nietzsche tells the story of the emergence of morality alongside autonomy, responsibility, '*the right to make promises*' and 'the idea that every injury has its *equivalent* and can actually be paid back, even if only through the *pain* of the culprit.'[22] Dodd stresses how Nietzsche 'portray[s] capitalism as an economic system defined not by a system of production or exchange but by its moral economy of debt'.[23] For Nietzsche, Christian morality turns debt into guilt by internalizing punishment-as-revenge, a process that forms what Nietzsche calls *bad conscience*. When this violence is re-externalized, Nietzsche calls this *ressentiment*. Nietzsche critiques the *Lex talionis*, the ancient Babylonian and Biblical law of 'retaliation' *not* for its violent excesses but for *limiting* violence to exact equivalents ('an eye for an eye'):

> [E]verywhere and from early times one had exact evaluations, *legal* evaluations, of the individual limbs and parts of the body ... some of them going into horrible and minute

detail. I consider it as an advance, as evidence of a freer, more generous, *more Roman* conception of law when the Twelve Tables decreed it a matter of indifference how much or how little [flesh] the creditor cut off.[24]

Ancient Roman debtors could be put to death, or their debts could be forgiven. However, the Christian and late Roman demand for equivalence (monetary or otherwise) homogenized and quantified qualitative relations, and while it did lay the foundations for a monetary calculus, it also foreclosed the possibility of noble pardon, generosity, forgiveness or oblivion – robust qualities of one who, like Caesar, knows how to forget. For Elizabethans, the ancient history of the creditor-debtor relation was further modified by the more recent tradition of the *wergild* ('man price'), which, for Ingham and Graeber, further illustrates how 'money has its origins in law.'[25] Jacobethan revenge tragedy syncretized tensions between Senecan and Christian limitations on revenge, the former stressing equilibrium and the avoidance of anger, ire and wrath, the latter leaving vengeance to God ('Vengeance is mine. I will repay.').[26] However, all of these prohibitions merely generated crueller fantasies of transgression, producing a fascination with exact revenge vis-à-vis the meticulous quantification of debts (e.g. 'a pound of flesh'). This obsession with exact vengeance, for Nietzsche, defines and constitutes the roots of modern morality. In this sense, all Jacobethan tragedy, when read didactically from the point of view of Christian morality, is revenge tragedy. We see this moralized vengeance in Brutus's injunction to the conspirators: 'Let's be sacrificers but not butchers … Let's kill him boldly, but not wrathfully' (2.1.165, 171). Sacrifice, like tribute or tax, is a finite, standardized and regulated unit of account. The moral Brutus will make sure to render unto Caesar *exactly* what is due Caesar.

G. Wilson Knight locates what might be called a Nietzschean bad conscience in Brutus, claiming 'He alone bears the responsibility of Caesar's death, since he alone among the conspirators sees – and so creates – its wrongfulness; he alone bears the burden of the conspiracy's failure. He only has a guilty conscience – anguished by an "evil spirit".[27] *Julius Caesar* is not widely recognized as a revenge tragedy, though many scholars – e.g. Norman Rabkin, Nicholas Brooke, James C. Bulman, W. Nicholas Knight and Alan Hager – have made this argument.[28] *Caesar* sits uncomfortably both inside and outside of the genre, mobilizing many of its requisite tropes but arranging them eccentrically. Critics categorizing *Caesar* as a revenge tragedy have noted that both Caesar and Brutus serve, in various ways, as the play's avenger. Hager goes as far as to argue that 'Brutus will simultaneously become Caesar's avenger and his punished murderer in his own suicide – and by the same sword.'[29] Brutus's suicide, his running upon his own sword, literalizes Nietzsche's figuration of bad conscience as the turning-inward of external punishments.

Such scenes motivate John Kerrigan's claim that 'Much revenge tragedy is structured by grim equivalence.'[30] Kerrigan locates the roots of this symmetry in the forensic rhetoric of the courtroom, in revenge tragedy and retributive justice's shared language of 'mimetic againness': re-venge, re-tribution, re-taliation, re-ciprocity, re-storation (of honour), re-cognition (*anagnorisis*).[31] He cites Simon Weil, who argued: 'The desire for vengeance is a desire for essential [albeit imaginary] equilibrium.'[32] Kerrigan links this 'equilibrium' to psychic equilibrium, but it's just as easy to discern a parallel with the formative assumptions of neoclassical economics' general equilibrium theory, the theory that, if everyone paid the (ideal) price, markets would stabilize. Craig Muldrew warns us of anachronistically finding Adam Smith's logic of rational self-interest within a world still governed by 'credit relations, trust, obligation and contracts.'[33] However, we can see the emergence and transformation of proto-capitalist debt relations taking shape through the language of revenge and 'reckoning'. Muldrew notes that 'the verb "reckon" referred to the action of two people coming together to compare their respective debts, and to determine how much each actually owed to the other.'[34] Reckoning provided a way to literally 'get even'.

Linda Woodbridge's *Money and the Age of Shakespeare*, a collection of essays authored by proponents of the New Economic Criticism, describes the late sixteenth century as a period awash in reckoning schools and manuals. Luca Pacioli's work, published in 1588, introduced Elizabethans to double-entry bookkeeping, which replaced counters with the Venetian system of 'reckoning by pen' in columns for debtor and creditor.[35] The logics of reckoning, equilibrium of obligation and double-entry bookkeeping structure the calculi of debt and revenge in *Caesar*. This logic is especially evident in Brutus's language. Though Knight argues that ultimately 'Brutus' ship of "honor" dashes upon the hard rocks of finance', we might notice how Brutus figures honour financially throughout the play.[36] Brutus is obsessed with debt repayment and equilibrium. His cost–benefit analysis determines not that he 'loved Caesar less, but that [he] loved Rome more' (3.2.21–2). In the market-place, Brutus reckons his debt to Caesar in balanced rhetorical equations – two successive tetracolons (i.e. two parallel sets of four juxtaposed cola or clauses of identical length and shape). The debt of the first tetracolon is reckoned by the second:

As Caesar loved me, I weep for him; as he was fortunate, I rejoice at it; as he was valiant, I honour him: but as he was ambitious, I slew him. There is tears, for his love; joy, for his fortune; honour, for his valour; and death, for his ambition.

(3.2.24–8)

Brutus, here, strives for a Stoic equilibrium of obligation (his Stoicism is Shakespeare's invention), describing retributive violence as though it were a transaction structured within the Elizabethan marketplace. He does not want to be a revenger, to give in to wrath, to tip the scales. As he kills himself, Brutus's apostrophe strives to quantify and cancel his debt to Caesar: 'Caesar, now be still / I killed not thee with half so good a will' (5.5.50–1). The rhyme of this couplet, itself a form of the 'mimetic againness' Kerrigan calls 'phonic revenge', serves as a final reckoning, achieving the equilibrium which will allow the play's tensions to settle.[37]

Caesar reckons differently. Nietzsche's writings are full of praise for Caesar, whose generosity makes him one of the 'finest type'.[38] Plutarch tells of a young Caesar captured and ransomed by pirates. These pirates, who demanded 'twenty talents' for his release, held Caesar captive for thirty-eight days. Caesar, laughing at his captors' valuation, generously outbid them by promising fifty.[39] When Caesar punishes – and he did eventually execute his captors – he does so without rancour, bad conscience or *ressentiment*. Caesar has been widely recognized for his *excessive* and *disproportionate* forgiveness, pardon and mercy. After fighting with Pompey against Caesar, both Brutus and Cassius benefited from such clemency. In his reading of Nietzschean tragedy, Gilles Deleuze argues that 'a true renaissance is needed in order to liberate the tragic from all the fear and pity of the bad listeners who gave it a mediocre sense born of bad conscience'.[40] When Nietzsche claims 'It is I who discovered the tragic', his boast generously gifts us 'tragic joy' – a joy that, Caesar-like, cancels debts, affirms the present and donates to the future.[41]

Such generosity was still possible within ancient Rome's fiscally structured economy – one without banks, wage labour or depersonalized, transferable debt – where money was explicitly tied to sovereignty, martial violence and the exchange of bodies.[42] Ancient coin was backed by a sovereign promise, which was further backed by the violence of an army. As Antony stands above Caesar's body, presented to the citizenry *in the market-place*, he reminds his audience how Caesar 'hath brought many captives home to Rome, / Whose ransoms did the general coffers fill' (3.2.89–90). Money enters society through soldiers and conquest, who, through massive and massively expensive armies, were increasingly expanding and creating new provinces.[43] Roman provinces were forced to pay tribute to Rome in Roman coins; raw metal would not suffice. Soldiers could offer conquered people these special tokens. So tight was the connection between martial violence and value that the word 'soldier' itself 'comes from the Roman "solidus", the gold coin in which they were paid'.[44] Some conquered peoples, however, became slaves, working in Roman mines to produce yet more coin. Graeber, adapting a term coined by Ingham, dubs this heroic economy the 'military-coinage-slavery complex' in order to signify the connection between coinage, violence and bodies.[45]

Between the second and first centuries BCE the amount of silver coin circulating in Roman territories increased tenfold.[46] However, in the final decades of the Republic, the supply of silver coin rapidly dwindled.[47] In response, Caesar introduced gold coinage to supplement this deficit. This huge change occurred just two years prior to Caesar's death.[48] When Caesar dies, however, Rome loses its central stakeholder – the constant by which all variables are measured. When Antony discovers Caesar's dead corpse, we can hear him struggle to calculate his grief amidst the crisis of currency that inevitably comes as a result of the sovereign's death. He asks 'Are all thy conquests, glories, triumphs, spoils, / Shrunk to this little measure?' (3.1.149–50). We should note, here, the inadequacy of the 'measure' in the face of such heterogeneous – even figurative – forms of value. The ancient *manubia*, ambiguously valued spoils of war, are beyond calculable 'measure'. Antony asks to die at the swords of the conspirators, worthy swords 'made rich / With the most noble blood of all this world' (3.1.155–6). Within the tradition of the *wergild*, in addition to the 'man price', medievals calculated what they called 'honour price', the price paid to restore another's diminished honour. We learn from David Graeber that, in medieval law, only in the sovereign's body are 'honour price' and 'man price' the same.[49] This special exception, the one that founds money's constitutive tie to royal prerogative, was strong in the ancient world but would be progressively obscured throughout the seventeenth century as the English came to see money as a private commodity.

Antony's funeral oration preserves the link between price, value and the sovereign's blood. Antony's real trick, though, will be to make dead Caesar's corpse continue to produce value in the literal market-place. His eulogy ends with language of accounting and financial speculation; making the private public, Antony bequeaths Caesar's 'private arbours' as 'common pleasures' (3.2.239, 241). He urges the citizens to take up this currency of the sovereign's body, to 'go and kiss dead Caesar's wounds / And dip their napkins in his sacred blood, / Yea, beg a hair of him for memory, / And, dying, mention it within their wills, / Bequeathing it as a rich legacy / Unto their issue' (3.2.133–8). In order to make this value even more explicit, Antony tells the crowd of Caesar's promise, written in his sealed will: 'To every Roman citizen he gives ... seventy-five drachmas' (3.2.234–5). Rome's level of monetization, like Elizabethan England's, could not keep pace with its citizens' needs. Antony's 'seventy-five drachmas' promised to stem the receding tide of liquidity, stimulating the economy and reorganizing political alliances.

What's critical, here, is Antony's speculative faith in the future and his right to make promises. Nietzsche directs his critique of the promise-making animal at those for whom responsibility comes by way of bad conscience; however, for generous and noble figures, Nietzsche tells a different story. Antony, like Caesar, presents such a noble type, a type who finds 'beggary in the love that can be reckoned' (*Antony and Cleopatra* 1.1.15). Antony's generosity shatters the Christian economy of revenge by participating in the excessive economy of the gift. Antony's speech, following Brutus's moralized reckoning, recognizes the sovereign's bounty. Antony has been studying Caesar's power to *produce*, rather than merely *manage*, economies. In Act I, Antony notes that 'When Caesar says, "Do this", it is performed' (1.2.10). In the market-place, Caesar's will, a written bond, allows Antony to exit Rome's financial and political crisis. Unlike Brutus's moralized and backward-looking vengeful reckonings, Antony eschews austerity, understanding economics as generous, performative and future-oriented. In his reading of Nietzsche, Peter Sloterdijk could be describing Caesar's funeral when he writes: 'History splits into the time of the economy of debt and the time of generosity. Whereas the former thinks of repayment and retaliation, the latter is interested only in forwards-donating'.[50] For Brutus, time, given shape by debt, brings in his revenges. For Antony, time is 'a delay in the future proliferation of generosity.'[51]

Caesar's death marks a turning point for coinage. During the turbulent final years of the Republic, people worried about the purity of coins. Romans were more conscious than we are about how money's value derived from the stability of a central stakeholder. During civil war, the value of coins as metal (i.e. metallism) became more stable than their tenuous link to a shifting political authority (i.e. nominalism). Antony must play upon his audience's complicated allegiances to and understandings of both metallism and nominalism. The term 'metallism' refers to a system wherein money's value is guaranteed by the value of its metal content (e.g. coin) or its symbolic relationship to such precious metals (e.g. the gold standard); these metals serve in many ways as money's 'referent'. Alternately, 'nominalism' refers to a system which guarantees money's nominal or face value by connecting this value to the promise of a sovereign authority and the latter's ability to make law and mobilize bodies in labour or violence (e.g. 'fiat' money). Metallism sees money's value as natural and private; nominalism sees money's value as conventional and civic. Beginning with Octavian/Augustus's reign, Romans stopped weighing coins; they simply counted them, trusting their nominal value and inspecting only for forgery.[52] We learn from Ingham that by the time of 'the death of Augustus in [14 CE], Rome's '"sound money" was accepted over an area larger than any before or after until the nineteenth century'.[53] Evidence of standardized Augustine coins have been found across the provinces, from Asia, to Syria, to Egypt, all of which suggests the triumph of imperial prerogative and an increase in the centralization of monetary authority.[54]

Shakespeare's Antony, in his funeral oration, preserves and strengthens the Roman tradition of monetary nominalism by rhetorically securing the link between coin and sovereign authority. He must assure the marketplace of coin's 'constant', 'true-fixed and resting quality' (3.1.60–1). To do so, Antony must embrace what new scholarship calls 'performative economics'. When Nixon took the US off the gold standard in the 1970s (metallism's death knell), economists had to negotiate similar insecurities around the money form, insecurities that persist for today's goldbugs. Like Antony, today's economists are turning to performative theories of economics. The concept of 'performativity', introduced by J. L. Austin during his 1955 lectures at Harvard, forms the basis of 'speech act theory', a framework wherein, over and above what it 'means' or 'represents', language is studied according to its rhetorical and material effects – the way *saying* often constitutes *doing*. Likewise, performative economics analyses how money and other economic technologies *produce*, rather than merely *represent* or *refer to*, civic capacities, resources and relations. Michel Callon, an anthropologist and perhaps the most prominent scholar in the field of performative economics, describes this field's premise: 'Economics is not just about "knowing" the world, accurately or not. It is also about "producing" it. It is not (only) about economics being "right" or "wrong" but ... about it being "able" or "unable" to transform the world.'[55] Antony is able. Caesar's word is his bond, and his promises will draw upon this authority to secure a new economy. We learn from Plutarch that, during the Battle of Philippi, Antony and Octavian increased the scope of their promising economy, '[promising] that every common soldier should receive for his pay five thousand drachmas.'[56] The proscription scene in Shakespeare's play only tells part of this grim reckoning, the part legible within early modern economics. Plutarch tells the Roman version, wherein the triumvirs 'did not limit themselves to the forfeiture of the estates of such as were proscribed, defrauding the widows and families, nor were they contented with laying on every possible kind of tax and imposition.'[57] They assassinated family members, arranged marriages and even robbed the funds held by the vestal virgins. All of this, though, had to be ratified by marriages – rather, the exchange of women.[58] Antony, of course, has Cicero's head and right/writing hand cut from him, and 'when he had satisfied himself with the sight of them, ordered them to be hung up above the speaker's place in the forum.'[59] Of this proscription, Plutarch writes: 'I do not believe anything ever took place more truly savage or barbarous than this composition'.[60] If this is vengeance, it is full retribution without equivalence or balanced scales.

Testing our mettle

During the reigns of Henry VIII and his son Edward VI, the sixteenth century witnessed the 'Great Debasement' between 1542 and 1551.[61] In addition to the regular shaving and clipping of coins by citizens, the royal mints mixed precious metals with increasing amounts of baser metal; these practices produced coins whose metal value was a fraction of their nominal value (i.e. 'debasement'). The debasement caused prices to nearly double by mid-century. At the beginning of her reign, between 1560 and 1561, Elizabeth initiated 'the great Elizabethan recoinage', in which debased currency was withdrawn from circulation and replaced by coin with a nominal value equal to the value of its metal content – once again reconnecting monarchical sovereignty with the metallic value of coin. That the monarch's face appeared on coins guaranteeing their 'face value' points up the power of royal prerogative to constitute value.[62] In fact, Henry's violation of the English commitment to nominalism was the exception that proved the rule of English law, a law passed down from strong Anglo-Saxon and Roman traditions of nominalism.

Desan notes how, 'While continental jurists developed arguments assimilating coin to metal, English common law debt would preserve monetary "nominalism".'[63] In the wake of the debasement, however, Desan illustrates how, legally, metallism 'figured as a kind of protest', stirring new debates about the nature of money. She claims that in the last fifteen years of the sixteenth century, nominalism was 'more controversial than at any earlier moment.'[64]

These debates may help us understand Cassius's desire for Brutus to assay his own 'mettle', a term figuratively straddling credit and coin. In Act I, Cassius asks Brutus to compare the names of 'Brutus' and 'Caesar': 'Write them ... Sound them ... Weigh them, [Brutus] is as heavy; conjure with 'em, / "Brutus" will start a spirit as soon as "Caesar"' (1.2.143–6). As soon as Brutus exits, Cassius comments that the gold, 'noble' coin that is Brutus is made of 'mettle [which] may be wrought / From that it is disposed' (1.2.307–8). Here, the base Cassius, whose very name sounds like 'cash' (a resonance already alive to early moderns), equivocates between two very different aspects of money: 1) commodity money with weight; speech act theory would refer to the metal weight anchoring coin's promise as its 'constative' dimension – the dimension in which money either truly or falsely refers to a commodity in the world – and 2) money's capacity to 'conjure'; speech act theory would refer to this as the 'performative' dimension – the dimension wherein money either does or does not shape the world. Ultimately, Brutus's name will not conjure the same value as Antony's promise of 75 drachmas. The performative and nominal aspects of money allow Antony to capitalize on the financial crisis of Caesar's death. Brutus's Stoic constancy and his commitment to the ostensibly 'true' value of his mettle leave him bankrupt and exiled.

In exile, Brutus and Cassius struggle to garner political and economic support. If we look at how Shakespeare alters Plutarch, we can see how his additions reflect contemporary anxieties about the money form, anxieties palpable in Elizabethan courts where, as Muldrew has shown, between

1580 and 1640 debt litigation reached an all-time high.[65] We can see this litigiousness in the argument between Brutus and Cassius before the Battle of Philippi. Plutarch does mention that the argument involved the punishment of Lucius Pella for embezzlement; however, in Plutarch, honour and consistency, rather than money, form the substance of the debate.[66] Shakespeare injects money into the argument, which now centres on Cassius withholding money from Brutus, a minor detail in Plutarch. Brutus demands a reckoning, to which Cassius replies, indignantly, that he feels 'Checked like a bondman; all his faults observed, / Set in a notebook, learned and conned by rote / To cast into [his] teeth' (4.3.96–8).

Brutus then disavows this reckoning, becoming nostalgic for an antique Roman money form, one deriving value directly from sovereign bodies. He says: 'I can raise no money by vile means. / By heaven, I had rather coin my heart / And drop my blood for drachmas than to wring / From the hard hands of peasants their vile trash / By any indirection' (4.3.71–5). A sovereign does not borrow coin; a sovereign is the source of coin. But such forms of monetary integrity had already begun to erode. Shakespeare charts their dissolution in *Richard II*. We can see, here, how Brutus echoes John of Gaunt's dying jeremiad against the 'inky blots and rotten parchment bonds' already in use to extort the gentry (*Richard II* 2.1.64). The author of such 'vile means' was known to be Lord Burghley, Elizabeth's Lord Treasurer.[67] Cassius mirrors Brutus's nostalgia, outbidding him by offering himself as sacrifice, saying 'here, my naked breast: within, my heart / Dearer than Pluto's mine, richer than gold / If that thou beest a Roman take it forth. / I that denied thee gold will give my heart. / Strike as thou didst at Caesar' (4.3.100–3). Both are unprepared and will commit suicide in the face of the seventeenth century's new economy.

The criminalization of debt

Graeber's study of debt illustrates how the early modern period inaugurates 'a turn away from virtual currencies and credit economies and back to [the] gold and silver' standards of the Roman Empire.[68] The growing insistence that coin serve as the exclusive unit of account and means of exchange in early modern England altered the elaborate local credit economies of those living below the money floor, those for whom coin's smallest denominations represented a half-day's labour.[69] Desan notes how 'Population growth, increased urbanization, rising prices, and more extensive monetization – all pushed up the demand for coin during the Queen's reign … [yet] the expanding currency had not kept pace.'[70] This change held huge consequences, chief among which was the way the instantaneous, anonymous transactional logic provided by coinage displaced intergenerational networks of personalized credit. Graeber describes how, within an infrastructure of vast inequality, coin created the illusion of equality. Graber joins a host of scholars arguing that, when early modern finance transformed 'patronage into debt relations', this established 'a certain formal, legal equality between contractor and contractee'; Graeber defines such emergent forms of debt as 'the agreement between equals to no longer be equal', which he calls 'the most ruthless and violent form of equality imaginable.'[71] Yet, debt's violence is one to which we've slowly become accustomed.

And if this was not brutal enough, coin and credit were becoming *moralized*. Those who could use coin were (save the pirates and criminals) exclusively the landed gentry and wealthy merchant class (who were also, occasionally, pirates and criminals). As a result, over time, 'the use of coins … had come to seem *moral* in itself.'[72] As coin displaced local credit relations, these relations of credit and debt, formerly a way of life, became increasingly suspect. The late sixteenth century, consequently, witnessed the beginning of a widespread 'criminalization of debt'.[73] Cue the moral revengers.

With this in mind, we can understand why so many of the scenes in *Caesar* reflect growing anxieties around the marketplace and the hegemony of coin as the preferred form of liquidity. When Antony encounters the conspirators standing above Caesar's freshly murdered corpse, he can only say, 'My credit now stands on such slippery ground' (3.1.191). Only in Elizabeth's newly arranged market, with its loosening of feudal ties, could such a claim make so much sense to so many. Antony's 'slippery ground', here, is both the literal blood of Caesar and the figurative authority which grounds currency in the sovereign's body. Making what is perhaps his fatal flaw, Brutus grants Antony permission to 'produce [Caesar's] body in the market-place' (3.1.228).

But we should note the strange ceremony by which Antony and the conspirators make this 'deal'. In the *Lives* of Brutus and Antony, Plutarch tells of days during which speeches were given, alliances were made and acts of oblivion were passed, before finally Antony offered the life of his son 'as hostage', securing the life of Brutus, so that the factions might break bread and sup together.[74] Omitting this traffic of bodies, Shakespeare, instead, dramatizes a much more modern transaction. Antony offers his *hand* to each conspirator. This shaking of hands is quite a bit of stage 'business'. Early modern 'handshake deals' were conducted in person, orally, and rooted in trust and credit.[75] When Cassius then asks Antony, 'What compact mean you to have with us?' (3.1.215), 'compact' might suggest negotiations with paper, a response to Antony's handshake deal. The word 'compact', in Shakespeare, often describes a written or 'sealed' document.[76] The 'compact', like Derrida's *pharmakon*, was a dangerous supplement, as 'compact' meant both 'truce' and 'conspiracy'.[77] As a paper document, it promised, by a new form of proxy, the establishment of a *deal*. We witness a similar transition from orality to literacy when Caska strikes the first blow to Caesar, exclaiming, like one signing a bond, 'Speak, hands, for me' (3.1.76). Similarly, the proscription scene provides a striking example of a radical redistribution of wealth enacted through ink and parchment, the media of contemporary forms of credit and future forms of credit money.

Shakespeare's Brutus, unlike Plutarch's, despises such oaths, bonds and contracts. Much has been made of Brutus's monologue disavowing the need for such vows. He pleads with the conspirators to 'not stain / The even virtue of our enterprise, / Nor th'insuppressive mettle of our spirits, / To think that or our cause or our performance / Did need an oath' (2.1.130–4). Brutus here represents the growing distaste Protestant gentlemen had for such trappings. Graeber tells us that 'The landed gentry and wealthy merchants, who eschewed handshake deals, would often use cash with one another, especially to pay off bills of exchange drawn on London markets.'[78] After Caesar's death, Brutus, ever austere and uncomfortable with immoral debts, points to the limitations of the hand, telling Antony, 'You see but our hands / And this the bleeding business they have done' (3.1.167–8). Hands do bleeding business. Brutus would rather 'coin his heart' or cash in the 'mettle of his spirit', a seemingly paradoxical term that combines Brutus's metallism with the empty metaphysics underwriting it.

The early modern period was increasingly fascinated by the way the market and the theatre produced what Shakespeare elsewhere calls the 'excellent dumb discourse' (*Tem* 3.3.39) of comportment, faces and hands. Agnew notes the proliferation of manuals and guides on gesture, decorum and contracts – guides that only made such handshake deals more suspicious. Agnew writes: 'With decisions of purchase and sale increasingly removed from the immediacy of the traditional marketplace, commercial transactions had already begun to take on the perceived character of a script drafted elsewhere and enacted by proxy.[79] Shakespeare's audiences, witnessing an explosion of debt litigation, were becoming increasingly suspicious of such oral vows and promises. According to Ingham, 'The widespread use of the bill of exchange ... undoubtedly hastened the transition from oral to written contracts'.[80] Some of these contracts, private bills of exchange, became detached, over time, from the merchants who used them – even the content of the exchange – creating a vast paper network of circulating, transferable, *private* bills of credit. This private money, escaping and obscuring the sovereign's monopoly on currency, circulated antagonistically in relation to an increasing, yet still insufficient, quantity of public coin.[81]

After the Restoration, Charles II began to subsidize, rather than charge for, the minting of coin, with the result that 'coin appeared to be silver or gold without more, a natural product rather than an artifact of sovereign power.'[82] Here we see a return to and naturalization of metallist ideology. Nietzsche provides perhaps the best account of such historical amnesia when he writes: 'Truths are illusions which we have forgotten are illusions; they are metaphors that have become worn out and have been drained of sensuous force, coins which have lost their embossing and are now considered as metal and no longer as coins.'[83] The Restoration also ushered in a now largely forgotten compromise between and integration of private and public forms of money (private bills and public coin).[84] When a group of forty merchants agreed to lend him £1.2 million, William III handed over his monopoly on public currency, granting the merchants, in addition, the right to make his new debt transferable. In this way, the Bank of England was formed, the first bank in Europe to issue such debt as national currency.[85] Were this debt repaid today, England's monetary system would collapse.[86] Ingham explains: 'In effect, the *privately* owned Bank of England transformed the sovereign's *personal* debt into a *public* debt and, eventually in turn, into a *public* currency.'[87] Graeber stresses: 'The fact that money was no longer a debt owed *to* the king, but a debt owed *by* the king, made it very different than what it had been before. In many ways it had become a mirror image of older forms of money.'[88] *Julius Caesar* inaugurates the turn of the seventeenth century, when these changes will occur, but all of the technologies that would later coalesce around the Bank of England were already fully formed in the sixteenth century.[89] During this time, money, like punishment in Foucault's genealogy, was slowly decoupled from the body of the sovereign. Instead, money's authority started to seem to dwell within the coin itself, making money appear more like a private commodity than ever before. Coins came to seem transparent, their tie to sovereignty obscured through a trick of finance. As Desan boldly claims, "The revolution [in money's design] occurred in early modern England. The revolution changed the way political communities create money. It changed how they, or how we, pay for money, how we think about human agency, how we define the market and its relationship to the public. The revolution in money's design, I argue, inaugurated capitalism."[90]

I would like to conclude by glancing at the Janus-faced structure of Calphurnia's dream. I want to consider how this dream prefigures the revolutionary shift in sovereignty's relation to currency, the shift wherein money transforms into 'a mirror image' of its older form. Calphurnia describes a statue of Caesar, a concretized form of sovereignty that, coin-like, produces liquidity from its body. Do the citizens take their due, as Caesar fears, or, as Decius suggests, does the sovereign distribute wealth to all, like the stomach in *Coriolanus*'s 'fable of the belly'? Like so many of the scenes examined above, this figure works emblematically to represent two views of the money form. This two-sidedness continues today. Dodd describes a contemporary rift between European scholars, 'who tend to view all money as a token of *debt* (derived from one's debts to society), and Anglo-American scholars, who regard all money as a form of *credit*, i.e. an obligation *from* society to the individual.'[91]

Nearly a half-century after the gold standard, we would do well to remember what Antony sees yet Brutus (and orthodox economists) cannot – that money is neither neutral, nor transparent, neither natural, nor a private commodity anchored in precious metals. Economics is performative, not constative; it performs, even when detached from its referent. Money performs inventively, shaped by the past yet radically open to the future. But in order to know the full possibility of the future, we have to labour to rewrite neoliberal finance's mythical narrative of the past. Though we live in a world beyond metallism, we still live in a world of bad conscience, a world full of resources and opportunities bitterly guarded by the gatekeepers of morality. Poverty, scarcity, austerity and revenge continue to haunt our collective futures. We can see the roots of such moral economies active throughout *Caesar*, but they're most legible today within the moralized economy of the Eurozone, with the economies and peoples of Southern Europe, Greece in particular, expected to internalize larger, systemic failures. Likewise, the systemic privatization of higher education in the US has pushed student loan debt to unprecedented heights, producing a demoralized and indebted generation. Neoliberal economics claims that the fault – for these 'lost ventures', these defaults – lies not in the state – no longer willing to pay 'ambition's debt' – but within students themselves. History, however, shows us that finance is a human technology we can design, not an intractable 'tide in the affairs of men'. Immediately following Caesar's death, Anthony persuaded the senate to pass an 'act of oblivion' whereby Caesar's noble acts would remain in effect, his faults forgotten.[92] After the Restoration, parliament passed a similar Act of Oblivion forgiving those guilty of various crimes during the Civil War and Interregnum. Overcoming a long history of moralized debt and austerity politics – a history pious in its *ressentiment* and violent in the impersonal exactitude of its shadowy bookkeeping – will require a Caesar-like generosity and a robust and excessive willingness to forget the bottom line, strike debt and invent a future. With the bounty that is already ours, we can indeed 'lift up Olympus' (3.1.74).

6

New Directions: What Should Be in that Caesar: The Question of Julius Caesar's Greatness

John E. Curran, Jr.

It is difficult to disagree with the distinction, offered by a recent editor of the play, that with *Julius Caesar* 'Shakespeare is more interested in Caesarism – a political strategy, an ideology, a movement in history – than in Caesar himself'.[1] However, though Shakespeare does not grant his Caesar many lines, at the hub of the play's inquiry into 'Caesarism' is the issue of his nature as an individual. One of *Julius Caesar*'s more remarkable effects is the double-sided way its sense of historical inevitability seems to tell on the characters. When Brutus muses that 'Between the acting of a dreadful thing / And the first motion, all the interim is / Like a phantasma or a hideous dream' (2.1.63–5),[2] he seems to feel pulled gravitationally into what we universally recognize as one of the world's all-time pivotal events, unfree to do anything with the helpless, dream-like interim leading up to it; but all at once, he seems to regard the process he is in as originating in his own 'motion', and not irrevocable until the dreadful thing has been acted. Perhaps the interim that weighs on Brutus's mind is dream-like to him because he somehow senses its lack of true contingency, but then again, perhaps because, from Brutus's perspective, truly anything might happen. *Julius Caesar*'s handling of 'Caesarism' is enriched by this ambiguous relationship between the play's characters and its unambiguous dramatic irony. We absolutely know as they cannot that the hand of fate is on them, for Julius Caesar has his ordained, world-historical role to play, and the conspirators have theirs, and their drama is destined to sum up, for all time, the conflict between the republican and the royal political visions. But do the characters comply meta-theatrically with these over-determined roles or behave as though self-determined? We know 'Caesarism' is a fact of life, to be debated, and lauded or loathed; but just how futile, the play forces us to ask, was resistance to it? And this problem has much to do with that of the quality of Caesar himself. That is, did those who attempted and failed to prevent 'Caesarism' from defining Western life rightly or wrongly assess what sort of person Julius Caesar truly was?

Was Caesar really different and better than other men? Cassius complains that Caesar 'doth bestride the narrow world / Like a colossus' (1.2.134–5), and effectively conveys 'Caesarism' as a massive fact of life, the hugeness of which stands to redefine all terms and rewrite all rules. But to what is this statue-comparison, however comprehensible in this way, actually referring? Is 'Caesarism' the contemplation of exaggerated artifice, or an unavoidable reaction to the presence of a giant? And which proposition emerges as the more foolish to deny? Shakespeare is, of course, very ambidextrous very often, but nowhere more so than here in *Julius Caesar*, pushing on us this question of the dictator's true specialness; indeed, despite Caesar's short time onstage, the play poses the question more intently and complexly than do other contemporary plays on the subject, and goes much further in factoring it into the analysis of 'Caesarism'. And it is a question on which the play encourages us to be doubtful – unlike its Romans, whose various attitudes are all suspicious. '[W]hat should be in that "Caesar"', demands Cassius; indeed, what? The play challenges us to refrain from hasty judgement as to whether Caesar's worth is substantive or accidental, and whether he deserves to be held exceptional, as a political phenomenon, as a historiographical authority and as an individual human mind.

As a political phenomenon, Caesar was most often placed in one of two overly simplistic categories: tradition had labelled him a Worthy or a Tyrant. He was a fixture of the Nine Worthies of medieval lore – Joshua, David, Judas Maccabeus; Hector, Alexander, Caesar; Charlemagne, King Arthur, Godfrey of Bouillon – heroes who incontrovertibly stood out over all others in derring-do and constructive leadership.[3] Shakespeare's England would have received this idea from many sources, prominent among which would be Caxton's preface to his edition of Malory, where the readiest and most secure way to elevate Arthur is grouping him with the Worthies: 'For it is notoyrly known through the universal world that there be nine worthy and the best that ever were.'[4] However, this basic view, approaching Caesar's political significance from the standpoint of his well-earned membership in the most elite of fraternities, could be rendered in much more sophisticated ways; some decades after Shakespeare's play, even Milton, defending tyrannicide, would have to exempt Caesar, recognizing him as worthiest to rule ('dignissimus').[5] At the other pole stood the Tyrant conceptions of Caesar influenced by the first-century poet Lucan, whose sensationalistic verse history portrayed Caesar's war with Pompey and liaison with Cleopatra as emanating from a bestial, compulsive drive to consume and destroy. Lucan's horror at Caesar's temerity was captured for Elizabethans in the playwright Christopher Marlowe's translation of the poem's first book;[6] the 'restles generall' cannot stop himself from rushing to deprive Rome of freedom, his own free will giving way to savagery: 'here, here (saith he) / An end of peace; here end polluted lawes; / Hence leagues, and covenants; Fortune thee I follow, / Warre and the destinies shall trie my cause' (226–30).

In near-contemporary dramatic renditions of Caesar this dichotomy between the Worthy and the Tyrant tends to be applied; even where plays allow for differing attitudes, they tend to alternate between extremes. Cued by Lucan, and by conventions of the stock Tyrant figure,[7] several dramas cast Caesar as the Tyrant by dint of his grasping for control when subject to control himself, from effeminizing powers of inner id and outer Fortune, and this is to diminish Caesar in terms not only of negativity, but of commonness as well. Opening Kyd's translation of Garnier's *Cornelia*,[8] Cicero laments sententiously how 'Equals are euer bandying for the best' (1.35), framing the civil war as wearisome repetition of a common problem. Consequently, to Cornelia, Caesar is fearful not in himself but because Fortune has consistently advanced him, and the Chorus while it cannot allay her fears can try to remind her that he is likely riding for a fall – probability rules him, as anyone (3.1.55–60). Chapman's *Caesar and Pompey*,[9] lionizing Pompey and especially Cato as Stoic sages, emphasizes Caesar's enslavement to Fortune to the point where he feels it himself. Sunk in worry before the oncoming showdown, he confronts the very real possibility of defeat as a shattering of his distinctiveness, and thus of his excuse for having 'ransack'd all the world': it simply cannot be that Nature could 'lift arts thus far up in glorious frame / To let them vanish thus in smoke and shame' (2.5.1–23). However, in more even-handed dramas, too, Caesar is categorized as a reiteration of a pattern. In the anonymous *Caesar's Revenge*,[10] the spirit of Discord pegs Caesar as merely the beneficiary of luck: 'Though *Caesar* be as great as great may be / Yet *Pompey* once was euen as great as he' (2.Ind.). Even when the Romans extol Caesar, it is in categorical terms, as they affirm him a Worthy; in him 'all is comprehended' – he is comparable to Hercules, Achilles, Alexander and Hector

(3.2). Similarly, *The Tragedy of Julius Caesar*, the final of Sir William Alexander's four *Monarch Tragedies*,[11] leaves Caesar open to debate because his marks *a* case of the common tension between individual achievement and public good. Caesar sees himself as a 'Phoenix', paradoxically, because he can now count himself to have 'equall'd' Alexander the Great and 'all that went before' (2.1.319–26); on the other side, Decius Brutus is indignant that 'He (to himselfe a slave) would make *Rome* thrall' (2.2.880).

The debate over Caesar which Sir William presents, setting a conqueror's worth against a dictator's threat to the state, has often been observed at work in *Julius Caesar*,[12] but not often observed is how that debate is inflected by the play's handling of Caesar's specialness. Not only can the play accommodate either view, the Worthy or the Tyrant, but also this multi-facetedness is compounded in how the play's special-versus-ordinary dialectic underwrites but also transcends the political alignments. That is, both Caesarism and anti-Caesarism hold Caesar ambiguously special and non-special.

That Caesar actually should be a colossus obviously bolsters the monarchical side. As Warren Chernaik points out, Caesar's actual conquests are scarcely mentioned in the play,[13] which begins with anguish that his triumph is against Pompey, not foreign enemies (1.1.34–5). In a way, the glory of Caesar's deeds comes across all the more resoundingly for this muting of it: in lieu of Sir William's Caesar's harping on the unmatched significance of subduing Gaul (2.1.335–48), Shakespeare's Caesar needs no boasting, on his own part or by proxy. Moreover, he caesar needs no comparison to anyone. Within the 'Worthies' discourse he is an exemplar of a rarefied type, but a type none the less, and by leaving his conquests unspoken but understood, he can come off as all the more a Worthy – or as not a Worthy at all but a class by himself.

From another direction, however, the case for Caesarism benefits from his not being very special as a person. From the first scene, we are met with a division between man and meaning, between, as Michael McCanles put it, 'the objective Caesar – the neutral facts about the man himself – and the carefully projected public image of the superhuman conqueror'.[14] However, the perceived gap between the public image and the person is part of what makes that image so compelling. Caesar is becoming an icon, a sign that the empire dawning is inevitable and irresistible.[15] The meaning is much larger than the man, and that meaning seems both inexplicable and incontestable, of overwhelming momentum as a political force and as a conceptual one. Hence the interpretation proffered by Caesar himself of the astounding prodigies being witnessed, that they 'Are to the world in general as to Caesar' (2.2.28–9), and hence Brutus's befuddlement at the offstage popular applause for Caesar's rejection of the crown. It were easier to digest for Brutus if, as he assumes (1.2.79–80, 131–3), the entranced crowd could be imagined as pleading for a hero-king. But they are not. Instead they celebrate something they seem to know not what. With a theatrics rhetorically effective even *for* its conceptual vagueness, Caesar moves Rome to invest him with kinglike mystique by affirming nothing, only divesting himself of any kinglike mystique. No wonder Brutus presses Caska not only to report the Lupercal spectacle, but also to account for it, break down the 'manner of it', and no wonder Caska could just as easily be hanged (1.2.233–4). With regard to Caesar the person, what does Rome respond to, other than an impersonal aura of awesomeness?

For the anti-Caesarians, meanwhile, arguing Caesar's tyranny would seem predicated on his being common. Here, Caska would write off Caesar's Lupercal display as 'mere foolery' (1.2.235), mere showmanship, explicitly because it is an attempt to conceal Caesar's true, basely tyrannical intent, but implicitly because of an objection similar to Cassius's, that 'Caesar' is crafted histrionics with no correspondence to flesh-and-blood. He is no icon, but an idol, one crying out for iconoclasm.[16]

And yet, too, both the conspirators' sense of urgency before the deed and their rationalization after it depend on Caesar's specialness. Cassius would have it that Caesar's largeness in the people's minds originates *in* their minds, which have fallen away from the modus operandi of the mentality of true Romans: 'What trash is Rome? / What rubbish, and what offal? when it serves / For the base matter to illuminate / So vile a thing as Caesar?' (1.3.108–11). The comparison of reputation to combustion, with Caesar's brightness generated not from himself but from dulled popular thinking, like garbage set aflame, strikingly expresses the superficiality of Caesarism – but the metaphor is soon undone. He and Caska agree that their enterprise requires the deep-penetrating persuasiveness of Brutus, since, says Caska, 'that which would appear offence in us / His [Brutus's] countenance, like richest alchemy, / Will change to virtue and to worthiness' (1.3.158–60). If the Romans' minds are 'base matter' in esteeming Caesar, it is base matter so well integrated, so stable and settled in its current state, that nothing short of alchemy will be needed to produce a different form of combustion. The hint is that the highest opinion of Caesar is 'base' not so much in being trash as in being *basic*, elemental and essential. Turning this opinion into approval of his murder will demand extravagant rhetorical pyrotechnics, measures extremely intricate and delicate, and under suspicion of fraudulence.

Indeed Brutus, we soon see, needs to practise a kind of ideological alchemy on everyone, including himself. His Act 2, Scene 1 'It must be by his death' soliloquy concedes that no sign has appeared of a Caesar whose 'affections swayed / More than his reason' (2.1.20–1); the only way to pigeonhole him as a common Tyrant will be to stress the probability that everything about him will change, and he will transmute into commonality and tyranny. Sadly, for the purposes of exposition and justification, 'the quarrel / Will bear no colour for the thing he is' (2.1.28–9). Regarding the existing Caesar, there is no *colour* to be had, no exculpatory explanation – no way to 'spin' actions against him. The recourse then must be convolution and obfuscation, and not merely in that the colour's basis must be an imaginary, prospective future Caesar; the case must also posit a haze of self-contradiction on the uncommon versus the common. Caesar is an uncommon hero uncommonly self-controlled, but 'common proof' (2.1.21) warns us that ambition lurks within modest appearances and metastasizes with promotion; the uncommonly good carriage must be reread as indicating commonly bad motive. Moreover, the common, proper response to such a Tyrant ought to be, especially for true Romans, the most strenuous resistance – a 'purpose necessary and not envious', as Brutus says to his fellows (2.1.177). But how can proper anti-Tyrant protocols be applied to an as-yet-non-tyrant whom everyone adores *but* the envious? Brutus must argue the assassins as being *constrained* to move and hence doing the only reasonable thing, and simultaneously as moving on the most abstract and theoretical of promptings, stretching themselves to foresee and forestall a danger unlike any other. A logical colour remaining thus elusive, Brutus the alchemist avoids logic and tries to transmute base matter into gold using distinctions hollow but high-sounding: he tells the masses, 'as he was valiant, I honour him: but as he was ambitious, I slew him' (3.2.25–7). What Caesar 'is' forces his opponents to deal in rhetorical alchemy, which seems to indicate his specialness. Brutus must suggest that this emergency warranted unwarranted action, being, sui generis: 'not that I loved Caesar less, but that I loved Rome more' (3.2.21–2).

That Brutus and Cassius finally cannot formulate 'reasons / Why and wherein Caesar was dangerous' (3.1.221–2) might well speak to Caesar's being uniquely beyond criteria for judgement – but it might do no such thing. It might be that branding Caesar a common Tyrant is actually much simpler than Brutus makes it. Similarly, it may be that what seems a Caesarian control over the story issues naturally from Caesarian excellence, or it may be far otherwise, from a suppression of alternative storytelling modes.

The play opens on this note. When Murellus complains about the citizens' stony hearts (1.1.33–52), as they are comfortable enough with the calamity of Caesar's ascendancy to 'cull out a holiday' from it, he is also complaining about neglect of the right retrospective vision. He demands, 'Knew you not Pompey?'; they certainly *did*, and their worship of him then should translate into an entirely different understanding of the unfolding of events than they have now. The tide of Caesarism, to Murellus, seems to reorient knowledge of the past. For him, Pompey it was who stood *for* Roman values and *as* Rome's darling, so that embracing his killing, and his killer, as heroic is equivalent to embracing that killer's rewriting and distorting of the record. Pompey had a history, and the people's love of him helped validate and further set down that history, and now that history is obscured in favour of another – one which, to Murellus, is degrading to both Rome and to the historical truth. However, if a degradation, this new history, wherein the people cannot know Pompey as they knew him, and wherein instead they know and propagate general knowledge of Caesar triumphant, is fast becoming *the* history. Such is painfully driven home with Caska's mention of how Murellus and his compatriot Flavius 'are put to silence' (1.2.285).

Ugly though this silencing of alternative history seems, we must wonder: *does* the new history degrade the truth? Was Julius Caesar a historiographical tyrant? Given the pre-eminence of Caesar's Commentaries as an indispensable part of the humanistic education, it would seem fairly easy to divorce his historiographical specialness from the question of his role in history. T. W. Baldwin proved long ago the high probability 'that if Shakespeare completed grammar school, he had read Caesar'; indeed, as far as exposing students to the best authors was concerned, 'We may regard Sallust and Caesar as universal'.[17] The Renaissance's schoolmaster, Erasmus himself, endorsed the singularity of Caesar the author, in the *De Ratione Studii* placing him on a shortlist of those every learner of Latin should read; in the *Ciceronianus*, the arch-humanist's critique of Ciceronians, who would raise Cicero to a status above all other writers, entails pointing to Caesar, who far surpassed him in propriety and elegance.[18]

For almost any literate sixteenth-century person, Caesar was a unique Worthy in being the historian of his own worthiness; even while the medieval romanticizing of his name was still resonating, in the Renaissance Caesar's fame took on a much more realistic and much less fanciful aspect, as, love or hate the politician, one had to admire the writer's gravitas and perfection of decorum. He had sung his own praises *without* singing them, by employing a straightforward, mature, just-the-facts style to describe the momentous events in which he had taken part. The weight of Caesar's Commentaries virtually guaranteed a view of their author's singularity: they must be read and their *sprezzatura* must be imitated, and their content must be believed.

For Englishmen, this historiographical dimension of Caesar's specialness took on a peculiar poignancy, for the Caesarian dominion over historical epistemology keenly affected their power of national storytelling. As a side-story of his account of his campaigns against the Gauls, Caesar told of how he had undertaken two expeditions to the terra incognita of Britain, learning a little something of its barbaric people and successfully beginning the process of subjugating them. This side-story effectively became the opening chapter of English history, owing both to the monolithic presence of the Commentaries and to the absence of any native competitor, beyond the hyper-enthusiastic and hyper-imaginative medieval Welshman Geoffrey of Monmouth (Galfridus). Geoffrey's *Historia Regum Britanniae* purported not only to fill in the gap of more than a millennium's worth of knowledge about the ancient Britons, but also to set the record straight about Caesar's invasions in particular; just as Caesar was *not* to be held as the original source of information on Britain, so too was his adventure there *not* the easy, casual conquest over a lot of savages he had made it sound like. He actually went to Britain regarding it as a rival Trojan-derived civilization almost on a par with Rome itself, and was twice humiliated there before winning Britain only by dint of British infighting. For support Geoffrey cites a line from Lucan, on how Caesar showed his back to the Britons.[19] They are magnified by their stout resistance to such a singular personage, and yet also by how they prove him not truly to be such; just as Lucan would reveal Caesar's tyranny against Rome and Romanitas, so would Geoffrey elaborate on Lucan to reveal the historiographical usurpation Caesar had committed against Britain.

Furthermore, despite the transparency of Geoffrey's aims and despite Caesar-the-historian's nearly unmatched predominance, the twelfth-century monk's protest against the mighty conqueror could in Shakespeare's time still stir English hearts. Humanistic education and humanistic advancements in historiography made Geoffrey pale beside Caesar, but the Galfridian ideal of alternative, native voices, of feeling enabled to challenge an imperialistic, monologic authority for ownership of the story, did not quickly dissipate. To this a later Shakespearean play, *Cymbeline*, testifies. As the Roman emissaries attempt to claim the tribute due them because of Caesar's conquest of Britain, King Cymbeline's vicious Queen is roused to push forward a competing narrative: 'A kind of conquest / Caesar made here, but made not here his brag / Of "Came, and saw, and overcame:" with shame / (The first that ever touch'd him) he was carried / From off our coast, twice beaten' (Cymbeline 3.1.23–7).[20] She is a villain from the start, and the play ends with her and her viewpoint disavowed in favour of a dignified rather than slavish capitulation to Rome; nevertheless, her speech shows Shakespeare's awareness of how the Galfridian ideal of historiographical independence could strike a chord.

Shakespeare does not overtly bring this awareness to bear on *Julius Caesar*, but the concern about subverting Caesar's right to dictate memory of the past is not confined to Murellus. Antony's funeral oration overwhelms that of Brutus in large part because it proposes to the Romans a clear and basic means of framing what has happened, and even offers evidence for it, with the mantle Caesar wore warring on the Nervii (3.2.168–71) and, finally, with Caesar's will. Brutus's oration's paradoxes, nuances and abstractions cannot keep up with the 'plain, blunt' Antony's posture of merely rehearsing what has taken place (3.2.211); against Brutus's imaginative exercise in divining Caesar's prospective ambition, Antony sets the generally-witnessed fact of Caesar's thrice-rejected crown (3.2.94–100). Antony's exordium, citing the *sententia* that 'The evil that men do lives after them: / The good is oft interred with their bones' (3.2.76–7), is calibrated to be undone by the content of his speech; the crowd's hearing the plain, blunt what-has-happened will guarantee their assent to Caesar's good living after him, and their interring of his potential ambition. Hence the exordium is more than an *occupatio* device, disclaiming a purpose of glorifying Caesar. It also lays the groundwork for viewing Caesar as exceptional as an object of remembrance, since the *sententiae* of memorializing are inapplicable to him. To wit: for Caesar alone, good far, far outlasts evil in retrospect, even as a *consequence* of a lack of polishing his story. The plain, blunt historical truth yields the irrefutable conclusion of Caesar's singularity: 'Here was a Caesar: when comes such another?' (3.2.243). There is a certain parallel to be made, then, between the plain, blunt funeral oration by Antony and the plain, blunt Commentaries by the man it implicitly but powerfully praises. And yet, Shakespeare does not seem to encourage us to react like this crowd. 'He would not take the crown; / Therefore 'tis certain he was not ambitious', declares the Fourth Plebeian (3.2.113–14); we might sympathize with their inability to respond for very long to Brutus's strained logic, but surely we dislike the reductiveness of their logic here. Could it not be that much more has happened than Antony refers them to, awareness of which would impede this too-easy, too-certain 'therefore'? And even if all facts do prove Caesar a unique Roman, should we not at least suspect that his form of anti-Roman ambition might be unique as well?

Like the Caesar of the Commentaries, Antony has parlayed a plain, blunt style into seizure of historiographical control, over both the matter to be read and the manner in which it is to be read. Perception of and revulsion at the germination of this control lie at the heart of Cassius's bitterness towards Caesar. Perhaps recalling the Galfridian argument of Britain as Rome's sister Trojan civilization, fully Rome's equal in the legacy of their common ancestor Aeneas, Cassius analogizes himself to Aeneas, and the helpless Caesar, whom Cassius once saved from drowning, to the helpless, carried Anchises (1.2.110–15). By Shakespeare's time, of course, the Virgilian connection between Caesar and Aeneas was completely standardized: in *The Faerie Queene*, when the Troy-descended knight Paridell relates Rome's founding and names Aeneas's son as 'Iulus', Spenser tells us nothing new. However, his Paridell is a blackguard, and his best knight, Britomart, is there to admonish him that he has omitted part of the story – the Galfridian part about Troy-descended Britain, and how it can 'dare to equalise' Rome.[21] Similarly, in trying to displace Caesar as an Aeneas-figure, Cassius dares to equalize him, by telling a counter-history unfairly unheard. Like Britomart's stance towards Paridell, Cassius convicts Caesar not so much of lying, as of neglecting the whole truth and of fostering the biases facilitated by ignorance of that whole. If the people knew the Caesar-story Cassius knows, from the dictator's almost drowning to his being shaken by a fever in Spain – ''Tis true, this God did shake' (1.2.121), bearing it 'As a sick girl' (1.2.128) – their historical 'therefores' would be different. Their conclusions would either be uncertain, or certain, as Cassius's and Britomart's are, in positing natural equals. Hearing Cassius here, especially in light of Murellus in Act 1, Scene 1, we must see validity in being uncertain. It is hard at the very least not to ask why purveyors of Pompey the Great's glory should be marginalized and silenced, why stories illustrating Caesar's ordinariness should not be told, and why Cassius, or indeed any leading Roman of the Republic, should not be able to analogize himself to Aeneas just as convincingly as Caesar can. And yet, simultaneously, being certain about the counter-history smacks of absurdity. If Cassius like Britomart brings us to valid doubt about the officially-sanctioned history, he also has something of the childish fury of Cymbeline's Queen. They protect not the truth from obscurity, but themselves from rankling feelings of inferiority.

How unfounded are such feelings? Perhaps no one should enjoy the Caesarian privilege of storytelling, and protest against such privilege is good in itself. But perhaps this protest flies in the face of the fact of Caesar's voice being unlike any other. Of this, the very existence of Brutus at the time *Julius Caesar* depicts makes for quiet but strong evidence – and in the play he does not simply exist, but takes centre stage. The play's reticence on Caesar's actual accomplishments can help build a sense of the colossal, and so can its making little of Caesar's pardoning Brutus even after he sided with Pompey. This Caesar doesn't need to boast, nor to hold over others' heads that they breathe at his discretion. In Sir William's drama the conqueror is made to trumpet his own 'clemency' towards the republicans he beat at Pharsalia (2.1.479–515), and Brutus is made heavy by his cognizance of his 'debt' to 'that great mans grace' (3.1.1127–42); in *Caesar's Revenge* an entire scene (1.2) is devoted to Caesar's granting Brutus his life: the amazed Brutus wonders 'To what a pitch would this mans vertues sore / Did not ambition clog his mounting fame'. But in Shakespeare an issue has not been made of Brutus owing Caesar his life, which makes the debt to Caesar, and Caesar's untroubled cancelling of it, loom all the greater in the case for Caesar's unique fairness. Antony casts Caesar as living out and dying in peculiarly generous sentiments, a view corroborated by Brutus's mere presence there. The 'Ingratitude' Antony decries, 'the most unkindest cut of all' (3.2.179–84), is in this light especially damning of the counter-narrative: Brutus has taken Caesar's life because of abstractions and prospective fears, whereas in factual history Caesar gave Brutus his life, disallowing ideological fear in favour of forgiveness and love. Why *not* entrust such a singular person, so above grudges against his foes, with singular storytelling power? Roger Ascham's *Scholemaster*, grading Caesar the writer with the highest marks, makes just this connection: his books were so 'perfectly done', that not even 'his greatest enemies could euer find the least note of parciality in him (a meruailous wisedome of a man, namely writing of his owne doinges)'.[22]

Thus, however insufficient his self-criticism as a conqueror and as a reporter, Caesar in each capacity was renowned to be objective and even indulgent towards others, despite formidable incentives to be far otherwise; this graciousness is certainly reflected in North's Plutarch.[23] In The Life of Caesar, the great biographer stresses the lavishness of Caesar's treatment of Brutus in the wake of Pharsalia: 'For *Caesar* did not only saue his life, after the battell of PHARSALIA when *Pompey* fled, and did at his request also saue many moe of his friends besides: but furthermore, he put a maruellous confidence in him' (p. 739). The confidence seems all the more to be marvelled at, that is, for its emergence in place of the distrust that would afflict just about any other civil-war winner. And something very like this marvellous confidence enables Caesar to write his rightly famous memoirs. North's Plutarch includes a Comparison of Alexander the Great with Julius Caesar, and the latter is credited with nearly incredible success as a writer, by any standard, but all the more given the tumultuous environment of writing: 'in the middest of his continuall troubles, he did reade, meditate, spake, wrote, and left behind him the goodliest booke that a martiall man, and one that entertaineth the Muses, can deuise to take in his hands' (p. 748). Whatever the dangers of the moment, he was composed enough to compose brilliantly, for all times, the history of that moment. And so in each case, giving Brutus life and giving posterity the Commentaries, Caesar's is a mind refusing to become discomposed by any base considerations.

This immunity to fears and this kindness to foes, as an actor in *and* as a commentator on history, both flow into a key concept the Comparison soon discusses: 'His magnánimitie weighed more, then any other vertue they could note in him: which is as much as if one would say, that *Caesar* outweighed all the other Captaines of the GREEKES and ROMAINES'. Whatever the 'daungers' surrounding him, even 'by some of his owne people', he 'weighed them not'; decisive and nearly always victorious on the battlefield, he consistently 'vsed moderation, gentlenesse, and humilitie in his victories': in fact, Caesar's 'gentlenesse is so much spoken of, that men iudge that that was one of the occasions of his death'. Whatever his excesses – on which the Comparison is explicit, remarking how Caesar 'distained his life with a continuall violent desire to subdue his countrie' (p. 745) – Caesar's mind was the very essence of magnanimity, a courageous generosity and a generous courage that applied itself regardless of circumstances. It could even apply itself alongside or despite his voraciousness and rapaciousness.

That Caesar's mind generated its own special, super-heroic mixture of generosity and fortitude was an idea of him that could not have been lost on Shakespeare. Of the many experts on magnanimity one might choose, Thomas Rogers seems as lucid as any: 'Magnanimitie is a certain excellencie of the minde, placing before her eyes at all times vertue and honor, and to the attaining of them bends all her cogitations and studyes'. Such a mind is incapable of the non-virtuous thought, the thoughts of fear or cruelty, bound to visit any other mind in extremes: 'if he be in aduersitie he mourneth not, in prosperitie he insulteth not'. More positively, the magnanimous man 'sets th'example of Caesar before his eyes, and is to nothing more redy then to mercifulnes', and he 'looueth to emulate the best' – 'He is of the best nature, and therfore as nigh as he can, hee will be the best man'.[24] It was a commonplace that for Caesar in particular, magnanimity expressing itself in emulation, the striving not merely for political supremacy but for ever higher splendour, and to exceed the glory of the most glorious of all, was intrinsic to cogitation; with success merely 'still kindling more and more in him, thoughts of greater enterprises', as North's Plutarch noted, 'This humour of his was no other but an emulation with himselfe as with another man, and a certaine contention to ouercome the things he prepared to attempt' (p. 737).[25] Even readers of Marlowe's Lucan might perceive something of this special-and-higher-thinking mind, the energies of which would seem communicated in his magnetic effect on his men. In Marlowe's astonishing wording, a representative soldier, poised to transgress the Rubicon and violate the sacred Republic beyond, gives voice to the unbreakable spell Caesar's sheer charisma has cast: 'Love over-rules my will, I must obay thee, / *Caesar*, he whom I heare thy trumpets charge / I hould no *Romaine*'; 'What wals thou wilt be leaveld with the ground, / These hands shall thrust the ram, and make them flie, / Albeit the Citty thou wouldst have so ra'st / Be *Roome* it selfe' (Lucans First Booke, 360–87).

And yet, dramatic portrayals of Caesar did not exactly capture a mind thinking singularly, even when they referenced his magnanimity. Unsurprisingly, Chapman's Caesar's claim to magnanimity is debunked: referring to his rival's epilepsy, Pompey insists that 'your disease the gods ne'er gave to man / But such a one as had a spirit too great / For all his body's passages to serve it ... Goats are of all beasts subject'st to it most' (1.2.244–56). His ambitious thoughts are not only debasing – they make for a diagnosable illness, a kind of constipation of mental waste-fluid. In *Caesar's Revenge*, aspiring thoughts do not debase him, but still fail to distinguish or elevate Caesar. Congratulated for rejecting the crown, Caesar stipulates that what drives him is not so much magnanimous, Roman public-spiritedness as banal self-apotheosis: 'Of *Ioue* in Heauen, shall ruled bee the skie, / The Earth of *Caesar*, with like Maiesty' (3.4). His thoughts are high, but only in the vein of any prideful worldling. Closer to magnanimity is Sir William's Caesar, but not to singularity. Here, rather than making a singular hero of him, the possibly heroic quality of Caesar's thought mostly factors in to the discussion of his possibly tyrannical motivation, and goes not much further. Antony's paean to his master's magnanimity couches it as generally applicable *sententia* – 'True magnanimity triumphs o're all' (2.1.334) – and Caesar differentiates his unquenchable power-thirst from tyranny in that he feels what anyone would (2.1.391–4). Brutus tries to grant Caesar the benefit of the doubt, suggesting that 'His thoughts are generous, as his minde is great'; and yet, this speculation quickly turns to generalizing on how peace can oftentimes tame a man's 'High thoughts which *Mars* inspires' (3.1.1045–58). Cassius's rejoinder accuses Brutus of naivety, as he is measuring Caesar's mind by his own, and 'honest mindes are with least paine deceiv'd' (3.1.1061). They differ on what *kind* of mind Caesar has, whether it is the kind guided by compunction and benevolence, like Brutus's, or not. The clearest dramatic picture of Caesar's mind's specialness appears in Fletcher and Massinger's *The False One*, and this specialness is brought out through his love affair with Cleopatra. Though no paragon of piety, this Caesar exhibits an intensity of generosity and courage that not only subsists despite but even co-ordinates with erotic intensity. With this multi-dimensional intensity *The False One* is able to build up Caesar's uniqueness in contrast to that opposition of pleasure to virtue which commonly lays men low, including the Caesar of *Caesar's Revenge* (see 2.3) and, of course, Antony in almost any incarnation.

Julius Caesar's titular character is not afforded this means to appear bigger than others. And yet, even if we restrict our assessment to the little we see of Caesar, it still seems that to dismiss his bigness out of hand, like Cassius – 'Upon what meat doth this our Caesar feed / That he is grown so great?' (1.2.148–9) – were as rash as to assume it, like Antony, for whom the conspirators have shed 'the most noble blood of all this world' (3.1.156). As Ernest Schanzer put it, 'Shakespeare calls in doubt the validity of Brutus' image of Caesar, just as he calls in doubt Cassius' image, and later Antony's, so that the nature of the real Caesar remains an enigma'.[26] I would add, however, that a sliver of light is shed on this enigma by Caesar's image of himself. His constant mindfulness of keeping up the image of his surpassingly great heart dissociates him from true, interiorly genuine great-heartedness, as has been in many interesting ways described;[27] but on the other hand, that he *is* mindful suggests a mind knowingly operating under pressures both tremendous and un-shareable.

This Caesar vouchsafes that he knows he and he alone has to be Caesar with utter consistency, and this burden in itself perhaps does set him apart.

Three times this double-sense is made to infuse Caesar's utterances. The first qualifies his confession of worry to Antony about the malcontented political hunger, perhaps signalled by the leanness of Romans like Cassius: 'I rather tell thee what is to be feared / Than what I fear: for always I am Caesar' (1.2.210–11). As he shuffles offstage asking Antony to buzz in his one functioning ear about Cassius being dangerous (1.2.212–13), Caesar himself substantiates Cassius' accusation of Caesarian inflatedness. Old and feeble of body, Caesar is small and common of mind, agitated over circumstantiality in exactly the way magnanimity would preclude, and overeager to cover up this disparity, even in private conversation. And yet, the intimacy of the moment, Caesar having no call to strike a pose, suggests the *sponte sua* quality of the thought here, as though Caesar's mind automatically imposes the dictates of Caesar-ness on itself. His mind is vulnerable to the ordinary fears of a new-made Tyrant, just as his body is vulnerable to the ordinary physical weaknesses of a man in his age group – but thoughts stemming from this ordinariness are, as if by his autonomic system, naturally detected by and detached from his mind's conception of its own proper thought-parameters. His mind cannot not identify fear as alien to being Caesar, and relocate it from a current felt emotionally to an abstraction understood intellectually. This 'always' working process is in one way mere delusion, his fear expressed as all the more deep-set for the attempt to distance himself from it, but in another way it is indeed exceptional. No one else's mind checks itself this way, with such completeness and such determination.

In fact, no one else's mind works this way at all; only Brutus's *seems* comparable, and our second example proves that he does not feel the weight of Brutus-ness the way Caesar does Caesar-ness. Both Brutus and Caesar can be manipulated, as Cassius and Decius respectively note (1.2.306–21;

2.1.201–10), into certain actions if they are led to believe those actions convey proper Brutus-ness and Caesar-ness. But while the suitability of prospective action to Brutus-ness tortures the conspirator to near self-division, to the point where he is so affected that his wife can scarcely 'know [him] Brutus' (2.1.254), Caesar protects his mind's confidence in Caesar-ness with relentless integrity. When Calphurnia, entreating him to listen to her premonitions, says she 'never stood on ceremonies' (2.2.13), she seems to ask more of her husband than to take ceremonies seriously now – she seems also to be asking him to be less ceremonious, less adherent to the shield of what is appropriate for the demeanour of Caesar. However, whereas Brutus's wife breaks down his veneer, and wins his promise that she 'shall partake / The secrets of [his] heart' (2.1.304–5), Calphurnia while she seemingly transmits her fear to Caesar cannot shake his commitment to being 'always' Caesar. Remarkably, his stance of being incapable of acknowledging a survival instinct alters not at all from a change in interlocutors, from Calphurnia alone to Decius; truly, throughout this scene he bends himself to sound like Caesar is supposed to sound, whether in private, in semi-private/semi-public or, as his entourage arrives, fully in public. Especially telling is his reaction to the horrifying news of the augurers finding no heart in their sacrificial victim: to him, it must mean 'Caesar should be a beast without a heart / If he should stay at home today for fear' (2.1.42–3). Even while this, like the whole scene, exudes both fear and fear of looking fearful, it also insists on the existence of a heart, one with absolute command over what the mind can think. The policing of thought is here so all-encompassing as to produce hermeneutic contortions. No wonder Decius gets Caesar so easily to agree to the unlikeliest of interpretations of the most easily interpreted of prodigies – whatever the bloody statues portend, the reading which to accept precludes fear is 'well expounded' (2.1.91). Caesar is already all too disposed to accept the reading that will confirm the presence, and the dominion over thought, of his great heart. That heart is far from confirmed, and it may well seem that Caesar goes to the ultimate lengths to deny its absence, to everyone else and to himself. Nevertheless, the lengths themselves may indicate a different-thinking mind, one busily fusing interior life, private life and public life into a unified 'always Caesar'.

This fusion is asserted, third and finally, as Caesar is just about to be struck down: 'I could be well moved if I were as you: / If I could pray to move, prayers would move me. / But I am constant as the northern star, / Of whose true-fixed and resting quality / There is no fellow in the firmament' (3.1.58–62). We cannot miss the irony of this moment, in so far as it realizes Decius's suggestion about Caesar's predictability, he being so amenable to the flattery of being above flattery (see 2.1.206–7); here before the Senate, Caesar compounds this blindness by flattering *himself* for his anti-flattery. Caesar actually has many 'fellows', for many a Tyrant is marked by the self-flattering notion that he has no fellow, and that only he among men cannot be flattered. And yet, the constancy of his mind's commitment to Caesar-ness, as, 'Unshaked of motion' (2.1.70), it shuts out all the time all un-Caesarly thought, is what has *allowed* his movements to be predicted and what has brought him here, to the point of death. The irony turns back on itself: the success of Decius's prediction, and indeed of the conspirators' whole enterprise, rests on their ability to believe securely in Caesar's unwavering constancy in being Caesar. They, and indeed we, can enjoy such security with no one else in the play's world – certainly not with Brutus, who can never firmly decide if his life's main action is something Brutus would properly do. Caesar's mind can be counted on, in a manner true of no one else's we meet, to be unshakable in its generation of Caesar-like and suppression of unCaesar-like motions.

Since such constancy might amount not to magnanimity but to inane role-playing, a political 'method-acting' he performs even in his bedroom, the 'northern star' speech should not turn us all into nodding Antonys. And yet, we cannot discount Caesar's claim to a stellar human quality, either. It is entirely possible that we do not see more of Caesar because we do not need to in order to understand him: it is entirely possible that, although actually subject to the fear and selfishness unbecoming of Caesar, Shakespeare's Caesar's mind is constant in its reinforcement of proper Caesar-thought, and displacement of anything unCaesar-like. In effect, then, the play asks us to be magnanimous in pondering the question of his magnanimity. We need to be fair and restrained as to whether his truly was a mind like no other.

7

New Directions: The Death of the Roman Republic: Julius Caesar and Cicero

Warren Chernaik

To writers in the republican tradition like Milton and James Harrington, Julius Caesar was a charismatic, malign figure, responsible for the extinction of Roman liberty. An entirely different image of Julius Caesar, especially prevalent in the nineteenth and early twentieth centuries, presented him as a heroic figure and model of conduct, a force for order, rising above the squabbling of petty men. In a sense, the two versions of Caesar replicate the rival Caesars constructed by Cassius and by Antony in Shakespeare's play: 'Here was a Caesar: when comes such another?' (3.2.243). To Cassius, seeking to enlist Brutus as one of his fellow conspirators:

Upon what meat doth this our Caesar feed
That he is grown so great? Age, thou art shamed!

> Rome, thou hast lost the breed of noble bloods! ...
> When could they say till now, that talked of Rome,
> That her wide walks encompassed but one man?

In contrast, to Antony, addressing the Roman populace about the moment when 'great Caesar fell', and displaying to them Caesar's blood-stained mantle:

> O what a fall was there, my countrymen!
> Then I, and you, and all of us fell down,
> Whilst bloody treason flourished over us.
> (1.2.148–50, 153–4; 3.2.187–90)

Though Cicero plays only a minor role in Shakespeare's *Julius Caesar*, he is the central character in Ben Jonson's *Catiline*, a play performed in 1611 by Shakespeare's company, the King's Men. In this play, an unscrupulous, ambitious Julius Caesar is Cicero's enemy, secretly backing Catiline's conspiracy. In Jonson's version of Roman history, Cicero is the guardian of Roman liberty, where Caesar, like Catiline, embodies a danger to the vulnerable Roman state. This chapter examines the complex relationship between these two Roman figures, in Cicero's own writings as well as in these two plays and others. As with Caesar, the prevalent view of Cicero's character – exemplary Stoic philosopher, republican hero, demagogue or timeserver – has fluctuated according to changing times and changing circumstances.

In his own day and later, assessments of Julius Caesar tend to divide into two sharply opposed camps, strongly positive or strongly negative. One view, with its origins partly in Caesar's own writings (as in the famous tag *veni*, *vidi*, *vici*), sees him as a model of decisive action and as one of the greatest heroes of antiquity. Dante was unequivocal in his praise of Caesar and his hostility towards Brutus and Cassius, presented in the *Inferno* as, along with Judas Iscariot, the worst of all sinners. In the nineteenth century, Theodor Mommsen's monumental *History of Rome* (1854–6) devoted eleven pages to a sustained encomium of Caesar as a 'creative genius' dedicated to 'the political, military, intellectual, and moral regeneration' of the Roman nation. Napoleon, who believed that Caesar's authority expressed the will of the people and that 'the person of Caesar was the guarantee of the supremacy of Rome', was hailed as a new Caesar by his admirers, while Napoleon III wrote an adulatory *Histoire de Jules César*. In the twentieth century, Benito Mussolini, who modelled himself on Julius Caesar in his political career, considered Caesar 'the greatest of all men who have ever lived', whose 'murder was a disaster for mankind'.[1]

A rival view, seeing Caesar as a potential tyrant, threatening the extinction of Roman liberty, finds expression in Lucan's *Pharsalia*. In this poem Cato, who committed suicide rather than surrender to the victorious Caesar, receives the greatest praise. In his rise to power, Caesar is presented as a wholly destructive force, impatient of any restraint, inordinately ambitious and sweeping aside anything that stands in his path. Caesar's victory in the civil wars against Pompey is seen as inevitable, but deeply regrettable, in bringing about the death of Roman liberty. In the Florentine republicans as in Lucan, we find an active hostility towards Caesar, whose rise to power is seen as the decisive moment when the liberty of the Roman Republic and its traditions of virtuous citizenship are snuffed out. Machiavelli and Guicciardini considered Caesar a tyrant and usurper, who had hoodwinked the Roman people, 'unaware of the yoke which they themselves had placed on their necks' in surrendering a liberty never to be regained.[2] Caesar, according to Machiavelli, was worse than Catiline, since 'he who has done wrong is more blameworthy than he who has but desired to do wrong'. To seventeenth-century republicans like Harrington and Milton, 'the arms of Caesar ... extinguishing liberty' gave rise to 'those ill-features of government which ... are become far worse in these western parts'. In the writings of these sixteenth- and seventeenth-century republicans, Brutus, Cassius and Cato were praised and tyrannicide justified.[3]

The high point of Cicero's posthumous reputation was in the Renaissance, when for Petrarch and other humanists he was considered the greatest of writers of Latin prose, a model for imitation in style as well as a practical philosopher of equally widespread influence. During this period, Cicero, as a pedagogical model, exercised 'an intellectual dominance that would last for centuries, a position comparable only to that of Aristotle' in schools and in universities. This intellectual dominance, though not unchallenged, continued into the eighteenth century when Enlightenment figures like Montesquieu and John Adams saw Cicero as 'a model of civic engagement and effective oratory'.[4] To John Adams, Cicero provided an unfailing model from which 'you will learn Wisdom and Virtue':

> He did not receive ... office as Persons do now a days, as a Gift, or a Farm, but as a public Trust, and considered it as a Theatre, in which the Eyes of the World were upon him.

His son John Quincy Adams, who followed his father as president of the United States, addressed an audience of university students in 1810:

> Let us make this the standard of moral and intellectual worth, for all human kind; and in reply to all the severities of satire, and the bitterness of misanthropy, repeat with conscious exultation, 'we are of the same species of being, as Cicero'.[5]

Later in the nineteenth century, Mommsen's adulation of Caesar was accompanied by severe denigration of Cicero, and his hostile view of Cicero's character and career, as 'a politician without principles and a writer without originality', became the received view for some years afterward. The historian J. A. Froude, writing in 1879, shared this view, treating Cicero with scorn as an unprincipled timeserver, Caesar as a model statesman, a strong and dominant leader, and, like Mommsen, found precedents for 'our present struggles in the history of the past'.⁶ Mommsen never tires of heaping obloquy on Cicero as 'pusillanimous', an advocate willing to sell his services to the highest bidder, ruled by 'material interests' alone:

> As a statesman without insight, ideas, or purpose, he figures successively as democrat, as aristocrat, and as a tool of the monarchs, and was never more than a short-sighted egotist ... He was valiant in opposition to sham attacks, and he knocked down many walls of pasteboard with a loud din; no serious matter was ever, either in good or evil, decided by him ... In the character of an author ... he stands quite as low as that of a statesman ... abounding ... in words, poor beyond all conception in ideas.⁷

When the novelist Anthony Trollope wrote *The Life of Cicero* in 1880, it was largely an attempt to argue against the prevalent view of Cicero as weak and vacillating, lacking in 'sincerity' and as a writer and thinker, 'of the second order' at best: 'I may say with truth that my book has sprung from love of the man, and from a heartfelt admiration of his virtues and his conduct as well as of his gifts'. Where Mommsen and Froude castigated Cicero for alleged weaknesses of character, Trollope saw Cicero as a man of conscience, aware of his own imperfections, 'a man human as men are now' – indeed, a man very much like some of the principal characters in Trollope's novels, Plantagenet Pallister or Phineas Finn. To the Caesars of the world, in contrast, 'there is no right but his power, no wrong but opposition to it'. As for Cicero, as Trollope viewed him:

> It is because he was in truth patriotic, because his dreams of a Republic were noble dreams, because he was intent on doing good in public affairs, because he was anxious for the honour of Rome and of Romans, not because he was or was not a 'real power in the State', that his memory is still worth recording.⁸

Plays in the Early Modern period featuring Cicero as a principal character tend to be republican in their sympathies and to treat Caesar as a potential or actual tyrant. Thomas Kyd's *Cornelia* (1594), a closet drama closely translated from Robert Garnier's Senecan tragedy, is unequivocal in its representation of Caesar as tyrant and destroyer of Roman freedom, and is unusual for this date in its endorsement of tyrannicide. Caesar, who appears in only one scene, is an exemplum of the folly of trusting in earthly greatness, as he boasts of his 'matchless victories':

> There lyves no King (how great so e're he be,)
> But trembleth if he once but heare of mee ...
> Rome, speak no more of eyther *Scipio*,
> Nor of the *Fabii*, or *Fabritians* ...
> *Caesar* doth triumph over all the world,
> And all they scarcely conquered a nooke.[9]

In Acts 1 and 2, Cicero laments Caesar's victories as destructive of Rome's ancient traditions, as he seeks to console the distraught Cornelia, Pompey's widow. Though the episode is invented, Cicero did express similar sentiments in his writings about Caesar, military prowess and Roman liberty, and he supported Pompey in the civil war, while urging peace and reconciliation. In a lengthy speech Cicero argues that Rome the conqueror, once the home of virtue and honour, had become Rome the conquered. 'Poysoned Ambition' and pride have endangered a Rome 'whose power, / Could never have been curb'd, but by it selfe'. The vocabulary here is the standard republican contrast of 'ancient freedom' and shameful bondage:

> Carthage and Sicily we have subdude,
> And almost yoked all the world beside ...
> Yet now we live despoild and robd by one,
> Of th'ancient freedom wherein we were borne.
> And even that yoke that wont to tame all others,
> Is heavily return'd upon our selves.[10]

In Acts 1 and 2, at the very moment when Caesar has gained supreme power backed by his army, both the Chorus and Cicero predict that, like any tyrant, Caesar will be overthrown. In a choral ode predicting that 'another *Brutus*' fighting 'in Romes defence' will arise as he did against 'unjust *Tarquin*' and 'free our Towne from tyrannie', the republican language is more or less that of sixteenth-century resistance theory ('servile thrall', 'tyrannous proud insolence'). The choral ode suggests that it is the abuses of tyrannous monarchs that bring about their deserved downfall. A later passage in a speech by Cicero in Act 3, closely following Garnier, openly justifies tyrannicide, asserting that Caesar will not be able to 'hold us in this servitude' much longer:

> *Caesar* thou shalt not vaunt thy conquest long …
> Nor shalt thou bathe thee longer in our blood …
> Think'st thou to signiorize, or be the King
> Of such a number, nobler then thy selfe?
> Or think'st thou Romains have such bastard harts,
> To let thy tyranny be unreveng'd?

In a vision prefiguring Caesar's assassination, Cicero can 'see' Caesar's 'stab'd and torne' corpse, and views the scene with approval.

> And many a Romaine sword already drawne,
> T'enlarge the libertie that thou usurpst.
> And thy dismembered body (stab'd and torne,)
> Dragd through the streets, disdained to be borne.[11]

In a play written (or translated) five years before Shakespeare's *Julius Caesar*, the motif of bathing in blood is deployed to the opposite effect from Shakespeare, presenting Caesar, not the conspirators, with bloody hands. Rather than the torn mantle of Caesar being displayed by Antony to prompt the crowd's revenge, here Cicero envisages the corpse of Caesar dishonoured after death, reduced to offal.

Robert Garnier wrote *Cornélie* in 1573, the year after the St Bartholomew's Day Massacre, and in a preface described this Roman play as 'propre aux malheurs de nostre siècle'. A moderate Catholic opposed to the violent anti-Huguenot policies of the Duke of Guise (who may be aimed at in the preface's comments on 'l'ambicieux discord' destructive of the 'grande République' of Rome), Garnier in several plays with Roman settings comments indirectly on the France of his own day. The play's approval of tyrannicide seems at variance with later plays by Garnier that counsel obedience even to a bad king.[12]

Sir William Alexander's *Tragedie of Julius Caesar* (1603), another closet drama, is more balanced in its treatment of Caesar, emphasizing his magnanimity and clemency, as well as his pride and overweening ambition.

> I moovd that warre which all the world bemones,
> Being urged by force to free my selfe from feares:
> Still when my hand gave wounds, my heart gave grones,
> No Romans blood was shed, but I shed teares.

Caesar, according to the play's Argument, was 'a man of a loftie minde, and given to attempt great things', yet, 'driven with a delight of soveraigntie', he sought supreme power, 'tending to tyrannie'. Even his enemies in the play pay tribute to Caesar's good qualities, praising him as 'worthy for his virtuous deeds', while arguing 'I owe him much, but yet my country more'.[13] Cicero, like Shakespeare's Cassius, sees Caesar as the enemy of freedom. In a colloquy with Decius Brutus, Cicero describes Caesar as ambitious, with 'his thoughts all bent to tyranny' even as a young man, at the time when, as consul, Cicero saved Rome from Catiline's treason. As in Jonson's *Catiline*, Caesar is presented as complicit in Catiline's conspiracy.

> And he that still striv'd tyrannie t'embrace,
> Was thought conjoynd with *Catilin* to bee;

And had wise *Catos* counsel taken place,
Had with the rest receiv'd his death by me.[14]

When the conspirators meet in Act IV, they decide, as in Shakespeare, not to invite Cicero to join them. Where Shakespeare's Brutus says dismissively of Cicero, 'For he will never follow anything / That other men begin' (2.1.150–1), here Brutus, though agreeing that, once the deed is done, Cicero by his eloquence could defend the tyrannicide before the people, argues that Cicero's weaknesses of character make him unfit to carry out such a bold deed. Though Cicero is a patriot and 'none *Caesar* more dislikes, nor likes us more', nevertheless:

Yet to his custodie Ile not commit,
The secrets of our enterprise so soone,
Men may them selves be oftentimes not fit,
To doe the things that they would wish were done.
  He still being timorous, and by age growne worse,
Might chance to lay our honour in the dust,
All cowards must unconstant be of force,
With bold designes none fearefull breasts can trust.
(*Tragedie of Julius Caesar*, 4.1, Sig. Y4)[15]

Alexander's play, unlike Shakespeare's, ends with the assassination (offstage, narrated to Calphurnia by a messenger) and with a final Choral Ode on the vicissitudes of fortune. There is no funeral oration, no crowd violence, no battle between the forces of Brutus and Cassius and those who seek to avenge the death of Caesar. Cicero, commenting on how 'great sprites must doe great good, or then great ill', sees in Caesar a mixture of 'vertues' and 'imperfections':

Then whilst he by the rules of reason liv'd,
When lawfully elected by the State,
What glorious deedes by *Caesar* were atchiv'd,
While all the world as wonders may relate.

> But when of right he buried all respects,
> As blind ambition had bewitcht his minde,
> What harme ensued by pitifull effects.
> We at the first, he at the last did finde.
> (*Tragedie of Julius Caesar*, 5.1, Sig. Cc1)

In its balance of sympathies and its dramatic structure (with two characters, in a succession of scenes, representing opposing sides in a debate), Alexander's play gives equal space to Caesar and to those who seek to 'redeeme the state' from 'bondage'. One extremely odd example of equivocation about tyrannicide occurs in a speech by Brutus in Act 3. In lines strikingly at variance with the general drift of the play, Brutus is made to say that the conspirators' projected actions are praiseworthy only because Caesar is a usurper and not a 'lawfull' hereditary monarch.

> If *Caesar* had bin borne, or chusde our Prince,
> Then those that durst attempt to take his life,
> The world of treason justly might convince.
>   For still the states that flourish for the time,
> By subjects should b'inviolable thought;
> And those no doubt commit a monstrous crime,
> That lawfull sovereignty prophane in ought.[16]

The tyrannicide Brutus is turned into an apologist for divine right monarchy, urging non-resistance to established monarchical authority. It is possible that Alexander, seeking preferment under James I, softened any dangerous implications of the received narrative.

Cicero's own remarks on Caesar, in *De Officiis*, his letters and his speeches, consistently saw Caesar as dangerous because of his great gifts: 'such lofty spirit and greatness of mind very easily breed a defiant and excessive lust for supreme power'. In *De Officiis*, a work of practical ethics that was extraordinarily influential in the Renaissance, Cicero deplores 'the shameless conduct of Gaius Caesar':

> He undermined all laws, divine and human, in order to establish that dominance which his erroneous belief had targeted for himself. What is distressing ... is that the ambition for civil office, military command, power and glory is usually nursed by men of the greatest and most outstanding talent. So great precautions must be taken to ensure that no wrong in such circumstances is committed.[17]

Tyrannicide, he argues, is honourable: tyrants deserve to be 'banished from human society', 'excised ... from the body of humanity which we all share'. A passage that does not name Caesar but clearly refers to him speaks of 'the man who lusted to become king of the Roman people and lord of all the world': 'it is dishonourable to become king in a state which was free and which ought to be free' (*De Officiis*, III.32, 83, pp. 94, 112).

As a man whose gifts were for oratory, in the civic arena, rather than in leading troops in battle, Cicero argued for the primacy of civil over military accomplishments. Again and again, Cicero called attention to his vigilance in defending the state at the time of Catiline's conspiracy, when as Consul he preserved the liberties of Romans.

> Most people think that the achievements of war are more important than those of peace, but the opinion must be corrected. For many men have sought occasions for war from the mere ambition for fame ... Did not arms yield to the toga, when I was at the helm of state? For never was the republic in more serious peril ... As the result of my counsels and my vigilance, their weapons slipped suddenly from the hands of the most desperate traitors ... What achievement in war, then, was ever so great?[18]

A similar view of Cicero as watchful sentinel is central to Jonson's *Catiline* and to Cicero's *In Catilinam*, I–IV, a major source for Jonson's play. Cicero, never sparing in his own praise, frequently reminded his Roman audience in his orations of his role as Rome's saviour. In his *Philippics* attacking Antony, at the very end of his career, he speaks of himself as once again compelled to defend Rome, by his words and his political acumen, against another would-be tyrant.

> I defended the State in youth, I will not desert it in old age; I despised the swordsmen of Catiline, I will not dread yours.[19]

At the time of his election as Consul in 63 BC, Cicero was conscious of his vulnerable position as being a 'new man', an outsider, not from one of the ancient patrician families and thus held in suspicion both by the conservative Senators (or *optimes*) and by those like Caesar and Catiline who sought support by appealing to the multitude and had little respect for Roman traditions. Cicero's election as Consul, his actions in putting down Catiline's conspiracy and the personal disasters that followed, when his enemies, including Caesar, had him exiled from Rome, in fear of his life, are the subject of two novels by Robert Harris, *Imperium* (2006) and *Lustrum* (2009), both of which find parallels to Cicero's career in the world of twentieth- and twenty-first-century politics, where high principles are shaded by compromise and shifting loyalties. Just as it is possible to see in the Rome of Shakespeare's *Julius Caesar* a version of England in the 1590s, so Harris, an experienced political journalist as well as a novelist, portrays a Rome similar in some respects to contemporary England.[20]

Cicero was aware of the dangers emanating from the ambitious Julius Caesar early in Caesar's career, before he had gained a reputation as a great, victorious general. Later, when the demagogue Clodius unleashed mobs and, with Caesar's backing, procured Cicero's exile, Cicero, feeling 'utterly lost', lamented 'the hopelessness of his situation'. After he returned to Rome, recognizing that 'the state of affairs was not to my liking' under the First Triumvirate of Caesar, Pompey and

Crassus, Cicero tried to establish cordial relations with the powerful Caesar despite their mutual distrust, and retired from active involvement in politics for the greater part of fifteen years.[21] In 50 BC, at a time when Caesar and Pompey, each with an army at his disposal, were contending for power and Caesar, Consul for the second time, seemed to be fortune's darling, Cicero wrote to Atticus about the difficulties in choosing the right course of action.

> Do you think they will be afraid of having a despot, when they never have objected to having one so long as they were left in peace? ... Do I approve of a man being allowed to stand for the consulship who has retained his army beyond the prescribed date? ... Did I approve of his being granted ten years of military command? ... But the source of all these evils is one and the same: we ought to have resisted him while he was still weak – and it would have been easy. Now he has eleven legions ... As the cow joins the cattle-herd, I shall join the patriots, or so-called patriots, even if they stampede to destruction. I can see what is the right course in these damnable straits. No one can tell what will happen when the fighting breaks out; but anyone can tell that, if the patriots lose, Caesar will be no more merciful than Cinna was in killing off the nobility.
>
> (*Letters,* tr. Wilkinson, 102–3)

During the period of his forced retirement, Cicero wrote a series of philosophical works which gained him a great reputation during the Renaissance, including *De Republica* in 52–4 BC and *De Officiis* in 44 BC. As he says in a letter:

> Only let us keep our resolve, to live together in pursuit of our studies ... If no one avails himself of our services, at any rate to read and compose 'Republics', and if we cannot guide the State from the Senate-house and Forum, at least to guide it from the study and library, as the great thinkers of old used to do.[22]

In old age, attacking Mark Antony in the *Philippics* with the same eloquence as in confronting Catiline twenty years earlier, Cicero praises the slaying of Caesar as a 'glorious deed': 'all good men, as far as their own power went, slew Caesar'. In these powerful orations, he presents himself as consistently, throughout his career, the guardian of Roman liberty. As he says in the peroration of *Philippic* VI:

> That the Roman people should be slaves is contrary to divine law ... Matters have been brought to a crisis; the issue is liberty ... Other nations can endure slavery; the assured possession of the Roman people is liberty.[23]

In *Catiline* (1611), Jonson depicts Cicero as 'the careful magistrate', with 'industry and vigilance' working for 'the public good', and Catiline and his associates as unremittingly wicked, willing to destroy Rome in their lust for power and personal aggrandizement:

> CAT. Is there a beauty here in Rome you love,
> An enemy you would kill? What head's not yours?
> Whose wife, which boy, whose daughter, of what race,
> That th'husband or glad parents shall not bring you, And
>   boasting of the office?[24]

Like Shakespeare's *Julius Caesar*, *Catiline* is closely based on classical sources – the historian Sallust's *Bellum Catilinae* for Acts 1–3 and part of Act 5, Cicero's speeches against Catiline, *In Catilinam*, for Act 4 and part of Act 5. Unlike *Julius Caesar*, Jonson's play was not a success. According to Leonard Digges, writing in 1640:

> So I have seen, when Caesar would appear,
> And on the stage at half-sword parley were
> Brutus and Cassius; O, how the audience
> Were ravished, with what wonder they went thence,
> When some new day they would not brook a line
> Of tedious though well-laboured *Catiline*.

In the 1611 Quarto, Jonson includes a combative preface and dedication to the Earl of Pembroke complaining of 'so thick and dark an ignorance as now covers the age'. He says of the theatrical audience, scornfully, 'neither praise nor dispraise from you can affect me', addressing himself, as in a number of his poems, not to the 'many', but to 'a few'.[25]

Jonson, like Sallust, presents Catiline's rebellion as a disease infecting Rome, just punishment for 'guilty states' suffering 'the plagues ... which they have deserved'. Sallust, writing in the last days of the Roman republic, between the death of Julius Caesar and the accession of Augustus, begins his narrative with general reflections on the decline of Rome, corrupted by greed and 'the ambitious desire of superiority' from its original republican virtues. Jonson adapts passages from Sallust in the Choral Ode ending Act 1 of *Catiline*:

> Rome now is mistress of the whole
> World, sea and land, to either pole,
> And even that fortune will destroy
> The power that made it: she doth joy
> So much in plenty, wealth, and ease,
> That now th'excess is her disease.[26]

In one major respect, Jonson departs from Sallust, in presenting Julius Caesar as implicated in Catiline's conspiracy and then, once Catiline's plot has failed, abandoning his former protégé. His immediate source in writing *Catiline*, as several scholars have pointed out, is the edition of Sallust published in Basel in 1564, which includes not only Sallust's Latin text, but Cicero's *In Catilinam* I and IV, and, along with other commentaries, an extended Latin narrative by the Italian humanist Felicius Durantinus that, in effect, rewrites Sallust's account of Catiline's conspiracy to correct Sallust's alleged bias and deficiencies.[27] As well as giving a more prominent role to Cicero as the saviour of Rome, virtually single-handed, Felicius presents Caesar as Catiline's secret ally. In Jonson's play, following Felicius, Caesar is an intriguing, dissembling

Machiavel, who, in clandestine meetings with Catiline, encourages him to 'Be resolute / And put your enterprise in act', and consistently denigrates Cicero's attempts to preserve the Roman republic against its enemies. The advice he gives to Catiline immediately before the conspirators' meeting shows Caesar to be deeply cynical in his advocacy of 'policy': might makes right, and moral considerations are irrelevant.

> CAESAR   Let 'em call it mischief;
> When it is past and prospered, 'twill be virtue.
> They're petty crimes are punished, great rewarded
> ... For they that win do seldom receive shame
> Of victory, howe'er it be achieved
> ... Come, there was never any great thing yet
> Aspired but by violence, or fraud.[28]

Caesar and the villainous Catiline share the conviction that 'conscience' is no more than 'folly', appropriate to 'a religious fool ... a superstitious slave' (3.3.28–30). Sallust, unlike Jonson, characterizes Caesar in favourable terms, describing the claim that Caesar was involved in the conspiracy as 'false', and praising Caesar's 'greatness of mind', 'curtesie and gentleness' and 'valor and good conduct' in war.[29] In Jonson's play, Caesar and his allies express their scorn of Cicero as a 'new man', a 'mere upstart / That has no pedigree', and claim that the fears and rumours of 'turbulent practices' and 'dangers' to the Roman state have been invented by Cicero to serve his own ends (2.1.119–20; 3.1.50–1, 92–7).

Twentieth- and twenty-first-century critics have frequently expressed doubts about the methods Jonson's Cicero uses in combating Catiline and his fellow plotters. The most common charge is expediency, the use of morally questionable means to bring about desired ends. Cicero himself comments on his use of surveillance and a network of spies and informers, as well as the employment of agents who may be cowardly, mercenary and base, bribed sometimes with 'offices' at his disposal: ''Tis well if some men will do well for price; / So few are virtuous when the reward's away'.[30] Harris's *Lustrum*, in which few of the characters ever act from pure motives, even when their intentions are good, places a great emphasis on expedient compromise, suggesting at one point that Cicero might have forged documents to implicate Catiline and his associates. Jonson's distinctions between the virtuous and vicious, the defenders of Roman liberty and the would-be tyrants and destroyers, are more clear-cut. But the problematical aspects of Cicero's actions are brought out again and again by Jonson. In a Choral Ode at the end of Act 4, Jonson raises questions about how to interpret the actions of political leaders in a time of crisis. The Roman populace, as represented by the Chorus, is in the grip of contradictory rumours, hopes and fears, swinging wildly from one extreme to another.

> One while we thought him innocent,
> And then w'accused
> The Consul for his malice spent
> And power abused.
>
> (4.7.44–7)

In the eyes of the troubled Roman citizens, beset with uncertainties, the actions of Cicero, as magistrate entrusted with protecting the state against possible enemies, can appear benevolent, necessary to secure public order, or an abuse of power, sinister and underhanded. Though the Chorus argues that it is important to 'give to every noble deed / The name it merits', the clear implication is that the names assigned to the deeds of public figures bear no absolute, unchanging significance, but vary according to circumstances:

> And call their diligence deceit,
> Their virtue, vice,
> Their watchfulness, but lying in wait,
> And blood the price.
>
> (4.7.6–3, 66–7)

The Tragedy of Marcus Tullius Cicero, published in 1651 at a time when the theatres were closed, is uncompromisingly republican in its stance, with many passages by the Chorus and public-spirited characters idealizing the early republic and portraying the present state as diseased, descending into servitude. In the opening scene, the ghost of Julius Caesar, sent 'from the black womb of hell' and gleefully contemplating blood, plague and slaughter, predicts of Rome:

> A heavier hand
> Shall make thee stoop to sovereign command
> And kiss the yoke, though sullied first and dyed
> In thine own gore.[31]

Antony and Octavius, contending for power though in temporary alliance under the Second Triumvirate, are both potential tyrants. Antony is transparently villainous, hating the virtuous Cicero and the very name of liberty, where Octavius, a dissembler, has momentary qualms, but is ultimately ruled by the relentless pursuit of absolute power.

> He that aspires to govern without check
> Must set his foot against his father's neck.
>
> (4.2.20–1)

Marcus Cicero and his brother Quintus disagree as to how to treat the rising power of Octavius. As Quintus, consistently both more practical and less willing to compromise, says at one point, warning that 'hopes of better times' are delusory:

> Rome has had a long succession
> Of state usurpers: when this Hydra's head
> Is cut away, another may bud forth.
>
> (1.4.40, 42–4)

Both Octavius and Antony are presented as heirs to Caesar, not in any legitimate sense, but as manifestations of the desire for power, bringing about the inevitable demise of liberty.[32] Octavius says, in a clear parallel to Caesar's crossing the Rubicon and to the axioms in Machiavelli's *The Prince*:

> If it be denied, I am determined
> To march myself to Rome, and gain by force
> What fair means cannot win.
>
> (3.2.20–2)

A choral ode at the end of Act III, in describing the rise of Octavius to power, would seem to suggest some contemporary parallels in the context of 1651, lamenting the destruction of liberty by a powerful figure, who dissembles his true motives and is backed by an army:

> But this young minion of blind chance
> Like a sky-climbing eagle still will tower
> Until he shall himself advance
> Unto a sovereign independent power.
>
> Heavens! If it be your sacred pleasure
> To put a period to our liberty,
> Oh, let the scepter bear some measure,
> That being servile we may yet seem free.
>
> (3.13.62–8)

Though it is possible that this play was written earlier than 1651, the lines appear to be directly applicable to Cromwell, and, like the play as a whole, to express the attitude of diehard republicans like Ludlow, Overton and Lilburne, who considered Cromwell to be yet another tyrant under a new name.[33]

In Act IV, a Soothsayer summoned by Cicero predicts that 'Romans must expect the yoke':

> Then, fathers, hear your dismal fate.
> Your freedom shall be lost, your State
> Converted to a monarchy.
>
> (4.4.15–17, 30)

In a series of speeches, Marcus and Quintus Cicero, contemplating suicide now that 'there's no hope of cure', agree that "tis a noble death / Not to survive one's country's liberty' (4.4.44–5; 4.5.167). Acts 4 and 5 are unrelentingly pessimistic, in presenting a series of debates on the ethics of suicide, followed by the proscription of Cicero and other republicans, several of whom (including Quintus and his son) are shown displaying their piety and virtue in facing torture and death at the hands of the soldiers. What survives, the play suggests, is virtue, while the victors show their vicious natures in their triumph. Antony and his wife Fulvia desecrate the severed head of Cicero ('Is this that Cicero's head that thundered so / In our tribunals? Ha, is this that mouth / Was wont to spit such lightning?') – unlike Julius Caesar, who is said to have wept when presented with Pompey's head. On receiving this 'kingly present', Antony *'rolls Cicero's head as if it were a ball'*, and the savage Fulvia cuts off Cicero's tongue:

> ANTONY Do Fulvia stab it, give it as many wounds
> As Julius Caesar had, whose horrid murder
> That worm extolled as a heroic deed.
>   (5.8.5–7; 5.10.4, 22–4)

More explicitly than any other play depicting this period of Roman history, *The Tragedy of Marcus Tullius Cicero* equates the death of Cicero with the death of Roman liberty, seen as inevitable.

Shakespeare's characteristic approach, very different from that in *Catiline*, Kyd's *Cornelia*, or *The Tragedy of Marcus Tullius Cicero* – and, for that matter, from Cicero's orations *In Catilinam* or from Cicero's comments on contemporary affairs in his letters – is argument *in utramque partem*, an 'unclosed argument', putting both sides of a case and doing equal justice to each. In *Coriolanus*, Act 1, Scene 1, neither Menenius nor the disgruntled Roman citizens can be said to win the argument, and the same can be said of the confrontation between Coriolanus and the citizens later in the marketplace, with their incompatible assumptions about *virtus* and heroism, the responsibility of the individual to the commonwealth, and the roles of the senatorial class and the plebeians in the recently established Roman republic. Some of the same elements of debate, with different views juxtaposed, are present in Alexander's *Tragedie of Julius Caesar*, though without much emotional involvement or depth. Argument *in utraquem partem* allows for the possibility of treating any position with a degree of irony, as an instance of the power of self-delusion, or revealing the fissures in the dominant ideology of republican or imperial Rome. Throughout *Julius Caesar*, Roman values, including the principles of republicanism, are held up to scrutiny.

In Shakespeare's *Julius Caesar*, the word 'Roman' is a highly charged term, implying possession of moral qualities – constancy, fidelity, perseverance, self-discipline – or a claim that others lack such qualities. When, early in the play, Cassius attempts to persuade first Brutus and then Caska to join the conspiracy, each mention of 'Rome' or 'Roman' suggests that to be a true Roman is to be a republican. 'Noble', a term repeated again and again in the play, is to Brutus, Cassius and their fellow conspirators a term partly moral and partly class-based: republicanism, in its distrust of the fickle 'rabblement', with their 'Sweaty nightcaps' (1.2.243–4), is the political philosophy of the Roman aristocracy. In addressing the superstitious Caska, seeking to shame him into demonstrating 'those sparks of life / That should be in a Roman', Cassius contrasts a degenerate modernity and a heroic Roman past in the manner of Sallust and Tacitus:

> For Romans now
> Have thews and limbs like to their ancestors;
> But woe the while, our fathers' minds are dead,
> And we are governed with our mothers' spirits:
> Our yoke and sufferance show us womanish.
>
> (1.3.57–8, 80–4)[34]

Brutus's 'Th'abuse of greatness is when it disjoins / Remorse from power' (2.1.18–19) is an axiom equally applicable to the characterization of Julius Caesar, 'the man who lusted to become king of the Roman people', in all the plays we have discussed, and to Cicero's treatment of Caesar in *De Officiis* and in his correspondence.

> Anyone who says this ambition is honourable is a lunatic; it justifies the extinction of laws and liberty, and regards the squalid and accused subjugation of them as magnificent.[35]

But in Shakespeare's play, Caesar's actual or potential tyranny, rather than being demonstrated over and over again in the action, is open to question, as different characters present rival interpretations of his character and behaviour. We do not even know whether, in the ceremony on the Lupercal, he wants to be crowned. Shakespeare gives us two conflicting versions of the offer of the crown, one by the hostile, cynical Caska and the other, after the assassination, in Antony's funeral oration. To Antony, seeking to sway the crowd in Caesar's favour, the refusal of the crown is presented as genuine, a proof that Caesar was no potential tyrant, but a virtuous, modest man, dedicated to the public welfare, rather than personal aggrandizement.

> You all did see, that on the Lupercal
> I thrice presented him a kingly crown,
> Which he did thrice refuse. Was this ambition?
> Yet Brutus says, he was ambitious,
> And sure he is an honourable man.
> I speak not to disprove what Brutus spoke,
> But here I am to speak what I do know.
>
> (3.2.96–102)

What Antony is doing here, with consummate skill, is precisely calculated 'to disprove what Brutus spoke', to dismantle Brutus's case against Caesar as a danger to the liberty of

Romans. By giving Caesar so few lines to speak, making him a character spoken about rather than speaking and acting, Shakespeare presents Caesar as enigmatic and opaque, a blank sheet for others to write upon.

What distinguishes Shakespeare's play from Roman plays like *Cornelia* and *Catiline* is the pervasive irony to which the well-meaning statements of the characters are subjected. When Caesar says, 'I am constant as the Northern star' (3.1.60), and when Brutus pretends that they will be able to kill Caesar without shedding blood, as priests of a republican religion performing a sacrifice, the irony is apparent. In what may be the most familiar lines in the play (other than 'Friends, Romans, countrymen, lend me your ears'), Cassius, skilled in the arts of persuasion, says to Brutus:

> Men at some time are masters of their fates.
> The fault, dear Brutus, is not in our stars
> But in ourselves, that we are underlings.
>
> (1.2.138–40)

The subsequent action of the play can be said to prove a contrary thesis: that men are at no times masters of their fates, though they think they are. There is no point in the play where Brutus and his fellow conspirators are more deeply mired in self-delusion than when they bathe their hands in Caesar's blood, vainly predicting that future ages will honour them as 'the men who gave their country liberty' (3.1.118). What Brutus and Cassius fail to realize is that the physical manifestation of the blood-stained hands and clothing, shockingly visible in a stage production, negates the cries of peace and liberty, brands them as murderers and suggests that more blood will be shed before the end of the play. What encloses and limits characters who erroneously think they are acting freely is an overarching dramatic irony: events have consequences, but not those intended by men and women acting out a script in which they have been assigned parts.

Critics still continue to disagree about the politics of *Julius Caesar*, the play's treatment of liberty, public order and the patterns of history in depicting the rise and fall of Caesar. One traditional view, more popular half a century ago than today, sees the play as illustrative of Shakespeare's (and the critic's own) ideological conservatism, his belief in the sanctity of order. The neoconservative Allan Bloom, writing in 1964, like the English and American critics represented in Peter Ure's 1979 Casebook, confident that 'certain important virtues can only be possessed by a few', saw Shakespeare's play as a homily against disorder, illustrating the 'social chaos' and anarchy that inevitably followed tyrannicide. Ideologically, such a view bears some similarities to the idealization of Caesar to be found in Mommsen and others in the nineteenth and early twentieth centuries, with its longing for a strong leader, bringing order and security to a troubled state.[36] More recently, Andrew Hadfield in *Shakespeare and Republicanism* (2005) has claimed *Julius Caesar* as 'a work on a conspicuously republican theme', illustrating 'how clearly republicanism had set the political agenda in Shakespeare's England'. Hadfield's book reflects the recent critical interest, in works by Quentin Skinner and others, in the survival of a republican or Neo-Roman tradition in the Early Modern period. Yet several essays and the editors' introduction in *Shakespeare and Early Modern Political Thought* (2009) present Shakespeare as deeply sceptical about some of the principal tenets of republicanism or even as hostile to republicanism. Far from being a committed republican or, like the imagined Shakespeare of an earlier generation, a committed conservative, the 'unremittingly bleak' Shakespeare of these essays does not appear to believe in anything, other than that in 'a dangerous and corrupt political world' the virtuous individual's primary concerns must be 'survival and self-interest'.[37]

With *Julius Caesar*, as with any other play, productions as well as critical accounts will often be governed, consciously or unconsciously, by critical assumptions widely held at particular times. Laurence Olivier's film of *Henry V*, produced in 1944 at the time of a war against fascism, inevitably saw the play as patriotic and heroic, while productions during the Vietnam or Iraq War were unlikely to follow a similar approach. Productions of *Julius Caesar*, at different times, have seen Brutus as an idealist and man of conscience, a Roman Hamlet or as a dissembling politician, ruled by self-interest, more Claudius than Hamlet. The challenge for any critic or producer is to avoid narrowing a play down to fit a particular dogmatism, in the hope of doing justice to a play's complexity. In the tradition of *in utraquem partem*, Shakespeare can dramatize ethical and political issues relevant to his own time and our own, but always as questions to be left unresolved, not as recommendations aimed at governing conduct.

8

Resources for Teaching and Studying *Julius Caesar*

Jeremy Lopez

Julius Caesar is among the most familiar of Shakespeare's plays and until quite recently it was – and had been for more than a century – the single play students were most likely to encounter in school. The fact that the play has little or no sex in it, that it can do double-duty as a literary text and a history lesson about ancient Rome and that it seems to celebrate timeless civic virtues (freedom, representative government, courageous resistance to tyranny, etc.) all made it an obvious choice for the secondary-school classroom in the first half of the twentieth century. Before the twentieth century – and before the establishment of the English literature curriculum that we still follow today – *Julius Caesar* was a standard text excerpted in British and American schoolbooks meant to teach students the conventions of classical oratory and rhetoric. When, at the end of the nineteenth century, English literature became a part of the university curriculum in its own right, it did so partly by way of Shakespeare – and Shakespeare was introduced to the curriculum partly by way of *Julius Caesar*. In 1874, Harvard University announced that its entrance exams would require students to write an essay on 'standard authors as shall be announced from time to time.' The texts announced for the first such exam included Shakespeare's *Julius Caesar*, *The Tempest* and *The Merchant of Venice*. Not surprisingly, Harvard's entrance-exam list precipitated a systematic effort in American high schools to undertake the teaching of Shakespeare.[1] The play has been ubiquitous ever since, though it seems to have been replaced, in the last 30 years or so, by *Romeo and Juliet* as the play most frequently taught in schools – students and teachers nowadays being more comfortable with the sexual dimension of Shakespeare's literature. It also may be the case that *Julius Caesar*'s academic past has caught up with it: the play has been a standard school-text for so long that it now seems like nothing more than a school-text. I will confess that I avoided teaching *Julius Caesar* until quite recently in my career. I thought that it was, and assumed that my students would think that it was, boring.

Is *Julius Caesar* boring? This is a question the teacher of the play – and, indeed, of any Shakespeare play – must reckon with head-on as he or she prepares to explore its language and form with young people for whom both are necessarily, inevitably alien and baffling. In the largest sense, the answer must be a qualified Yes, because the contemporary reader's experience of Shakespeare is almost always framed by the institution of the school. Even Shakespeare knew that school was boring, as we see from his description of one of the seven ages of man:

> ... the whining schoolboy, with his satchel
> And shining morning face, creeping like snail
> Unwillingly to school.
> (*As You Like It*, 2.7.145–7)[2]

What was school like for the Elizabethan schoolboy? What did he carry in his satchel – what was he forced, unwilling, to read? Latin, mostly: Ovid, Cicero, Seneca, Virgil and, of course, Julius Caesar's own account of his wars in Gaul. The

Elizabethan schoolboy would have become deeply familiar with the content and the style of these authors by means of meticulous, tedious grammatical analysis and soul-killing rote-memorization exercises. For schoolboys in Shakespeare's time, was Julius Caesar boring? Yes.

In her introduction to the 2012 Norton edition of *Julius Caesar*, Susan Cerasano writes that

> [g]enerations of English schoolboys had translated Caesar's *Gallic Wars*, as well as Cicero's orations addressing Cataline's thwarted conspiracy and other aspects of contemporary politics during the period when Caesar ruled the Roman Republic. There were, as well, references to Caesar and his time in the writings of many classical authors whose works were standard reading for sixteenth-century students.[3]

Cerasano's argument is that the familiarity of Caesar meant that Shakespeare could create a 'larger-than-life presence who could easily take over the Globe stage.' The opposite argument, however, could just as easily be made: perhaps the author of any play about Julius Caesar in the period (and there were several) would have had to struggle mightily to show an audience something new or surprising. The ubiquity of Caesar in Shakespeare's time might be analogized to the ubiquity of Shakespeare in ours. Teachers know that *Julius Caesar* has a particular formal and linguistic character, and that it is one of Shakespeare's most fascinatingly strange plays. To most students, however, *Caesar* is just another alleged masterpiece that they are compelled to lug around in their satchels. By the time Shakespeare sat down to write his play, sometime in 1598 or 1599, late sixteenth-century English audiences at theatres of all sorts (university, court and public) had seen at least half a dozen other plays about Caesar – including, as recently as 1594–5, a two-part tragedy (no longer extant) called *Caesar and Pompey*, performed at the Rose Theatre. Moreover, Thomas North's very popular translation of Plutarch's *Lives*, which was the primary source for Shakespeare's play, had gone through two editions. If you were going to write a play about Julius Caesar at this point, you had to figure out a way to make it new.

Whether or not Shakespeare succeeded in making Caesar new is something of which we can never be certain: as with most plays of the English Renaissance, there is little evidence by which to judge *Julius Caesar*'s popularity. None the less, whatever people thought of the play in its own time, it has become a ubiquitous cultural presence in ours. 'Et tu, Brute?'; 'Friends, Romans, countrymen'; 'The Ides of March': these are phrases from the play which people speak and understand even if they don't know exactly where they're from – and not because the phrases are particularly poetic or meaningful, but because for several generations nearly every person with a secondary-school education was expected to read *Julius Caesar*. Now that *Julius Caesar* is no longer an inevitable presence in the classroom, the teacher's task is to figure out how to make it seem exciting and resurgent – how to make it seem like more than an assemblage of famous quotations. To do this is no small feat, considering the play's episodic structure and its often deliberately formal rhetorical quality. In the pages that follow I attempt to provide some strategies, and to suggest some critical readings, for making *Julius Caesar* seem strange, unfamiliar and unexpected – not simply a lesson in history and rhetoric whose component parts must be learned and mastered, but a deliberately difficult, fragmented poetic and theatrical event whose meaning demands the ongoing, active participation of a critically engaged reader.

Teaching history and form

I think the main problem students have with *Julius Caesar* is that they do not feel like it is actually about 'real people'.

Everyone knows that Julius Caesar once walked the earth, but the image most people most readily call to mind when they hear his name is probably the image of a marble bust: a monochromatic, motionless, disembodied head. In such an imagining, Caesar is not so much a historical figure as a weighty symbol of the idea of History itself. The play can sometimes suggest that Shakespeare had this weighty symbolic idea in mind – most particularly when characters speak of themselves in the third person:

> CAESAR   What can be avoided
> Whose end is purposed by the mighty gods?
> Yet Caesar shall go forth, for these predictions
> Are to the world in general as to Caesar.
>
>   (2.2.26–9)

Or:

> BRUTUS Brutus had rather be a villager
> Than to repute himself a son of Rome
> Under these hard conditions as this time
> Is like to lay upon us.
>
>   (1.2.172–5)

In these passages Shakespeare seems to make use of a deliberately artificial idiom. No one talks like this, in real life *or* in plays! The artificiality is probably intended to suggest what is true of the play as a whole: that all of its main characters are aware of themselves as actors in a great historical drama that will have ramifications for centuries to come.

> CASSIUS ... How many ages hence
> Shall this our lofty scene be acted over
> In states unborn and accents yet unknown?
>
>   (3.1.111–13)

These are Cassius's words immediately following the assassination of Caesar. The character anticipates the theatrical performance in which the actor participates – and this could be a performance in Shakespeare's time or in ours. Cassius's self-referentiality is a more vivid and exciting version of Caesar's and Brutus's occasional, rather stilted references to themselves in the third person.

But as much as Shakespeare's characters in this play seem able to see themselves from the outside, or from a retrospective distance, they are also completely caught up in their own present moment. Some of the 'reality' of the characters can be seen in those moments where Shakespeare shows that they do not have any special knowledge of the course of historical events, but rather are entirely at the mercy of those events. Brutus is perhaps the best example, and the most useful to the teacher. Conventionally imagined as a taciturn, sagacious, far-sighted revolutionary, Brutus is actually, in Shakespeare's play, passionate, conflicted and often over-confidently myopic. Indeed, it is almost possible to see the structure of the play as grimly comic in representing Brutus's failed revolution as a series of disastrous and obvious mistakes. No sooner has Brutus been persuaded – to some extent flattered – by Cassius into taking on leadership of the conspiracy, than he makes a fatal error in its planning: while all the other conspirators think that Antony should be killed along with Caesar, Brutus insists that to do so will compromise the moral authority of the conspiracy. After the assassination, Brutus compounds his error by allowing – again over the objections of his fellow conspirators – Antony to speak at Caesar's funeral. Once the civil war is fully underway, Brutus makes the decision to meet Antony's army in battle rather than allow Antony's forces to wear themselves out coming to him. Just before the battle, Brutus tells Cassius both that he will never commit suicide – to do so would fly in the face of his Stoic philosophy – and that he will never allow himself to be carried in triumph to Rome. The paradox suggests that Brutus is secretly certain that victory is the only possibility; in a devastating tragic irony,

Brutus finds himself, just a few scenes later, literally begging his friends to help him kill himself. There is something like comedy – subtle, cruel comedy – in the way Shakespeare uses history against his characters, giving them enough foresight to see themselves as the instigators of a great historical drama, but not enough to see what is happening, or about to happen, in their present moment. Students will find much material for rewarding interpretation if directed to pay attention to such perspectival shifts – not only with Brutus, but also with Cassius (who always gives Brutus good advice but makes a grave error in judgement at the battle of Philippi), with Caesar (who constantly talks of his awareness of death's inevitability, but has no inkling of a conspiracy that involves almost every other character around him) and with others.

Is the Brutus of Shakespeare's play the Brutus of the history books on which Shakespeare based the play? What about the other characters – the 'lean and hungry' Cassius, the dyspeptic Caska, the carousing and duplicitous Antony, the Caesar who is subject to fainting fits and so on? The answers to these questions are to some extent a matter of interpretation; fortunately for us, the materials on which to base interpretation are readily available. *Julius Caesar* is somewhat unusual among Shakespeare's history plays in that it is based almost entirely on a single source – the histories of Caesar, Brutus and Antony as recorded in Plutarch's *Lives* – and follows that source quite closely. Almost all modern editions (as noted below) reprint the excerpts from Plutarch (that is, from Thomas North's sixteenth-century English translation) which correspond to the action represented in Shakespeare's play.[4] North's Plutarch is vividly written and easy to read, and it provides many fascinating historical details that can illuminate, or help a student to interpret, Shakespeare's play. Take, as just one example, the account of the assassination in the history of Caesar's life:

> ... Caesar turned him nowhere but he was stricken at by some, and still had naked swords in his face, and was hacked and mangled among them, as a wild beast taken

of hunters. For it was agreed among them that every man should give him a wound, because all their parts should be in this murder. And then Brutus himself gave him one wound about his privities. Men report also that Caesar did still defend himself against the rest, running every way with his body. But when he saw Brutus with his sword drawn in his hand, then he pulled his gown over his head and made no more resistance ...

Students should ask themselves: is the action described above what is implied by – or what we are to imagine when we read – Shakespeare's laconic stage direction, *'They stab Caesar'*? In that direction there is no hint of chaotic struggle, of the wild beast taken by hunters; there is no indication that Brutus stabs Caesar near the genitals, nor that Caesar makes a physical gesture of surrender by pulling his gown over his head when he realizes that Brutus is one of the conspiracy.

Of course, Shakespearean stage-directions are rarely very detailed, and Shakespeare may simply have assumed that his actors would perform the assassination as it was described in the popular historical source. He could certainly count on many of his spectators to have read Plutarch, and these spectators (like modern movie-goers watching films based on popular books) would probably have been interested to see what they had read turned into live action on the stage. But throughout his historical works, Shakespeare does not as a rule seem to have been too concerned about replicating historical detail exactly. The actors in the original production of *Julius Caesar* almost certainly did not wear historically accurate togas and sandals, but rather Elizabethan clothing that would more immediately and clearly signal social status to a contemporary audience. Shakespeare and his contemporaries brought their own very modern sensibilities to the dramatization of historical events, and wrote their plays for modern audiences.[5] The assassination scene that Plutarch describes in his life of Caesar certainly might have gripped an Elizabethan audience, but it is entirely possible that

Shakespeare and his company came up with an alternative staging that they preferred. Indeed, Plutarch himself provides at least one alternative to the description quoted above. In the history of Brutus's life, we hear that Caska stabbed Caesar first, but not very effectively; as Caesar was trying to flee, he saw Brutus's drawn sword and so threw his gown over his face and allowed himself to be stabbed.

> Then the conspirators thronging one upon another because every man was desirous to have a cut at him, so many swords and daggers lighting upon one body, one of them hurt another; and among them Brutus caught a blow on his hand because he would make one in murdering him ... [6]

The final detail of Brutus getting his hand cut is very theatrical, and I am surprised to say that I've never seen or heard of a theatre company making use of it. It seems like the kind of ironic, quasi-symbolic detail Shakespeare would have liked, but of course there is no evidence for it in the play-text. The play-text provides only three words, '*They stab Caesar*', and, in these three words, the opportunity for students to triangulate their sense of what kind of violence has been building up throughout the first two acts with, on one hand, the multiple perspectives provided in Plutarch and, on the other, their own imagining of what the scene should look like. It is only through such triangulations, which might take the form of a written critical exercise or an actual in-class staging of the scene (or both), that the play can continue to speak beyond its own historical moment.

Thus far my suggestions for making *Julius Caesar* more vivid to students for whom it might seem forbidding, or even boring, have had to do with the play's main characters. By drawing students' attention to the fallibility or even the incompetence of nearly mythical figures like Brutus and Caesar, or by giving students access to the historical narratives out of which Shakespeare constructed his play, a teacher can suggest that even the most familiar historical narrative is never finished being written – that the lives of great historical figures are in a constant state of flux and reinterpretation. I want to conclude this section by shifting my focus slightly, and suggesting that a productive and exciting site for interpretation is in the lives of *Julius Caesar*'s many minor characters.

Cicero. Flavius and Murellus. The Cobbler. The Camp Poet. Lepidus. Varrus and Claudio. Clitus, Dardanius, Volumnius, and Strato. Cinna the Poet. These are the names of characters who are given the opportunity to speak in only one scene each. Each fulfills, in his few lines, an essential and vivid dramatic function: Cicero, undaunted by the terrible storm and apparently supernatural events that occur on the night the conspirators meet, gives explicit voice to the play's ongoing concern with subjective interpretations of visible phenomena; the hapless Lepidus allows us to see Octavius's and Antony's ruthless ambition for what it is; the scene with the Cobbler dramatizes subversive (or perhaps uninformed and self-destructive) popular support for Caesar as he enters triumphantly into Rome; the scene with Cinna the Poet dramatizes the violence unleashed within and upon the citizenry of Rome in the aftermath of Caesar's assassination; and so on. Alongside the list of characters who speak in only one scene, we could create a list of characters who speak in only two or three scenes, and whose very few lines are of great and obvious significance: Calphurnia; the Soothsayer; Artemidorus. Alongside this list, we might create yet another list of characters whose presence in the play seems disproportionate to their importance: Brutus's wife Portia, who appears in only two scenes and remains on the margins of the play's great events; and Brutus's servant Lucius, a character invented by Shakespeare (that is, he is not in Plutarch), who seems to be almost constantly at Brutus's side.

What I am trying to suggest with these lists is that Shakespeare's approach to character and character relationships in *Julius Caesar* is a deliberately fragmented one. It is not simply that Brutus, whose approximately 725 lines constitute more than one quarter of the play, speaks far more than any other character; Shakespeare's tragic protagonists tend to dwarf all the other roles in their plays – Hamlet speaks nearly half the lines in his. Nor is it simply that the play's three main characters, Brutus, Cassius and Antony, stand out against a numerous background of comparatively minor characters; this is also the case with many of Shakespeare's tragedies. What is peculiar about *Julius Caesar* is that, with very few exceptions, almost every character who speaks says something absolutely, demonstrably important to the thematic structure of the play, and yet very few of the characters who appear in the first part of *Julius Caesar* appear in the second – and that includes the title character himself! Shakespeare's dramatic vision of Caesar's Rome and the men (for the characters are almost all men) who lived and died in it might best be compared to a mosaic: the whole picture is created out of so many discrete, finely wrought parts placed carefully next to one another and your eye constantly moves back and forth between perceiving the shape of the whole and the contours of each individual part. The goal of all teaching of *Julius Caesar* should be to enable students to experience and appreciate this shifting perspective.

In Act 4, Scene 3, the complex, deeply personal argument between Brutus and Cassius begins with accusations and recriminations about what either man did or did not do with regard to another man named Lucius Pella who may or may not have taken bribes. Lucius Pella never appears in *Julius Caesar*, and the bribery controversy of which he is the centre is nowhere else mentioned; nor does it have any effect upon the events represented in the play. The industrious student who looks for Lucius Pella in North's Plutarch will find him, but will find very little more information than is given in the play. Pella is a negligible historical figure – merely, we might say, an excuse for a quarrel that is actually about something much more significant. What, then, is the quarrel about? What does Lucius Pella allow Brutus and Cassius to say that they otherwise could not? How, that is, does Shakespeare make use of this peripheral figure to dramatize something that is at the heart of one of the play's most important relationships? This is a challenging, interesting question, and representative of the kinds of serious questions students might be encouraged to ask about the many small characters in *Julius Caesar*, either in written exercises or by getting up on their feet and performing the scenes in which these characters appear. Why does Calphurnia appear at all in Act 1, Scene 2, if it is only to speak a single line? What kind of marriage do she and Caesar have, and why does Shakespeare give us a snapshot of their domestic life just before Caesar is killed? What purpose does the doggerel-speaking Camp Poet serve in the quarrel scene? How is our understanding of Brutus's character affected by his relationship with Lucius – that is, how would a moment such as Brutus's encounter with the ghost be different if it were not preceded by his conversation with the boy? And so on. In order to answer these questions, you have to think about even the most briefly appearing characters as real people. Shakespeare did; if he hadn't, he would not have troubled to dramatize their lives briefly intersecting with the world-making deeds of great men.

Modern editions, and teaching the text

The teacher of *Julius Caesar*, like the teacher of any Shakespeare play, is faced with an embarrassment of riches when deciding which modern edition to use. To my mind, the best edition for the high-school or undergraduate classroom is the Pelican, edited by William Montgomery with an introduction by Douglas Trevor. This edition, which is available as a slim single-text volume (2000) or as part of the *Pelican Complete Works* (2002), is notable for its judicious, unobtrusive footnotes: student readers can refer quickly to the bottom of the page in order to get the meanings of obscure words or phrases, and will not be overwhelmed by an excess of historical, textual and other information crowding out the text of the play. The Pelican's concise introduction provides a fine discussion of Shakespeare's use of Plutarch and of the play's place in the political and theatrical world at the turn of the seventeenth century. Other, similarly good, concise editions for teaching the play at the introductory level are the Folger edition, edited by Paul Werstine and Barbara Mowat (1992), and the Signet edition, edited by William and Barbara Rosen (1986). Both contain some introductory material that gives information about Shakespeare's life and theatre, and both include, at the back, some commentaries on the play by modern literary critics. The Folger edition has a very good annotated bibliography of further critical reading students might undertake on the play, on Shakespeare's works and language or on the political and theatrical world of Shakespeare's time.

For advanced undergraduates (that is, undergraduates who might be doing a research paper on the play, rather than reading it as part of a survey course) or for graduate students, I would recommend either the Norton Critical Edition, edited by S. P. Cerasano (2012), or the Arden 3 edition, edited by David Daniell (1998). Cerasano's introduction puts *Julius Caesar* in the context of the 'craze for Roman plays' (xiv) at the end of the sixteenth century, and shows how Shakespeare dovetailed the form of the Roman play with the popular seventeenth-century form of the revenge tragedy. Her introduction ends with a detailed performance-history for the play and a section called 'Elements of Production', which describes the various explicit and implicit dramaturgical necessities – noises, costumes, staging effects, etc. – of the play. The Norton edition also contains a wide-ranging selection of critical responses to the play from the eighteenth century to the present. Daniell's Arden edition, like all Ardens, features exhaustive footnotes and a comprehensive introduction. It gives a clear picture of the state of criticism on the play, and is an indispensible resource for any serious student of the play. In his introduction, Daniell makes a compelling argument that, in 1599, *Julius Caesar* was a 'new kind of political play combining fast action ... and compelling rhetoric. Julius Caesar and the people of Rome, patricians and plebeians alike, have an immediacy that can be felt: the recent history of Rome, and of Caesar himself, is rapidly (and unobtrusively) sketched' (1). The introduction also contains a good, rigorous but accessible discussion of the play's text.

There is only one authoritative early text of *Julius Caesar*, and that is the text printed in the 1623 folio of Shakespeare's works. All modern editions are based on this text, which is generally considered to have been printed from a slightly revised version of Shakespeare's manuscript. The folio text has few significant textual problems, cruxes or mysteries associated with it, and so all modern editions look pretty much the same. This makes *Julius Caesar* different from many other familiar Shakespeare plays: *Hamlet*, *King Lear*, *Othello*, *Romeo and Juliet* and *Henry V* (to name a few) all have at least two significantly different early texts, and there are often radical differences between modern editions. For example, the Pelican Complete Shakespeare contains a parallel-text edition of *Lear* (the Quarto and Folio texts on facing pages) as well as a conflated edition (a modern editor's 'best guess' about what Shakespeare might have wanted the play to look like); and the most recent Arden edition of *Hamlet* contains, in two volumes, all three early texts – the 1604 'good' Quarto, the 1623 folio text and the 1603 'bad' quarto. Teachers and students working on these plays quickly see that an understanding of a play's textual history, and an awareness of the differences between early texts, can both delimit and generate interpretations.

Julius Caesar provides only a few opportunities for developing interpretation out of textual history, and these are somewhat speculative since there is no other early text against which to compare the folio. Such speculation can nevertheless help students to understand the play's form in a new way. I will now briefly discuss three formal oddities of *Julius Caesar*, all of which originate in Act 4, all of which are odd in a similar way and all of which might be (but do not have to be) explained by imagining the play's textual history. I will first list the examples with which I am concerned:

1 At the end of Act 4, Scene 2, Brutus and Cassius decide to take their simmering quarrel out of public view and retire to Brutus's tent. 'Let Lucius and Titinius guard our door,' Brutus says, and the characters exit, ending the scene. At the very beginning of Act 4, Scene 3, Brutus and Cassius enter again, now quarrelling in earnest.

2 In the middle of Act 4, Scene 3, after the quarrel of Brutus and Cassius has ended, Brutus reveals, unexpectedly, that Portia is dead. He and Cassius speak about this for about 20 lines before Brutus says that they should 'Speak no more of her'. Their conversation is then interrupted by the entrance of Messala and Titinius, and Brutus discusses with them news he has recently received from Rome. Over the course of about 25 lines Messala gradually reveals that he knows Portia has died 'by strange manner', and Brutus reacts as though this is the first time he has heard the news.

3 At the end of Act 4, Scene 3, Brutus is visited by the ghost of Caesar, who tells him that he has come 'To tell thee thou shalt see me at Philippi'. While Brutus does say, in Act 5, Scene 5, that he has been visited by the ghost 'last night, here in Philippi fields', the visit is not something we see staged.

These examples are all similarly odd in that they involve some form of awkward repetition. In the segue between Act 4, Scene 2 and Act 4, Scene 3, Brutus and Caesar leave the stage only to return to it almost immediately. This is very unusual in the drama of Shakespeare and his contemporaries; if one or more characters enters to a new location after having just exited, there are almost always at least few lines spoken by other characters in between. The double report of Portia's death is an obviously awkward repetition: how does a reader (or the actor playing Brutus) explain to him or herself Brutus's apparent forgetfulness about information he's just heard? Finally, the promise the ghost of Caesar makes to Brutus that he will appear again seems to signal a climactic meeting between Brutus and the great man he murdered. But when that second meeting does happen, it happens out of the audience's view and Brutus seems almost to treat it as identically significant to the first:

The ghost of Caesar hath appeared to me
Two several times by night: at Sardis once,
And, this last night, here in Philippi fields:
I know my hour is come. (5.5.16–20)

The promised climax has become an anticlimax.

All of these formal oddities can, of course, be explained on the dramaturgical, thematic and structural terms of the play as we have it. In the shift between Act 4, Scene 2 and Act 4, Scene 3 Shakespeare might have imagined that Brutus and Cassius would move from one part of the stage, representing 'outside', to another part of the stage – which was perhaps adorned with a tent-like set-piece – that represented the 'inside' of the tent. In the double report of Portia's death, Shakespeare might have imagined that Brutus was, in front of less intimate friends than Cassius, trying not to reveal that he knew about and was distressed by his wife's death – trying not, on the eve of battle, to show any form of weakness before his soldiers. In handling the reappearance of Caesar anti-climactically, Shakespeare might have been working out in formal and dramatic terms an idea about history that the play does seem to contain: that portents and omens, so susceptible as they are to interpretation and misinterpretation, are only one small part of the forces men and women grapple with in trying to determine, and in coming to terms with, their own fates.

At the same time, all of these formal oddities *might* be explained in terms of an imagined history of textual transmission: they might be actual gaps in the 'ideal' *Julius Caesar* as Shakespeare wrote or imagined it, created in part by revisions to or deletions from the text between the time the play was written in 1598–9, the time it was performed in 1599 and the time it was printed in 1623. Perhaps there were a few lines between Act 4, Scene 2 and Act 4, Scene 3 (spoken, perhaps, by Lucilius to the soldiers) that were, by accident or design, omitted when the printer set up the text of the folio edition from an annotated manuscript. Perhaps Shakespeare meant for Act 4, Scene 3 to contain only one version of the news of Portia's death, but couldn't decide whether it was better to have Brutus report it himself or react to the report. And perhaps both versions remained in the manuscript used by the playing company, with one marked for the deletion, but perhaps the 'delete' marks were not noticed by the folio printers. Perhaps the first version of *Julius Caesar* did include a scene in which Brutus encountered the ghost a second time, and perhaps the actors (or even the playwright himself) thought 'Well, that didn't work very well' – or even 'The play is too long with that repeated meeting between Caesar and the ghost' – and so had Shakespeare convert it into a piece of reported information.

As my repeated use of the word *perhaps* indicates, everything I am saying here is completely speculative. Since there is no early text of *Julius Caesar* other than the folio, no modern editor would dare to write a few lines for Lucilius, delete one of the reports about Portia or add a second entrance-direction for Caesar's ghost. (The modern theatre tends to be a bit more daring in this regard, and directors often 'improve' the text in ways such as those I have listed. Students might be encouraged to demonstrate their own interpretations of the play by staging Act 4, Scene 3 with only one of the reports of Portia's death; or by making an argument for a moment in Act 5 where the ghost of Caesar might appropriately enter.) The hypothetical narratives of textual transmission and revision which I have created are plausible only because we have evidence to support them in other Shakespeare plays – in the two versions of *Henry V*, for example, one with the Chorus and one without. Presenting these hypothetical narratives to students can be a way of emphasizing the strange fluidity not only of Shakespearean texts, but of Shakespearean dramatic action in general.

The typical student reading *Julius Caesar* for the first time might well find it strange that Portia's death is reported twice in rapid succession, but not allow him or herself to acknowledge the strangeness: this is a Shakespeare play after all, and as such not only a historical artifact reliant upon unfamiliar conventions but also a certified masterpiece. If something seems strange and out of place (the student might think) the problem must be with the modern reader. Hypothetical narratives of textual transmission and revision offer such a student at least the beginnings of a method for identifying and acknowledging strangeness where it exists – and thus for taking on the project of interpretation *as* a modern reader. Whether or not they are the result of textual transmission and revision, the awkward repetitions discussed here are of a piece with the play's many formally awkward elements: its being split in half between Caesar and Brutus, for example, its proliferation of minor, only-seen-once characters or its sometimes labored dramatic language. Whatever its origins, even if it is exactly what Shakespeare wrote and wanted to see on the stage, the text that we have of *Julius Caesar* is a strange object, replete with surprising starts and stops, omissions and repetitions. The most productive interpretive engagements with it will acknowledge and embrace this strangeness from the start.

Julius Caesar on the screen and on the stage

There is really only one film version of *Julius Caesar* and that is the 1953 MGM film, directed by Joseph L. Mankiewicz and starring John Gielgud (Cassius), James Mason (Brutus),

Deborah Kerr (Portia) and Marlon Brando (Antony). Of course this is not the *only* film version of the play, but it is far and away the most well-known and probably the best. This is not to say that it is a particularly great film, that it is a particularly interesting interpretation of Shakespeare's play or that students – especially high-school students or undergraduates in an introductory-level course – will particularly like it. The film is in black and white and unabashedly filmed on a soundstage decorated to look like a rather unpopulous ancient Rome. Everywhere there are imposing white columns, staircases and walls, and these tend to make even the crowd scenes look somewhat empty. The acting is incredibly good but, in comparison to both more recent films (even Shakespeare films) and many popular films of the late 1940s and early 1950s, the pacing is quite slow – and feels even slower than it actually is if, as will be the case for most people watching the film, you already know what's going to happen (and exactly what's going to be said) from one moment to the next. With this film, as with the play itself, it can be hard to feel like you are watching something about real people; and it can be easy to feel bored. One moment where this is not the case is in Antony's funeral speech, where the charismatic Brando speaks with a fiery energy that the film generally keeps suppressed. In this scene you see both Brando acting like the movie star that he is and Antony seizing an opportunity to take control of events; it is a scene that gives reality and immediacy to the play's concern with what a teacher might call, rather abstractly, the power of rhetoric.

Personally, I would not ask students to watch the entire Mankiewicz film. Some might find it useful for helping them to visualize the action of the play, but these students might equally be helped by watching the two BBC film versions (one from 1969, the other from 1979), which are available for free on YouTube. Like the Mankiewicz film, the BBC productions were filmed on stages and can, in spite of the excellent acting, feel rather ponderous. Unlike the Mankiewicz film, the BBC productions make use of a complete text of the play, and so might provide some assistance to the student who finds it easier to understand Shakespeare's language when it is spoken aloud. Mankiewicz's film does not contain the scene with Cinna the Poet, the Camp Poet's entrance into the quarrel between Brutus and Cassius, the second report of Portia's death and numerous other short and long passages throughout the play. Nevertheless, I would also not recommend that a student watch either of the BBC productions in its entirety; it will be too boring. Somewhat more exciting, and certainly more contemporary-feeling than the BBC productions, is the 2012 video production (available on DVD) of Gregory Doran's 'African' *Caesar*, originally staged by the Royal Shakespeare Company in 2012. Set in modern-day Africa and performed by an all-black British cast, this production explicitly invites, and indeed challenges, the modern spectator to see that the play is about real people. Teachers and students will undoubtedly find much to discuss about how the setting, the casting and the strongly emphasized female characters create and encourage new, subversive interpretations of the play. Still, the entire conception of the video production is somewhat odd, as it moves between indoor scenes filmed on the stage of the Royal Shakespeare Theatre and outdoor scenes filmed in desolate areas of modern-day England. There is a great deal of energy in both the acting and the structure of the production as a whole, but it can be hard to see what it all adds up to. As often happens with Shakespeare on film, you feel like things might have been a bit clearer if you had been able to see a live performance.

For instructional purposes, then, film versions of *Julius Caesar* are best used in small pieces. You might recommend that students watch two or more versions of the same scene (Antony's funeral speech, for example) and discuss what the differences or similarities between them reveal about both the form of the play and changing interpretations of the play over time. YouTube contains an almost endless supply of clips from professional film and theatrical productions of *Julius Caesar* – the 2015 Shakespeare's Globe production, the 2012 Royal Shakespeare Company production, the 1970 film starring Charlton Heston, a 1960 television production starring William Shatner and so on – as well as from semi-professional, amateur and student productions, adaptations, parodies and mash-ups. Each of these, good or bad, provides an example of energetic engagement with the play, and as such can provide students a model through or against which to understand their own goals and priorities as literary critics.

Ideally, anyone studying *Julius Caesar* would also see a live theatrical production of it. There is, of course, no guarantee that a live theatrical production would not be boring or difficult to follow or unrewarding in any number of other ways. If, however, you are fortunate enough to take your students to see a good one, they might get to experience the particular exhilaration that comes from watching live actors, in real time, speak Shakespeare's heightened verse as they perform world-defining actions. These students might then be able to connect their feeling of exhilaration to particular, previously unthought of performance choices: a particular line-reading ('Et tu, Brute?' spoken with a grim chuckle, for example); a particular emphasis on or in a relationship (if, for example, Caesar and Calphurnia were shown to be very much in love); a startling special effect (perhaps the ghost of Caesar is genuinely frightening); or a comic turn from a minor character (Lepidus, for example). In the perhaps more likely event that your students end up seeing a not-very-good production of *Julius Caesar* they will nevertheless experience the play, on at least one level, just as Shakespeare's audience would have experienced it: as an act of present-moment communication about events in the distant past, which requires the audience to exert itself almost as much as the actors.

Julius Caesar is a difficult play to perform: if you produce it in togas and sandals it risks seeming artificial and distant, but if you update it so that it is an allegory of contemporary politics it risks seeming opportunistic and trivial. Desperate to stave off boredom, productions often resort to a vast array of theatrical gimmicks that can easily overload this rather spare play. I once saw a production that, in its programme notes and scenic design, drew explicit parallels between Caesar and a wide array of assassinated politicians; that was staged in the round; *and* that featured a woman playing the role of Caesar. It was exhausting. Because of the problems it presents simply in terms of establishing a convincing theatrical idiom, *Julius Caesar* is, on the contemporary stage, one of the less popular of Shakespeare's more familiar plays; you are much more likely, at any given moment, to see a production of *A Midsummer Night's Dream* or *Macbeth*. So most students will probably not see a production of the play while studying it. It is nevertheless possible, especially for advanced undergraduates or graduate students, to make use of the performance tradition, recent and past, in order to develop and flesh out their own interpretations. The archive that makes this kind of research and analysis possible is the archive of theatre reviews, both journalistic and academic. The internet makes available a huge number of newspaper and blog reviews of performances from the last two decades or so. Academic journals such as *Shakespeare Survey*, *Shakespeare Quarterly* and *Shakespeare Bulletin* have been running reviews of Shakespeare productions for well over 50 years; written by Shakespeare scholars who are trying to describe and analyse changing interpretative approaches to the plays, these reviews often give highly detailed accounts of set design, production concept, line-readings and other actorly or directorial choices. Theatre reviews can give students a sense of the kinds of things that Shakespeare scholarship has felt are important to notice about the plays, and can begin to give them some of the tools they need – an understanding of stage-craft, an ear for dialogue, the ability to visualize action while reading – to decide in more detail what kinds of things *they* think are important to notice about the plays.

Critical resources

As is the case with most of Shakespeare's plays, literally thousands of critical essays and books have been written about *Julius Caesar*. The graduate student and the fully fledged Shakespeare scholar learn and constantly refine the skill of sifting and making selective use of this material: you start with a visit to the library, or with a comprehensive online database such as the World Shakespeare Bibliography or the Modern Language Association bibliography; you select works either that you have been told are relevant to your topic of research or whose titles suggest that they might be; and as you create a topic-specific reading list you also create a more general list – one that will allow you to speak, as necessary, in an informed way about other critical approaches to the play you're working on. But what if you are not a Shakespeare scholar, or one in training, but rather an interested and enthusiastic high-school student or undergraduate? What is the value and use of the extensive, always expanding, critical tradition, and how on earth do you start to get some grasp on it?

As a teacher of Shakespeare at the high school, undergraduate and graduate levels over the past two decades, I have found that it is challenging and rewarding enough for students at all levels simply to learn how to read Shakespeare's plays closely and form their own interpretations. Acquiring the fluency with broader historical and theoretical contexts which is necessary to make productive use of criticism usually takes more time than is available in a single term. Literary criticism is almost always very boring to read, especially if you don't have a good sense of what its stakes are. So I do not generally recommend that students read literary criticism as they develop their own analytical and interpretative reading skills.

For the more advanced student whose analytical and interpretative reading skills are well-developed, and who is interested in getting some sense of the stakes of literary criticism, I would recommend starting with the chapter on *Julius Caesar* in Alexander Leggatt's book *Shakespeare's Political Drama*; accessible but also sophisticated, this is an excellent critical introduction to the play.[7] I would also recommend Leggatt's preface, which explains what he means, and what might be meant, by 'political drama'. Armed with Leggatt's lucid exposition of the play's thematic structure and an analytical approach to it, a student should be prepared to tackle, wholly or in part, one or more of the following studies that discuss *Julius Caesar* in the larger context of Shakespeare's representation of Rome: Maurice Charney's *Shakespeare's Roman Plays: The Function of Imagery in the Drama*;[8] Vivian Thomas's *Shakespeare's Roman Worlds*;[9] and Coppélia Kahn's *Roman Shakespeare: Warriors, Wounds, and Women*.[10] The student who is interested in getting this far into the criticism might be encouraged, subsequently or simultaneously, to read either or both of the superb performance histories of the play: John Ripley's *Julius Caesar on the Stage in England and America, 1599–1973*[11] and Andrew James Hartley's *Shakespeare in Performance: Julius Caesar*.[12] Both books provide a digest of some of the most important critical approaches to *Julius Caesar* over the past 400 years by describing changing theatrical approaches to the play during the same period.

For the student who desires, after reading any of the preceding books, to get more closely acquainted with *Julius Caesar* criticism, I would recommend moving on to one or more of the following essay collections: *Twentieth-Century Interpretations of Julius Caesar*;[13] *Julius Caesar: New Casebooks*;[14] *Julius Caesar: New Critical Essays*;[15] and *Bloom's Modern Critical Interpretations: Julius Caesar*.[16] Each of these is a single-volume collection of essays by modern literary critics, and each begins with an introduction that provides an analytical overview of the play and a brief survey of its critical history. I would not recommend any one of these volumes over another. The essays in Dean (*Twentieth-Century Interpretations*) might occasionally feel dated, but a number of them (Reginald Foakes's 'Language and Action in *Julius Caesar*', for example) are spectacularly good and very accessible. The numerous and diverse essays in Zander (*New Critical Essays*) will give students a very good idea of the current state of scholarship on the play, but some will seem quite arcane in their use of specialized theoretical language or their allusive engagement with long-standing critical problems. The point is not to read all of the essays in any one volume, and certainly not to read them all in sequence, but rather to 'read around', dipping into essays that seem interesting and seeing how far you can get. When you find one you like, or that makes you think in surprising new ways about the play – or about the 'boring' genre of literary criticism – the best thing to do is to peruse the footnotes and bibliography for suggestions of further reading. This is how you become a part of an ongoing critical tradition, and how you make use of that tradition to give new meaning to the play.

NOTES

Introduction

1. Caesar's victorious re-entry into Rome, which the people are celebrating at the beginning of the play, seems to draw on his defeat of Pompey's sons in Spain at the battle of Munda.

2. It was one of the sticking points of Elizabeth I's reign that England – like several other Protestant countries – in an act of nationalist defiance, did not adopt the Gregorian calendar (which was proposed by the then Pope Gregory XIII), which England continued to resist until 1752.

3. Ben Jonson is a good case in point. Though he is a consummate dramatist, Jonson's authorial voice is much easier to track, and when one reads his satires one tends to emerge with a good idea about who and what Jonson thought was stupid.

4. Macbeth's use of comedy is confined almost exclusively to the Porter scene between the murder of Duncan and the discovery of his body.

5. In Plutarch, several days pass between Brutus's speech to the crowd and Antony's, and Antony does not so much alter the crowd's sympathies single-handedly as he senses their dissatisfaction with the assassination, shifts his own position accordingly and rouses them to action.

6. It may say something about how we collectively remember ancient Rome that our cultural representations of it are frequently dominated by political intrigue and statesmanship.

7. This seems deliberate on Shakespeare's part since Brutus's stoicism is also largely his invention and contradicts the depiction of Brutus's philosophical pluralism which we see in Plutarch.

Chapter 1

1. Thomas Platter, *Thomas Platter's Travels in England, 1599*, edited and translated by Clare Williams (London: Jonathan Cape, 1937), 166.
2. Ben Jonson, *Timber: or Discoveries* (ll. 802–28) in *The Complete Poems*, ed. George Parfitt (London: Penguin, 1975; reprinted 1988), 373–458.
3. Ibid, l. 807.
4. Leonard Digges, 'Upon Master William Shakespeare' in *Ben Jonson*, ed. C. H. Herford, Evelyn Simpson and Percy Simpson, 11 vols (Oxford: Clarendon Press, 1925–52) XI, 496.
5. John Dryden, prologue to *Julius Caesar* in *Covent-Garden Drollery* (1672) excerpted in *William Shakespeare: The Critical Heritage*, ed. Brian Vickers, 6 vols (London: Routledge and Kegan Paul, 1974–81), I, 141–2 (142).
6. Margaret Cavendish, *Sociable Letters* (Letter 113), in *Critical Heritage*, I, 43.
7. Thomas Rymer, *A Short View of Tragedy* in *Critical Heritage*, II, 55.
8. Ibid., 56.
9. Ibid., 58.
10. John Dennis, *The Advancement and Reformation of Modern Poetry*, in *Critical Heritage*, II, 147.
11. Ibid.
12. Gerard Langbaine, *The Lives and Characters of the English Dramatick Poets* (London: Thomas Leigh, 1698), 3–4.
13. Ibid., 126.
14. Charles Gildon, *An Essay on the Remarks on the Plays of Shakespeare*, in *Critical Heritage*, II, 256.
15. John Upton, *Critical Observations of Shakespeare*, in *Critical Heritage*, III, 295.
16. Alexander Pope, in *Critical Heritage* II, 407.
17. Samuel Johnson, in *Critical Heritage*, 146.
18. Samuel Taylor Coleridge, *The Literary Remains of Samuel*

Taylor Coleridge, ed. Henry Nelson Coleridge, 4 vols (London: William Pickering, 1836), II, 139.
19 Ibid., 139–40.
20 William Hazlitt, *Characters of Shakspeare's Plays* (Boston: Wells and Lilly, 1818), 52.
21 Ibid., 56–7.
22 Charles Knight, *Studies in Shakespere* (London: George Routledge and Sons, 1868), 411.
23 Ibid., 419.
24 Ibid., 404.
25 Edward Dowden, *Shakspere: A Critical Study of his Mind and Art* (1875; reprinted London: Kegan Paul, 1909), 281.
26 Ibid., 282.
27 Ibid., 285.
28 Paul Stapfer, *Shakespeare and Classical Antiquity*, translated by Emily J. Carey (London: C. Kegan Paul, 1880), 330–1.
29 A. C. Bradley, *Shakespearean Tragedy: Lectures on 'Hamlet', 'Othello', 'King Lear', 'Macbeth'*, 2nd edn. (London: Macmillan, 1950), 81–2.
30 Ibid., 85.
31 Otto Rank quoted in Ernest Jones, 'A Psycho-Analytic Study of Hamlet' in *Essays on Applied Psycho-Analysis*, ed. Ernest Jones (London: The International Psycho-Analytical Press, 1923), 1–98 (70).
32 Jones, 71.
33 John Palmer, *Political and Comic Characters of Shakespeare* (London: Macmillan, 1962), 35–6.
34 M. W. MacCallum, *Shakespeare's Roman Plays and their Background* (London: Macmillan, 1910; reprinted 1967), 213.
35 H. B. Charlton, *Shakespearian Tragedy* (Cambridge: Cambridge University Press, 1948; reprinted 1961), 70.
36 G. Wilson Knight, *The Wheel of Fire: Interpretations of Shakespearian Tragedy* (Oxford: Oxford University Press, 1930; reprinted London: Methuen, 1965), 15.
37 G. Wilson Knight, *The Imperial Theme: Further Interpretations*

of Shakespeare's Tragedies Including the Roman Plays (Oxford: Oxford University Press, 1931; reprinted London: Methuen, 1965), 63.

38 Adrien Bonjour, *The Structure of 'Julius Caesar'* (Liverpool: Liverpool University Press, 1958), 3.

39 Ibid.

40 Matthew N. Proser, *The Heroic Image in Five Shakespearean Tragedies* (Princeton: Princeton University Press, 1965), 10–50; Gordon Ross Smith, 'Brutus, Virtue, and Will', *Shakespeare Quarterly* 10. 3 (1959): 367–79.

41 Ernest Schanzer, *The Problem Plays of Shakespeare* (London: Routledge and Kegan Paul, 1963), 34.

42 Ibid., 70.

43 E. A. J. Honigmann, *Shakespeare: Seven Tragedies, The Dramatist's Manipulation of Response* (London: Macmillan, 1976), 30.

44 Ibid, 31 and 53.

45 Maurice Charney, *Shakespeare's Roman Plays: The Function of Imagery in the Drama* (Cambridge, MA: Harvard University Press, 1961; reprinted 1963), 15–16.

46 Derek Traversi, *Shakespeare: The Roman Plays* (London: Hollis and Carter, 1963), 21.

47 Ibid., 22.

48 Norman Rabkin, 'Structure, Convention, and Meaning in *Julius Caesar*', *The Journal of English and Germanic Philology* 63. 2 (1964): 240–54 (246).

49 Ibid, 250.

50 James Emerson Phillips, *The State in Shakespeare's Greek and Roman Plays* (New York: Columbia University Press, 1940), 179.

51 Ibid., 186.

52 Ibid., 187.

53 John Dover Wilson, introduction to William Shakespeare, *Julius Caesar*, ed. John Dover Wilson (Cambridge: The New Cambridge Shakespeare, 1949), xxv.

54 Brents Stirling, *The Populace in Shakespeare* (New York: Columbia University Press, 1949), 31 and 149.
55 Ibid., 29 and 32.
56 Brents Stirling, *Unity in Shakespearian Tragedy: The Interplay of Theme and Character* (New York: Columbia University Press, 1956), 41.
57 Irving Ribner, 'Political Issues in *Julius Caesar*', *Journal of English and Germanic Philology* 56 (1957): 10–22 (10–11). See also, Virgil K. Whitaker, *Shakespeare's Uses of Learning: An Inquiry into the Growth of his Mind and Art* (San Marino: Huntington Library, 1953).
58 Ibid., 12.
59 Ibid., 18.
60 Allan Bloom with Harry V. Jaffa, *Shakespeare's Politics* (New York: Basic Books, 1964; reprinted Chicago: University of Chicago Press, 1981), 75–112.
61 T. J. B. Spencer, 'Shakespeare and the Elizabethan Romans', *Shakespeare Survey* 10 (1957): 27–38 (33).
62 J. Leeds Barroll, 'Shakespeare and Roman History', *The Modern Language Review* 53. 3 (1958): 327–43.
63 Geoffrey Bullough, *Narrative and Dramatic Sources of Shakespeare: Volume V, The Roman Plays* (London: Routledge and Kegan Paul, 1966).
64 Ibid., 57.
65 Michael Platt, *Rome and Romans According to Shakespeare* (Salzburg: Institut für Englische Sprache und Literatur, 1976), 181.
66 Ibid., 191.
67 Ibid.
68 Ibid., 186.
69 Ibid., 191.
70 Robert S. Miola, *Shakespeare's Rome* (Cambridge: Cambridge University Press, 1983), 76
71 Ibid.
72 Ibid., 113.

73 Vivian Thomas, *Shakespeare's Roman Worlds* (London: Routledge, 1989), 1.

74 Ibid., 71.

75 Geoffrey Miles, *Shakespeare and the Constant Romans* (Oxford: Oxford University Press, 1996), 1.

76 Ibid., 135.

77 Jan H. Blits, *The End of the Ancient Republic: Shakespeare's 'Julius Caesar'* (Durham: Carolina Academic Press, 1982; reprinted Lanham: Rowman and Littlefield, 1993), 33.

78 Ibid., 65.

79 Ibid., 81.

80 Alexander Leggatt, *Shakespeare's Political Drama: The History Plays and the Roman Plays* (London: Routledge, 1988), 140.

81 Ibid., 142.

82 Ibid., 144.

83 Ibid, 158 and 160.

84 Paul N. Siegel, *Shakespeare's English and Roman History Plays: A Marxist Approach* (Cranbury: Associated University Presses, 1986), 97.

85 Catherine Belsey, *The Subject of Tragedy: Identity and Difference in Renaissance Drama* (London: Methuen, 1985), 101.

86 Ibid., 101–2.

87 See Robert S. Miola, '*Julius Caesar* and the Tyrannicide Debate', *Renaissance Quarterly* 38. 2 (1985): 271–89 and Rebecca W. Bushnell, *Tragedies of Tyrants: Political Thought and Theater in the English Renaissance* (Ithaca: Cornell University Press, 1990).

88 Jonathan Goldberg, *James I and the Politics of Literature: Jonson, Shakespeare, Donne, and their Contemporaries* (Baltimore: Johns Hopkins University Press, 1983; reprinted Stanford: Stanford University Press, 1989), 165.

89 Ibid., 166.

90 Ibid., 168.

91 Wayne A. Rebhorn, 'The Crisis of the Aristocracy in *Julius Caesar*', *Renaissance Quarterly*, 43. 1 (1990): 75–111.

92 Richard Wilson, 'Shakespeare's Roman Carnival' in *New Historicism and Renaissance Drama*, ed. Richard Wilson and Richard Dutton (Harlow: Longman, 1992), 145–56 (147).

93 Ibid.

94 Ibid., 155.

95 Ibid., 156.

96 This approach is outlined in C. L. Barber, *Shakespeare's Festive Comedy: A Study of Dramatic Form and its Relation to Social Custom* (Princeton: Princeton University Press, 1959).

97 Naomi Conn Liebler, *Shakespeare's Festive Tragedy: The Ritual Foundations of Genre* (London: Routledge, 1995), 7–8.

98 Ibid., 91.

99 Ibid., 91–2.

100 Ibid., 104.

101 John Drakakis, '"Fashion it thus": *Julius Caesar* and the Politics of Theatrical Representation', *Shakespeare Survey* 44 (1992): 65–73 (72).

102 Ibid., 70.

103 Richard Burt, '"A Dangerous Rome": Shakespeare's *Julius Caesar* and the Discursive Determinism of Cultural Politics' in *Contending Kingdoms: Historical, Psychological, and Feminist Approaches to the Literature of Sixteenth Century England and France*, ed. Marie-Rose Logan and Peter L. Rudnytsky (Detroit: Wayne State University Press, 1991), 109–27 (117).

104 Harold Bloom, *Shakespeare: The Invention of the Human* (New York: Riverhead Books, 1998), 116.

105 Coppélia Kahn, *Roman Shakespeare: Warriors, Wounds, and Women* (London: Routledge, 1997), 1.

106 Ibid., 77.

107 Ibid., 89.

108 Ibid,, 101.

109 Mary Hamer, *Writers and their Work: William Shakespeare, 'Julius Caesar'* (Plymouth: Northcote House, 1998), 9.

110 Ibid., 20.

111 Ibid., 38–9.

112 Ibid., 32, 38.

113 Ibid., 41.

114 Ibid., 72.

115 Gail Kern Paster, '"In the spirit of men there is no blood": Blood as Trope of Gender in *Julius Caesar*', *Shakespeare Quarterly*, 40.3 (1989): 284–98 (284).

116 Ibid., 294.

117 Cynthia Marshall, 'Portia's Wound, Calphurnia's Dream: Reading Character in *Julius Caesar*', *English Literary Renaissance* 24.2 (1994): 471–98 (476).

118 Barbara Parker, 'The Whore of Babylon and Shakespeare's *Julius Caesar*', *Studies in English Literature 1500–1900*, 35. 2 (1995): 251–69 (251).

119 Barbara J. Bono, 'The Birth of Tragedy: Tragic Action in *Julius Caesar*', *English Literary Renaissance*, 24.2 (1994): 449–70.

Chapter 2

1   See Andrew James Hartley, *Julius Caesar* (Shakespeare in Performance series) (Manchester: Manchester University Press, 2014), 11. This book also contains further details of the productions discussed in this chapter. The other major source on the play's performance history is John Ripley's *Julius Caesar on Stage in England and America, 1599–1973* (Cambridge: Cambridge University Press, 1980).

2   See Hartley, 206–9.

3   The film was nominated for four Academy Awards including Best Picture, and won for Best Set Decoration. It also won two BAFTAs, a National Board of Review Award for Best Actor (Mason) and earned a nomination for Outstanding Directorial Achievement in Motion Pictures (for Mankiewicz) from the Screen Directors Guild.

4   Alex Matheson Cain, writing in *The Tablet* (5 December 1964).

5   Hartley, 134.

6   The Nazis themselves had a curious attitude to Shakespeare, viewing him as effectively German, a part of their own national heritage which had (somehow) to be rescued from the English. A lot of Shakespeare was staged under the Third Reich, most of it politically neutral, which goes some way to explaining how Jürgen Fehling, though unsympathetic to the Nazis himself, was able to direct a conspicuous expressionist production of the play at the Staatstheater in 1940 without dire consequences. Rudolph Hess saw the production and applauded it as well suiting Nazi ideology. Though Claus Von Stauffenberg who led the plot to assassinate Hitler in 1944 was caught in possession of a copy of the play in which Brutus's speeches were underlined, the play was not generally considered an endorsement of tyrannicide, prevailing attitudes seeming to treat it as a study in high-minded virtue rendered safe by its venerable classicism in the tradition of the British eighteenth century. When Fritz Kortner directed the show in 1955 at the Residenztheater in Munich, audiences apparently were keen to see a more obviously anti-Hitler production, but what they got was a study in the new anti-heroic naturalism, and the production was criticized (somewhat perversely) for its lack of grandeur. Some of that grandeur was restored by Peter Stein's 1992 production for the Salzburg summer festival at the Felsenreitschule, a throwback to quasi-Victorian classicism with lots of toga-draped supers, but critics thought it had little new to say.

Chapter 3

1   Joseph Candido, '"Time … Come Round": Plot Construction in *Julius Caesar*', in Julius Caesar: *New Critical Essays*, ed. Horst Zander (London: Routledge, 2005), 127–38 (127).

2   Ibid., 127, 132, 134, 135.

3   Julia Griffin, 'Shakespeare's *Julius Caesar* and the Dramatic Tradition', in *A Companion to Julius Caesar*, ed. Miriam Tamara Griffin (Wiley: Hoboken, 2009), 371–98 (384).

4   Ibid., 384–5

5   Ibid., 382.
6   Ian Donaldson, '"Misconstruing Everything": *Julius Caesar* and *Sejanus*', in *Shakespeare Performed: Essays in Honor of R. A. Foakes*, ed. Grace Ioppolo (Newark: University of Delaware Press, 2000), 88–107 (95, 93).
7   Ibid., 105, 96–7.
8   Robin Headlam Wells, '*Julius Caesar*, Machiavelli and the Uses of History', *SS* 55 (2002): 209–18 (217).
9   David Willbern, 'Constructing Caesar: A Psychoanalytic Reading', in Julius Caesar: *New Critical Essays*, ed. Horst Zander (London: Routledge, 2005), 213–26 (218).
10 Ibid., 216, 220.
11 Ibid., 218.
12 Dennis Kezar, '*Julius Caesar*'s Analogue Clock and the Accents of History', in Julius Caesar: *New Critical Essays*, ed. Horst Zander (London: Routledge, 2005), 241–55 (246, 250).
13 Ibid., 251–2.
14 John Roe, *Shakespeare and Machiavelli* (Cambridge: Brewer, 2002), 134.
15 Ibid., 154.
16 Ibid., 168–9.
17 Ibid., 169, 157.
18 Ibid., 166.
19 Wells, 212–14.
20 Ibid., 216.
21 Ibid., 215.
22 Hugh Grady, 'Moral Agency and Its Problems in *Julius Caesar*: Political Power, Choice, and History', in *Shakespeare and Moral Agency*, ed. Michael D. Bristol (London: Continuum, 2010), 15–28; 'The End of Shakespeare's Machiavellian Moment: *Julius Caesar*, Shakespeare's Historiography, and Dramatic Form', in *Shakespeare and Renaissance Literary Theories: Anglo-Italian Transactions*, ed. Michele Marrapodi (Farnham: Ashgate, 2011),119–36.

23 Grady, 'Moral Agency', 24.
24 Grady, 'The End of Shakespeare's Machiavellian Moment', 136; 'Moral Agency', 17.
25 Grady, 'Moral Agency', 24–5.
26 Warren Chernaik, *The Myth of Rome in Shakespeare and His Contemporaries* (Cambridge: Cambridge University Press, 2011), 96.
27 Adrian Phoon, '"A vision fair and fortunate": Ideology, Politics and Selfhood in *Julius Caesar*', *Sydney Studies in English* 30 (2004): 21–41 (40).
28 Ibid., 22–3.
29 Matthew Sims, 'The Political Odyssey: Shakespeare's Exploration of Ethics in *Julius Caesar*', in *The Hero's Journey*, ed. Harold Bloom (New York: Bloom's Literary Criticism, 2009), 95–105 (103).
30 Ibid., 99, 103, 105.
31 Jennifer Feather, 'To "Tempt the Rheumy and Unpurged Air": Contagion and Agency in *Julius Caesar*', in *Shakespeare and Moral Agency*, ed. Michael D. Bristol (London: Continuum, 2010), 86–98 (97).
32 Ibid., 87.
33 Ibid., 87, 96.
34 Lloyd B. Davis, 'Embodied Masculinity in Shakespeare's *Julius Caesar*', *EnterText* 3 (2003): 161–82 (165–7).
35 Ibid.: 167.
36 Eugene Giddens, 'Honourable Men: Militancy and Masculinity in *Julius Caesar*', *Renaissance Forum* 5 (2001): 1–34 (17).
37 Ibid.: 11, 21–2, 26.
38 Ibid.: 29, 34.
39 Parker, 'From Monarchy to Tyranny', 111–13.
40 Michael Platt, *Rome and Romans According to Shakespeare* (Salzburg: Institut für Englische Sprache und Literatur, 1976). See Daniel Cadman's chapter in this volume, pp. 36–7.
41 Anthony Miller, *Roman Triumphs and Early Modern English Culture* (Basingstoke: Palgrave, 2001), 128.

42 Ibid., 131.

43 Ibid., 132.

44 Ibid.

45 Wells, 'Uses of History', 211.

46 Suzanne Smith, 'Shakespeare and the Politics of Honor: Purpose and Performance in *Julius Caesar*', *Interpretation: A Journal of Political Philosophy* 33 (2006), 243–80 (266).

47 Ibid., 251.

48 Andrew Hadfield, *Shakespeare and Republicanism* (Cambridge: Cambridge University Press, 2005), 182–3.

49 Ibid., 172, 183.

50 David Hawkes, 'Shakespeare's *Julius Caesar*: Marxist and Post-Marxist Approaches', in Julius Caesar: *New Critical Essays*, ed. Horst Zander (London: Routledge, 2005), 199–212 (203).

51 Daniela Carpi, 'Law and Sedition in *Julius Caesar*', in *Shakespeare and the Law*, ed. Daniela Carpi (Ravenna: Longo, 2003), 103–15 (114).

52 Ibid., 110.

53 Ibid., 109, 105, 107.

54 David Colclough, 'Talking to the Animals: Persuasion, Counsel and Their Discontents in *Julius Caesar*', in *Shakespeare and Early Modern Political Thought*, ed. David Armitage, Conal Condren and Andrew Fitzmaurice (Cambridge: Cambridge University Press, 2009), 217–33 (218, 232–3).

55 Ibid., 225, 227. Colclough (ibid., 229–32) also interestingly proposes a passage from Christopher Goodman's *His Superior Powers Ought to Be Obeyed* (1558) as a possible source for a crucial sentence in Antony's oration.

56 Coppélia Kahn, '"Passion of some difference": Friendship and Emulation in *Julius Caesar*', in Julius Caesar: *New Critical Essays*, ed. Horst Zander (London: Routledge, 2005), 271–83 (273).

57 Ibid.

58 Ibid., 281.

59 Edward M. Test, '"A dish fit for the gods": Mexica Sacrifice in De Bry, Las Casas, and Shakespeare's *Julius Caesar*', *JMEMS* 41 (2011), 93–117.

60 Ibid., 104, 106–7.

61 Oliver Arnold, *The Third Citizen: Shakespeare's Theater and the Early Modern House of Commons* (Baltimore: Johns Hopkins University Press, 2007), 176.

62 Baines, 'Vicissitudes of Language', 147.

63 Maddalena Pennacchia, 'The Stones of Rome: Early Earth Sciences in *Julius Caesar* and *Coriolanus*', in *Questioning Bodies in Shakespeare's Rome*, ed. Maria Del Sapio Garbero, Nancy Isenberg and Maddalena Pennacchia (Göttingen: V&R Unipress, 2010), 309–25 (312).

64 Ibid., 312–13.

65 Ibid., 313.

66 Brents Stirling, *The Populace in Shakespeare* (New York: Columbia University Press, 1949). See Daniel Cadman's chapter in this volume, pp. 33–4.

67 Jerald W. Spotswood, '"We are undone already": Disarming the Multitude in *Julius Caesar* and *Coriolanus*', *TSLL* 42 (2000): 61–78 (61).

68 Ibid., 62.

69 Ibid., 70.

70 Ibid., 62–3.

71 Christine E. Hutchins, '"Who is here so rude that would not be a Roman?": England as Anti-Type of Rome in Elizabethan Print and *Julius Caesar*', *BJJ* 8 (2001): 207–27 (213).

72 Ibid., 214.

73 Jeffrey Edward Green, *The Eyes of the People: Democracy in an Age of Spectatorship* (Oxford: Oxford University Press, 2010): 131–2.

74 Ibid., 135.

75 Arnold, *Third Citizen*, 146.

76 Ibid., 146–7.

77 Ibid., 143.

78 Barbara L. Parker, 'From Monarchy to Tyranny: *Julius Caesar* among Shakespeare's Roman Works', in Julius Caesar: *New Critical Essays*, ed. Horst Zander (London: Routledge, 2005): 111–26 (119).

79 Naomi Conn Liebler, 'Buying and Selling So(u)les: Marketing Strategies and the Politics of Performance in *Julius Caesar*', in Julius Caesar: *New Critical Essays*, ed. Horst Zander (London: Routledge, 2005): 165–79 (166, 169).

80 Ibid., 168.

81 Ibid., 166, 176.

82 Alison A. Chapman, 'Whose Saint Crispin's Day Is It?: Shoemaking, Holiday Making, and the Politics of Memory in Early Modern England', *RQ* 54 (2001): 1467–94 (1468, 1481).

83 Ibid., 1489, 1477.

84 Ibid., 1490.

85 Christopher Holmes, 'Time for the Plebs in *Julius Caesar*', *EMLS* 7 (2001): 1–32; Richard Wilson, '*Julius Caesar*: Shakespeare's Roman Carnival', *ELH* 54 (1987): 31–44. See Daniel Cadman's chapter in this volume, p. 42.

86 Holmes, 'Time for the Plebs': 25.

87 Ibid., 24–6.

88 Ibid., 27.

89 Ibid., 23, 29.

90 Ibid., 29, 16, 2.

91 Claudia Corti, '"The three-fold world divided": *Julius Caesar* in the Light of *Theologia Platonica*', in *Shakespeare, Italy, and Intertextuality*, ed. Michele Marrapodi (Manchester: Manchester University Press, 2004), 176–93 (183).

92 Ibid., 183–6.

93 Ibid., 186, 189.

94 Nicholas Royle, 'The Poet: *Julius Caesar* and the Democracy to Come', in *Julius Caesar in Western Culture*, ed. Maria Wyke (Malden: Blackwell, 2006), 205–27 (206, 222, 214).

95 Mark Robson, 'The Hour is Unknown: *Julius Caesar*, et

cetera', in *Shakespeare and the Urgency of Now: Criticism and Theory in the 21st Century*, ed. Cary DiPietro and Hugh Grady (Basingstoke: Palgrave Macmillan, 2013), 188–209 (192–3).

96 Ibid., 196, 202.

97 Maddalena Pennacchia, 'Antony's Ring: Remediating Ancient Rhetoric on the Elizabethan Stage', in *Identity, Otherness and Empire in Shakespeare's Rome*, ed. Maria Del Sapio Garbero (Farnham: Ashgate, 2009), 49–59 (50, 56, 51).

98 Ibid., 57–9.

99 Barbara Joan Baines, '"That every like is not the same": The Vicissitudes of Language in *Julius Caesar*', in Julius Caesar: *New Critical Essays*, ed. Horst Zander (London: Routledge, 2005), 139–53 (139).

100 Ibid., 150, 148.

101 Ibid., 144.

102 David Lucking, *The Shakespearean Name: Essays on* Romeo and Juliet, The Tempest *and Other Plays* (Bern: Peter Lang, 2007), 133.

103 Ibid., 135.

104 John W. Mahon, 'Providence in *Julius Caesar*', in *Shakespeare's Christianity: The Protestant and Catholic Poetics of* Julius Caesar, Macbeth, *and* Hamlet, ed. Beatrice Batson (Waco: Baylor University Press, 2006), 91–110 (93).

105 Ibid., 93, 101.

106 Andreas Mahler, '"There is Restitution, no End of Restitution, only not for us": Experimental Tragedy and the Early Modern Subject in *Julius Caesar*', in Julius Caesar: *New Critical Essays*, ed. Horst Zander (London: Routledge, 2005), 181–95 (181).

107 Ibid., 189.

108 Ibid., 190–1.

109 Robert McCutcheon, 'The Call of Vocation in *Julius Caesar* and *Coriolanus*', *ELR* 41 (2011): 332–74 (373).

110 Ibid., 352–3.

111 Ibid., 354, 358.

112 See Daniel Cadman's chapter in this volume, p. 44–7.

Chapter 4

1   All references to Shakespeare's plays, other than *Julius Caesar*, are taken from Arden Complete Works: William Shakespeare, *The Arden Shakespeare Complete Works*, ed. Richard Proudfoot and others, rev. edn (London: Bloomsbury, 2011).

2   Anthony Munday, *A Second and Third Blast of Retrait from Plaies and Theaters*, translated by Salvian of Marseilles [electronic resource] (Imprinted at London: By Henrie Denham, dwelling in Pater noster Row, at the signe of the Starre, being the assigne of William Seres. Allowed by aucthoritie, 1580), 1, 105.

3   The text reads, 'The woman shal not weare that which perteineth vnto the man, nether shal a man put on womans raiment: for all that do so, *are* abominacion vnto the Lord thy God', followed by the note, 'd. For that were to alter the ordre of nature, & to despite God' (*The Geneva Bible, a facsimile of the 1560 edition*, n.p.: Madison, University of Wisconsin Press, 1969).

4   William Prynne, *Histrio-mastix* (London: Printed by Edward Allde, Augustine Mathewes, Thomas Cotes and William Iones for Michael Sparke, and are to be sold at the Blue Bible, in Greene Arbour, in little Old Bayly 1633), sig. $_5X_4^r$.

5   William B. Worthen, *The Idea of the Actor: Drama and the Ethics of Performance* (Princeton, NJ: Princeton University Press, 1984), 19; Stephen Gosson, *Playes Confuted in Fiue Actions* (London: Imprinted for Thomas Gosson dwelling in Pater noster row at the signe of the Sunne, 1582), sig. D8^v-EI^r.

6   Stephen Gosson, *The Schoole of Abuse* (Printed at London: for Thomas VVoodcocke, 1579), sigs. C_{1r}-C_{2r}.

7   *The Second Part of The Return from Parnassus*, in *The Three Parnassus Plays, 1598–1601*, ed. J. B. Leishman (London: Nicholson & Watson, 1949), 337.

8   The first recorded production of the play is 21 September

1599. See E. K. Chambers, *The Elizabethan Stage*, vol. 2 (Oxford: Clarendon Press, 1923), 364–5.

9   Heather James, 'Shakespeare's Juliet and Ovid's Myths of Girlhood', *Shakespeare Association of America Annual Meeting* (Vancouver, British Columbia, 1–4 April 2015).

10 This claim is supported by a reference to a production of *Julius Caesar*, most likely Shakespeare's at the Globe, by a traveller from Switzerland, Thomas Platter, who visited England from 18 September to 20 October 1599. He commented on the 'excellent performance' and the 'elegant and curious dance' staged afterwards, among other references to the play's performance around that time. See Chambers, 2.364–5 and Ernest Schanzer, 'Thomas Platter's Observations on the Elizabethan Stage', *Notes and Queries*, 3 (1956): 465–7.

11 Naomi Conn Liebler, '"Thou Bleeding Piece of Earth": The Ritual Ground of Julius Caesar', *Shakespeare Studies*, 14 (1981): 175. Liebler's discussion rightly centres on Shakespeare's uses of other Plutarch texts, but these sources do not explain the attitude towards clothing. Liebler discounts the influence of Ovid's *Fasti* because Shakespeare would not have had an English translation of the poem available (176). However, as many contemporary writers on the subject have agreed, Shakespeare would most likely have read *Fasti* in its original Latin.

12 Ovid, *Fasti*, ed. G. P. Goold and James George Frazer (Harvard University Press, Cambridge, Mass.: W. Heinemann, 1989), Book 2: 282–308.

13 All subsequent quotations from Shakespeare's *Julius Caesar* will be taken from the Arden Shakespeare, 3rd edn, ed. David Daniell (Walton-on-Thames, Surrey, UK: Thomas Nelson and Sons, 1998).

14 Martha Hale Schackford, 'Julius Caesar and Ovid', *Modern Language Notes*, 41, 3 (1926): 172–4. Schackford was the first to point out the references in Shakespeare's play to Ovid's *Metamorphoses* in 1926, but her analysis does not extend much beyond identifying the similar passages. Since then, not many scholars have noted the importance of Ovid's Book 15 in Shakespeare's treatment of Caesar, with the exception of my own work (see Lisa S. Starks-Estes, *Violence, Trauma, and*

Virtus in Shakespeare's Roman Poems and Plays: Transforming Ovid (Houndmills, Hampshire and New York: Palgrave Macmillan, 2014), 130, 138–9, 143.

15 All quotations from Arthur Golding's translation of *Metamorphoses* will be taken from Ovid, *Ovid's Metamorphoses: The Arthur Golding Translation, 1567*, ed. John Frederick Nims and Jonathan Bate (Philadelphia: Paul Dry Books, 2000).

16 Quoted in Geoffrey Bullough, *Narrative and Dramatic Sources of Shakespeare, vol. 5. The Roman plays: Julius Caesar, Antony and Cleopatra* (London: Routledge and Kegan Paul; New York: Columbia University Press, 1957–75), 83

17 Ibid., 83.

18 James O. Wood, 'Intimations of Actaeon in Julius Caesar', *Shakespeare Quarterly*, 24.1 (1973): 86.

19 Ibid., 87.

20 See Margaret Maurer, 'Again, Poets and Julius Caesar', *Upstart Crow: A Shakespeare Journal,* 28 (2009): 5–16, esp. 6. Gary Taylor also examines the association between Cinna the Poet and Ovid's Orpheus in 'Bardicide', in *Shakespeare & Cultural Traditions,* ed. Tetsuo Kishi, Roger Pringle and Stanley Wells (Newark: University of Delaware Press, 1994), 333–49.

21 David Kaula also examines the assassination as sacred ritual: see '"Let Us Be Sacrificers": Religious Motifs in Julius Caesar', *Shakespeare Studies*, 14 (1981): 197.

22 Jonathan Goldberg interprets these lines in relation to larger circulations of power in the play and in Jacobean England. See Jonathan Goldberg, *James I and the Politics of Literature: Jonson, Shakespeare, Donne, and Their Contemporaries* (Baltimore: Johns Hopkins University Press, 1983).

23 Paul Menzer, 'The Actor's Inhibition: Early Modern Acting and the Rhetoric of Restraint', *Renaissance Drama*, New Series, 35 (2006): 83–111.

24 This detail not included in Plutarch. See Bullough, 43.

25 Some of the following section on blood and martyrdom has been adapted from my book, *Violence, Trauma, and Virtus*, 129, 131–3, 135–7.

26 Caroline Walker Bynum, 'Violent Imagery in Late Medieval Piety', 15th Annual Lecture of the German Historical Institute, 8 November 2001, *Bulletin of the German Historical Institute* 30 (2002): 3. Available at http://www.ghi-dc.org/publications/ghipubs/bu/030/3.pdf (accessed 13 February 2016).

27 Bynum, 'Violent Imagery', 70.

28 See Caroline Walker Bynum, *Wonderful Blood: Theology and Practice in Late Medieval Northern Germany and Beyond* (Philadelphia: University of Pennsylvania Press, 2007), 3.

29 On poetry, see Bynum, 'Violent Imagery', 20–2, and Douglas Gray, 'The Five Wounds of Our Lord', *Notes and Queries* (1963): 163–4. On sermons and drama, see Margaret E. Owens, *Stages of Dismemberment: The Fragmented Body in Late Medieval and Early Modern Drama* (Newark: University of Delaware Press; Cranbury, NJ: Associated University Presses, 2005), 57–62.

30 Owens, *Stages of Dismemberment*, 57.

31 Bullough, *Narrative and Dramatic Sources of Shakespeare*, 5: 42.

32 For more on the contradictory meanings of blood in this play, see my discussion in Starks-Estes, *Violence, Trauma, and Virtus*, 131–3.

33 Jack Heller, '"Your Statue Spouting Blood": *Julius Caesar*, the Sacraments, and the Fountain of Life', in *Word and Rite: The Bible and Ceremony in Selected Shakespearean Works*, ed. Beatrice Batson (Newcastle upon Tyne: Cambridge Scholars Publishing, 2010), 79–85. Heller also reads these versions of Calphurnia's dream as indicative of religious sacrament. However, he sees the difference between the two as 'baptismal' and 'Eucharistic', relating to protestant as opposed to Catholic theological interpretations of Christ's blood and sacrifice.

34 Julia Reinhard Lupton, *Afterlives of the Saints: Hagiography, Typology, and Renaissance Literature* (Stanford, CA: Stanford University Press, 1996), 42–3.

35 Katharine Park, *The Secrets of Women: Gender, Generation, and the Origins of Human Dissection* (New York: Zone Books, 2006), 19.

36 Lupton, *Afterlives of the Saints*, 46.

37 See Jack Heller, 'Your Statue Spouting Blood', 79.

38 I elaborate on the importance of considering Julius Caesar as a specifically *male* martyr in *Violence, Trauma, and Virtus*, especially 137.

39 The Elizabethan/Jacobean use of the term 'personate', to mean 'acting', sparked a lively debate throughout the twentieth century, as it was seen to indicate a new acting style. One camp of critics argued that this acting style was formal or artificial, while the other countered that it was naturalistic, with the usage of the word 'personate' denoting 'true to life'. It is beyond the scope of this paper to outline this debate, but briefly, like Paul Menzer, I see this binary of artificial/naturalistic as a false one that really does not tell us much at all about the acting style of the time. Menzer, 'That Old Saw: Early Modern Acting and the Infinite Regress', *Shakespeare Bulletin* 2 (2004): 27.

40 Worthen, 17. Although Worthen describes the actor's alteration of self as 'metamorphosis', he does not explicitly mention Ovid.

41 Joseph R. Roach, *The Player's Passion: Studies in the Science of Acting* (University of Michigan Press, 2008), 42. Roach cites Thomas Heywood in his reference to the legend of Julius Caesar's stint as an actor, noted also below, from *An Apology for Actors* (New York and London: Garland, 1973), E4.

42 Roach, 42.

43 Roach, 28.

44 Thomas Heywood, 'The Prologue to the Stage, at the Cocke-pit' to *The Jew of Malta*, by Christopher Marlowe, in *Christopher Marlowe: The Complete Works, vol. 1*, ed. Fredson Bowers, 2nd edn (Cambridge and New York: Cambridge University Press, 1981), 259; Richard Flecknoe, *Love's kingdom* [electronic resource] (London: Printed by R. Wood for the author, 1664); Thomas Randolph, *The Jealous Lovers* [electronic resource] (Cambridge: Printed by Roger Daniel, printer to the Universitie of Cambridge: 1640. And are to be sold by Richard Ireland, 1640). Preface to *Jealous Lovers* (1632).

45 Robert Burton, *The Anatomy of Melancholy*, ed. Holbrook Jackson (New York: New York Review of Books, 2001), I.2, 257.

46 Thomas Beard, *The Theatre of Gods Iudgements: or, a Collection of Histories out of Sacred, Ecclesiasticall, and Prophane Authours*, translated by Jean de Chassanian (London: Printed by Adam Islip, 1597), 249. STC 1659. William Fulbecke, *An Historicall Collection of the Continuall Factions, Tumults, and Massacres of the Romans and Italians During the Space of One Hundred and Twentie Yeares Next Before the Peaceable Empire of Augustus Cæsar* (London: Printed by R. Field] for VVilliam Ponsonby, 1601), 170. STC 11412. John Drakakis also refers to these sources in his discussion of the play's defence against the anti-theatrical position, but he focuses primarily on the play as a subversive force in the way it stages contesting authorities. See '"Fashion it thus": *Julius Caesar* and the Politics of Theatrical Representation', *Shakespeare Survey* (1991): 71.

47 Heywood, *An Apology for Actors*, E4.

48 See Drakakis: 66.

49 I. G., Heywood, *An Apology for Actors*, 28.

50 John Weever, *The Mirror of Martyrs, or The Life and Death of Sir John Oldcastle* [electronic resource] (London: Printed by Valentine Simmes for William Wood, 1601), A3.

51 Leonard Digges, *Vpon Master William Shakespeare, the Deceased Authour, and his Poems* (Farmington Hills, MI: Gale Research, 1988), II.41–8.

52 T. G. (Thomas Gainsford), *The Rich Cabinet*, translated by Giovanni Della Casa (London: Printed by Iohn Beale for Roger Iackson and are to be sold at his shop neere Fleete Conduit, 1616), sig Q4^r. Thomas Nashe, *Works of Thomas Nashe*, ed. R. B. McKerrow (Sidgwick & Jackson, 1910), I, 212.

53 Francis Meres, *Palladis Tamia, Wits Treasury* (At London: Printed by P. Short, for Cuthbert Burbie, and are to be solde at his shop at the Royall Exchange, 1598), 282.

Chapter 5

1. Steve Hartsoe, 'Of Shakespeare and Financial Decisions,' *Duke Today*, 14 September 2012. Available at http://today.duke.edu/2012/09/forlinesclass

2. Ibid., n.p.

3. Ibid., n.p.

4. Christine Desan, 'Booms and Busts: The Legal Dynamics of Modern Money', *8 Lectures from Occupy Harvard Teach-In*. OpenCulture.com. 12 December 2011. Available at www.openculture.com/2011/12/eight_lectures_from_the_occupy_harvard_teach-in_watch_online.html

5. All citations from Shakespeare's plays will be from the Arden Third Series; Tony Cox, 'What Shakespeare Can Teach Us About Money', *Marketplace.org* (28 December 2012). Available at http://www.marketplace.org/topics/life/what-shakespeare-can-teach-us-about-money

6. Michael Bloomberg, 'The 2008 Time 100', *Time Magazine*, 12 May 2008. Available at http://content.time.com/time/specials/2007/article/0,28804,1733748_1733758_1736192,00.html

7. John Carney, 'Sandy Weill: I Fired Jamie Dimon Because He Wanted To Be CEO,' *Business Insider*, 4 January 2010. Available at http://www.businessinsider.com/sandy-weil-i-fired-jamie-dimon-because-he-wanted-to-be-ceo-2010-1

8. Hariett Rubin, 'Lessons in Shakespeare, From Stage to Boardroom,' *New York Times*, 10 November 2007. Available at http://www.nytimes.com/2007/11/10/business/10shakespeare.html

9. See Douglas Lanier, 'Shakescorps "Noir"' *SQ* 53.2 and Scott L. Newstok, 'A joint and corporate voice: Re-working Shakespearean Seminars', *SS* 1.66 (December 2013).

10. Marc Shell, *Poetry, Language, and Thought: Literary and Philosophic Economies from the Medieval to the Modern Era* (Baltimore and London: Johns Hopkins University Press, 1982), 2.

11. Jean-Christophe Agnew, *Worlds Apart: The Market and the*

    Theatre in Anglo-American Thought, 1550–1750, (Cambridge: Cambridge University Press, 1986), 46.
12. Ibid., 60.
13. Ibid., 82 (my emphasis).
14. Geoffrey Ingham, *The Nature of Money* (Cambridge: Polity Press, 2004), 107–33.
15. The 2 November 2011 walkout was part of a long tradition of walkouts protesting the orthodox economics curriculum. For a history of such walkouts, see Mike Beggs, "Occupy Economics," *Jacobin*, Issue 5: Phase Two (Winter 2012). Available at https://www.jacobinmag.com/2011/12/occupy-econ/
16. Nigel Dodd, *The Social Life of Money* (Princeton: Princeton University Press, 2014), 17–23. See also Desan, 'Booms and Busts', David Graeber, *Debt: The First 5000 Years* (Brooklyn: Melville House, 2011), 29, and Ingham, 22–4.
17. Dodd borrows this argument from Keith Hart. Dodd, 19.
18. Ingham, 9.
19. Graeber, 40.
20. Desan, 'Booms and Busts'.
21. Christine Desan, *Making Money: Coin, Currency, and the Coming of Capitalism* (Oxford: Oxford University Press, 2015), 8.
22. Friedrich Nietzsche, *On the Genealogy of Morals*, translated by R. J. Hollingdale, ed. Walter Kaufmann (New York, 1989), 57, 62–3.
23. Dodd, 145.
24. Nietzsche, *Genealogy*, 64. About this passage, Graeber comments, 'Nietzsche had clearly been reading too much Shakespeare. There is no record of the mutilation of debtors in the ancient world', 402.
25. Ingham, 93. See also, Graeber, 133–64.
26. John Kerrigan, *Revenge Tragedy: Aeschylus to Armageddon* (Oxford: Oxford University Press, 1996), 111–41.
27. G. Wilson Knight, 'The Eroticism of *Julius Caesar*', an excerpt from *The Imperial Theme* (1931), in *Shakespeare: Julius Caesar, A Casebook*, ed. Peter Ure (London: Macmillan, 1969), 150–1.

28 Vivian Thomas, *Twayne's New Critical Introduction to Shakespeare: Julius Caesar* (New York: Macmillan, 1982), 19.
29 Quoted in Thomas, 19.
30 Kerrigan, 115.
31 Ibid., 21.
32 Ibid., 7, 10.
33 Craig Muldrew, 'Interpreting the Market: The Ethics of Credit and Community Relations in Early Modern England', *Social History* 18.2 (May, 1993): 163.
34 Craig Muldrew, *The Economy of Obligation: The Culture of Credit and Social Relations in Early Modern England* (London: Palgrave Macmillan UK, 1998), 108.
35 Linda Woodbridge, *Money in the Age of Shakespeare* (New York: Palgrave Macmillan, 2003), 2.
36 Knight, 145.
37 Kerrigan, 199.
38 Friedrich Nietzsche, *Twilight of the Idols*, translated by R. J. Hollingdale (London: Penguin, 1968), 111.
39 Plutarch, *Plutarch's Lives, Vol. 2*, translated by John Dryden, ed. Arthur Hugh Clugh (New York: Modern Library, 1992), 199–200.
40 Gilles Deleuze, *Nietzsche and Philosophy*, translated by Hugh Tomlinson (New York: Columbia University Press, 1983), 17.
41 Quoted in Deleuze, 11.
42 Ingham, 106.
43 Graeber, 49–50.
44 Christine Desan, 'Creation Stories', *Harvard Public Law Working Paper* 13–20 (30 July 2013): 49.
45 Graeber, 229; Dodd, 95.
46 Ingham, 101.
47 W. V. Harris, 'A Revisionist View of Roman Money,' *The Journal of Roman Studies* 96 (2006), 18.
48 Ibid., 19.
49 Graeber, 173.

50 Peter Sloterdijk, *Nietzsche's Apostle*, translated by Steven Corcoran (Frankfurt: Semiotext(e), 2013), 59.
51 Ibid., 59.
52 Harris, 20; Desan, 'Creation Stories', 37.
53 R. Goldsmith, quoted in Ingham, 101.
54 Andrew Burnett, 'The Augustan Revolution Seen from the Mints of the Provinces,' *Journal of Roman Studies* 101 (November 2011): 10.
55 Michel Callon, 'What Does It Mean to Say Economics is Performative?' in *Do Economists Make Markets? On the Performativity of Economics,* ed. Donald MacKenzie et. al. (Princeton: Princeton University Press, 2008), 321.
56 Plutarch, 493.
57 Ibid.
58 Ibid., 492.
59 Ibid.
60 Ibid.
61 Ibid., 232.
62 Christopher Edgar Challis, *The Tudor Coinage* (Manchester: Manchester University Press, 1978), 226; Desan, 'Booms and Busts'.
63 Desan, *Making Money*, 9.
64 Ibid., 148.
65 Muldrew, 3–7.
66 Plutarch, 595.
67 For more on this, see *Richard II* (Arden edition), ed. Charles R. Forker, 489.
68 Graeber, 308.
69 Desan, *Making Money*, 9.
70 Ibid., 236; Graeber, 312.
71 Graeber, 191, 120.
72 Ibid., 335 (my emphasis).
73 Ibid., 334.

74 Plutarch, 489.
75 Graeber, 328.
76 Vivian Thomas, *Shakespeare's Political and Economic Language: A Dictionary* (London: Bloomsbury Arden Shakespeare, 2015), 68–9.
77 'compact, n.1'. OED Online. June 2015. Available at http://www.oed.com/view/Entry/37366 (accessed 13 July 2015).
78 Graeber, 329.
79 Agnew, 98.
80 Ingham, 119.
81 Ibid., 114–33.
82 Desan, *Making Money*, 238.
83 Friedrich Nietzsche, 'On Truth and Lies in a Nonmoral Sense', *Philosophy and Truth: Selections from Nietzsche's Notebooks of the early 1870s*, ed. and trans Daniel Breazeale (New York: Humanity Books, 1993), 84.
84 Ingham, 129.
85 Graeber, 339–40.
86 Ibid., 49.
87 Ingham, 128.
88 Graeber, 339.
89 Ingham, 121.
90 Christine Desan, 'Christine Desan's "Making Money",' Harvard Law School Library Book Talk, November 2014. Available at https://www.youtube.com/watch?v=bCdKI5dGn9c
91 Dodd, 94.
92 Plutarch, 489.

Chapter 6

1 Oliver Arnold, 'Introduction', in *Julius Caesar*, ed. Oliver Arnold (New York: Longman, 2010), xv–xliii (xix).
2 References to the play are from *Julius Caesar*, ed. David

Daniell (London: Arden, 2003). I have also consulted *Julius Caesar*, ed. T. S. Dorsch (London: Arden, 1966).

3   For the medieval tradition on Caesar see Almut Suerbaum, 'The Middle Ages', in *A Companion to Julius Caesar*, ed. Miriam Griffin (Chichester: Wiley-Blackwell, 2009), ch. 22. For an Elizabethan account see Richard Lloyd, *A brief discourse of the most renowned actes and right valiant conquests of those puisant Princes, called the Nine Worthies* (London, 1584).

4   William Caxton, Preface, in *Le Morte D'Arthur* Vol. 1, ed. Janet Cowen (London: Penguin, 1969), 3.

5   John Milton, *Pro Populo Anglicano Defensio*, in *The Works of John Milton* Vol. 7, ed. Frank Allen Patterson et al. (New York: Columbia University Press, 1932), 336.

6   References are from Christopher Marlowe, *Lucans First Booke*, in *The Complete Works of Christopher Marlowe* Vol. 1, ed. Roma Gill (Oxford: Clarendon Press, 1987), 93–111. For the republican overtones of Lucan's and Marlowe's sense of sublimity, see Patrick Cheney, *Marlowe's Republican Authorship: Lucan, Liberty, and the Sublime* (Basingstoke: Palgrave Macmillan, 2009), 42–9. For the effect of Lucan on Elizabethan–Jacobean republicanism see also William Blissert, 'Lucan's Caesar and the Elizabethan Villain', *Studies in Philology*, 53 (1956): 553–74; Paulina Kewes, 'Julius Caesar in Jacobean England', *The Seventeenth Century*, 17 (2002): 155–86; Andrew Hadfield, *Shakespeare and Republicanism* (Cambridge: Cambridge University Press, 2005), 53–65. For the Caesar references in Marlowe's Tamburlaine, see Lisa Hopkins, *The Cultural Uses of the Caesars on the English Renaissance Stage* (Aldershot: Ashgate, 2008), 55–77.

7   See Rebecca Bushnell, *Tragedies of Tyrants: Political Thought and Theater in the English Renaissance* (Ithaca: Cornell University Press, 1990), 56–69.

8   References are from *Cornelia*, in *The Works of Thomas Kyd*, ed. Frederick S. Boas (Oxford: Clarendon Press, 1901), 101–60.

9   References are from *The Tragedy of Caesar and Pompey*, in *The Plays of George Chapman: The Tragedies* Vol. 2, ed.

Thomas Marc Parrott (New York: Russell & Russell, 1961), 341–400.

10 References are from *The Tragedie of Caesar and Pompey or Caesars Reuenge* (London, 1607).

11 References are from *The Tragedy of Julius Caesar*, in *The Poetical Works of Sir William Alexander* Vol. 1, ed. L. E. Kastner and H. B. Charlton (Edinburgh: William Blackwood and Sons, 1921), 344–442.

12 For recent specimens see, pro-Caesar, Timothy Burns, 'Julius Caesar: The Problem of Classical Republicanism', in *Shakespeare and the Body Politic*, ed. Bernard J. Dobski and Dustin Gish (Lanham: Lexington, 2013), 49–77; for Tyrant-Caesar, Maurice Charney, *Shakespeare's Villains* (Madison, NJ: Fairleigh Dickinson University Press, 2012), 131–7. For the play's ambivalence, see Warren Chernaik, *The Myth of Rome in Shakespeare and His Contemporaries* (Cambridge: Cambridge University Press, 2011), 97.

13 Chernaik, 92.

14 Michael McCanles, *Dialectical Criticism in Renaissance Literature* (Berkeley: University of California Press, 1975), 188.

15 Mark Rose, 'Conjuring Caesar: Ceremony, History, and Authority in 1599', *English Literary Renaissance*, 19 (1989): 291–304.

16 Richard F. Hardin, *Civil Idolatry: Desacralizing and Monarchy in Spenser, Shakespeare, and Milton* (Newark: University of Delaware Press, 1992), 152–63.

17 T. W. Baldwin, *William Shakspere's Small Latine & Lesse Greeke*, 2 vols (Urbana: University of Illinois Press, 1944), 2, 564–72.

18 Erasmus, *De Ratione Studii* and *Ciceronianus*, in *Opera Omnia* Vol. I.2, ed. Jean-Claude Margolin and Pierre Mesnard (Amsterdam: North-Holland, 1971), 116, 642. For the importance of the *De Ratione*'s programme see Baldwin, 1, 75–93.

19 Geoffrey of Monmouth, *The History of the Kings of Britain*, ed. Michael D. Reeve (Woodbridge: Boydell, 2007), 79.

20 Reference is from *Cymbeline*, ed. J. M. Nosworthy (Cambridge, MA: Arden, 1960).

21 Edmund Spenser, *The Faerie Queene*, ed. A. C. Hamilton (London: Longman, 1977), III.ix.43.5, 44.9.
22 Roger Ascham, *The Scholemaster* (London, 1579), fol. 67.
23 References are from Plutarch, *The Liues of the Noble Grecians and Romaines*, translated by Thomas North (London, 1603).
24 Thomas Rogers, *A Philosophicall Discourse Entituled, The Anatomie of the Minde* (London, 1576), fols. 140–2.
25 On emulation, including a discussion of this passage, see Gordon Braden, *Renaissance Tragedy and the Senecan Tradition: Anger's Privilege* (New Haven: Yale University Press, 1985), 10–15.
26 Ernest Schanzer, 'The Problem of *Julius Caesar*', *Shakespeare Quarterly* 6 (1955): 303.
27 McCanles, 188–9. See also Geoffrey Miles, *Shakespeare and the Constant Romans* (Oxford: Clarendon, 1996), 129–44.

Chapter 7

1 Theodor Mommsen, *The History of Rome*, translated by W. P. Dickson, 5 vols. (London: Macmillan, 1913), V.305–8; Maria Wyke, *Caesar: A Life in Western Culture* (London: Granta Books, 2007), 79–87, 156–68, 172–80. For further discussion of the reputation of Julius Caesar as hero or tyrant in the Early Modern period, see Warren Chernaik, *The Myth of Rome in Shakespeare and his Contemporaries* (Cambridge: Cambridge University Press, 2011), 84–92.
2 Quentin Skinner, *The Foundations of Modern Political Thought*, 2 vols (Cambridge: Cambridge University Press, 1978), I. 83, 161–2.
3 Niccolò Machiavelli, *Discourses*, ed. Bernard Crick (Harmondsworth: Penguin, 1970), I.10; I.17, 135–6, 158; James Harrington, *The Commonwealth of Oceana*, ed. J. G. A. Pocock (Cambridge: Cambridge University Press, 1992), 8.
4 Anthony Grafton, 'Cicero and Ciceronianism', in *The Classical Tradition*, ed. Anthony Grafton, Glenn W. Most and Salvatore Settis (Cambridge, MA: Belknap, 2010), 194–7.

5   Margaret Malamud, 'Manifest Destiny and the Eclipse of Julius Caesar', in *Julius Caesar in Western Culture*, ed. Maria Wyke (Oxford: Blackwell, 2006), 148–51; Nicholas Cole, in *The Cambridge Companion to Cicero*, ed. Catherine Steel (Cambridge: Cambridge University Press, 2013), 337–8.

6   Grafton, 'Cicero and Ciceronianism', 194; Cole, in *Cambridge Companion*, 338–42. On Froude, see Frank M. Turner, 'British Politics and the Roman Republic', *The Historical Journal* 29 (1986): 592–3.

7   Mommsen, *The History of Rome*, IV. 470, 516; V. 133–4, 504–5. To Mommsen, Cicero 'had no conviction, and no passion; he was nothing but an advocate, and not a good one' (IV. 505). On Mommsen's praise of Caesar as the saviour of Rome and denigration of Cicero as 'the champion of a bankrupt republic', see *Cambridge Companion*, 338–40.

8   Anthony Trollope, *The Life of Cicero*, 2 vols (London: Trollope Society, 1993), I. 2–3, 17, 25–6, 34. Trollope says of Froude, 'his sketch of Caesar is one prolonged censure of Cicero' (I. 4), and for Trollope as well the two figures of Cicero and Caesar are contrasted throughout.

9   Thomas Kyd, *Cornelia* (London, 1594), Act 4, Sig. H1, H1ᵛ.

10 Ibid., Act 1, Sig. A1ᵛ, A2, A2ᵛ, A3. On republican motifs in *Cornelia*, see Curtis Perry, 'The Uneasy Republicanism of Thomas Kyd', *Criticism* 48 (2006): 535–55.

11 Kyd, *Cornelia*, Act 2, Sig. D2; Act 3, Sig. E3.

12 Robert Garnier, *Cornélie* (Paris, 1574), Sig. A3ᵛ–A4. Kyd wrote *Cornelia* a year before his death, after surviving arrest and torture for possession of allegedly treasonous and atheistic writings, evidently in the hand of his friend Christopher Marlowe. For Garnier and Kyd, see Howard Norland, *Neoclassical Tragedy in Elizabethan England* (Cranbury: Associated University Presses, 2009), 218–19, 228–31; and Perry, 'Uneasy Republicanism', 535–8.

13 Sir William Alexander, *The Tragedie of Julius Caesar*, in *The Monarchicke Tragedies* (London, 1607), Argument, Sig. P3; 2.1, Sig. R3.

14 Alexander, *The Tragedie of Julius Caesar*, II.ii, Sig. S4, S4^v, T2; III.i, Sig. V2.

15 In a letter to Atticus, Cicero's closest friend, written in 43 BC, Brutus criticizes Cicero as one who in spite of his 'past achievements' and writings against tyranny, is willing to 'cringe and serve' in his dealings with Octavius: *Letters of Cicero*, trans L. P. Wilkinson (London: Geoffrey Bles, 1959), 184–5.

16 *Tragedie of Julius Caesar*, 3.1, Sig. V2^v, V4-4^v. The passage is discussed in Paulina Kewes, 'Julius Caesar in Jacobean England', *The Seventeenth Century* 17 (2002): 155–60, bringing out its contemporary relevance, especially in light of the Gunpowder Plot of 1605.

17 Cicero, *On Obligations (De Officiis)*, trans P. G. Walsh, I. 26, 64 (Oxford: Oxford World's Classics, 2001), 11, 23.

18 Cicero, *De Officiis*, trans Walter Miller, I. 74, 77 (London: Loeb Library, 1913), 75, 79. Here the Loeb translation is closer to the Latin original than the one in World's Classics. In his own time and afterwards, Cicero has often been criticized for praising his achievements as Consul, and vanity seems to have been one of his faults of character.

19 Cicero, *Philippics*, II. 118, translated by Walter Ker (London: Loeb Library, 1957), 187.

20 Robert Harris, *Imperium* (London: Hutchinson, 2006): *Lustrum* (London: Hutchinson, 2009). Charlotte Higgins, reviewing *Lustrum* in the *Guardian*, 17 October 2009, says that 'the real triumph' of this novel is that, on a 'bedrock of historical veracity, Harris has built a story that is really about modern politics' – 'if you can imagine the thrustingly ambitious men and women of New Labour equipped with private armies'. In an interview, Harris commented: 'What has changed? Nothing at all' (interview with Claire Armitstead, Guardian Books Podcast, 16 October 2009).

21 *Letters of Cicero*, trans. Wilkinson, 43, 55.

22 To Varro, April, 46 BC, *Letters of Cicero*, ed. Wilkinson, 128.

23 Cicero, *Philippics*, II. 25-30, pp. 89–93; *Philippics*, VI. 19, 333, trans. Ker.

24 Ben Jonson, *Catiline His Conspiracy*, 1.1.474-8, 2.1.401;

3.1.33; 4.7.54, in *The Works of Ben Jonson* (Cambridge: Cambridge University Press, 2012), Vol. IV.

25 Introduction, *Catiline, Works*, IV.8; *Catiline, Works*, IV. 25-6. A commendatory poem by Francis Beaumont praises Jonson as one who has not 'itched after the wild applause / Of common people' (ibid., IV.27).

26 *Catiline*, 3.5, 59–60; 1.1. 545–50; Sallust, *The Conspiracie of Cateline*, trans. Thomas Heywood (London, 1609), Chapter 3, Sig. C1. On the idealization of the early Roman republic in Sallust and the corruption of republican Rome by ambition, greed and luxury, see *The Conspiracie of Cateline*, trans. Heywood, Chapter 3, Sig. B4-C2^v; and my discussion in *The Myth of Rome in Shakespeare and his Contemporaries,* 22–5.

27 See Blair Worden, 'Politics in *Catiline:* Ben Jonson and his Sources', in *Re-Presenting Ben Jonson,* ed. Martin Butler (Basingstoke: Macmillan, 1999), 152–73; and Patricia Osmond and Robert Ulery, 'Constantius Felicius Durantinus and the Renaissance Origins of Anti-Sallustian Criticism', *International Journal of the Classical Tradition* 1 (1995): 29–56.

28 *Catiline*, 3.3.1–2, 15–17, 21–3, 26–7. This passage is closely based on Machiavelli, *History of Florence*, as has been shown in a recent article by Domenico Lovascio, *N&Q,* 57 (2010), 411–13.

29 *The Conspiracie of Cateline*, trans. Heywood, ch. 16, 43, 54.

30 *Catiline*, 3.2.240, 245–6. For attacks on Jonson's Cicero as 'a flexible, even a compromised statesman, adept at bestowing flattery, gifts, and bribes', see Anne Barton, *Ben Jonson, Dramatist* (Cambridge: Cambridge University Press, 1984), 160–1; and Rebecca Lemon, *Treason by Words* (Ithaca and London: Cornell University Press, 2006), 139–41, 149–57.

31 *The Tragedy of that Famous Roman Orator Marcus Tullius Cicero* (1651), 1.1.37–40, in *Drama of the English Republic, 1649–60,* ed. Janet Clare (Manchester: Manchester University Press, 2002).

32 On Octavius and Antony as 'heir to Julius', see several speeches by Quintus in Act 3, Scene 3: e.g. 'The very name of Caesar seems to incite him' and 'What profit gain we by the overthrow / Of Antony, since for reward Octavius / Requires succession in his tyranny?' (3.3.58, 30–32)

33 See the comments on classical republicanism and Cromwell's rise to power in Janet Clare's introduction, *Drama of the English Republic*, 45–9.

34 On the use of the magic words 'Rome' and 'Roman' by various characters in *Julius Caesar*, see *The Myth of Rome in Shakespeare and his Contemporaries*, 79–84.

35 Cicero, *De Officiis*, trans. Walsh, III.83, 112.

36 See Allan Bloom with Harry V. Jaffa, *Shakespeare's Politics* (Chicago: University of Chicago Press, 1964), 80, 89, 104; and essays by Brents Stirling, Mark Hunter and J. F. Phillips in *Julius Caesar: A Casebook*, ed. Peter Ure (London: Macmillan, 1979).

37 See Andrew Hadfield, *Shakespeare and Republicanism* (Cambridge: Cambridge University Press, 2008), 95, 167; and *Shakespeare and Early Modern Political Thought*, ed. David Armitage, Conal Condren and Andrew Fitzmaurice (Cambridge: Cambridge University Press, 2009), 16, 155, 218. On the republican or Neo-Roman tradition of the 'free state', see Quentin Skinner, *Liberty before Liberalism* (Cambridge: Cambridge University Press, 1998).

Chapter 8

1 See Elizabeth Renker, 'Shakespeare in the College Curriculum, 1870–1920,' in eds Coppélia Kahn et al., *Shakespearean Educations* (Newark: University of Delaware Press, 2011).

2 This quotation is from the *Pelican Complete Works of Shakespeare*, eds A. R. Braunmuller and Stephen Orgel (Penguin: New York 2002). All quotations from *Julius Caesar* in this essay are from the Arden Third Series edition (London: Bloomsbury), ed. David Daniell (1998).

3 *Julius Caesar*, ed. S. P. Cerasano (Norton: New York, 2012), xii.

4 Teachers using editions that do not include excerpts from Plutarch can find these in Geoffrey Bullough, *Narrative and Dramatic Sources of Shakespeare*, vol. 5 (London: Routledge,

1964), and also on-line at Internet Shakespeare Editions: http://internetshakespeare.uvic.ca/Annex/Texts/Plutarch/intro/Intro/default/;jsessionid=08C92E28D5EEB69839494FB6C22ED449. (accessed 23 September 2015).

5 A famous anachronism in *Julius Caesar* is the striking clock at 2.1.190. Striking clocks were not invented until the Middle Ages.

6 See Bullough, 102.

7 Alexander Leggatt, *Shakespeare's Political Drama* (London: Routledge, 1989), 139–60.

8 Maurice Charney, *Shakespeare's Roman Plays: The Function of Imagery in the Drama* (Cambridge, MA: Harvard, 1961).

9 Vivian Thomas, *Shakespeare's Roman Worlds* (London: Routledge, 1989).

10 Coppélia Kahn, *Roman Shakespeare: Warriors, Wounds, and Women* (London: Routledge, 1997).

11 John Ripley, Julius Caesar *on the Stage in England and America, 1599–1973* (Cambridge: Cambridge, 1980).

12 Andrew James Hartley, *Shakespeare in Performance:* Julius Caesar (Manchester: Manchester University Press, 2014).

13 *Twentieth-Century Interpretations of* Julius Caesar, ed. Leonard F. Dean (New York: Prentice Hall, 1968).

14 Julius Caesar: *New Casebooks*, ed. Richard Wilson (Houndmills, Basingstoke: Palgrave, 2002).

15 Julius Caesar: *New Critical Essays*, ed. Horst Zander (London: Routledge, 2005).

16 *Bloom's Modern Critical Interpretations:* Julius Caesar, ed. Harold Bloom (New York: Chelsea House, 2009).

BIBLIOGRAPHY

The Second Part of the Return from Parnassus. In *The Three Parnassus Plays, 1598–1601*, edited by by J. B. Leishman. London: Nicholson & Watson, 1949.

Agnew, Jean-Christophe. *Worlds Apart: The Market and the Theatre in Anglo-American Thought, 1550–1750*. Cambridge: Cambridge University Press, 1986.

Alexander, Sir William. *The Tragedie of Julius Caesar*, in *The Monarchicke Tragedies*. London, 1607.

Alexander, Sir William. *The Tragedy of Julius Caesar* in *The Poetical Works of Sir William Alexander* Vol. 1, edited by L. E. Kastner and H. B. Charlton. Edinburgh: William Blackwood and Sons, 1921.

Armitage, David, Conal Condren and Andrew Fitzmaurice, eds. *Shakespeare and Early Modern Political Thought*. Cambridge University Press, 2009.

Arnold, Oliver. Introduction in *Julius Caesar*, ed. Oliver Arnold. New York: Longman, 2010.

Arnold, Oliver. *The Third Citizen: Shakespeare's Theater and the Early Modern House of Commons*. Baltimore: Johns Hopkins University Press, 2007.

Ascham, Roger. *The Scholemaster*. London, 1579.

Baines, Barbara Joan. '"That every like is not the same": The Vicissitudes of Language in *Julius Caesar*'. In Julius Caesar: *New Critical Essays*, ed. Horst Zander, 139–53. London: Routledge, 2005.

Baldwin, T. W. *William Shakspere's Small Latine & Lesse Greeke*, 2 vols. Urbana: University of Illinois Press, 1944.

Barber, C. L. *Shakespeare's Festive Comedy: A Study of Dramatic Form and its Relation to Social Custom*. Princeton: Princeton University Press, 1959.

Barroll, J. Leeds. 'Shakespeare and Roman History'. *The Modern Language Review* 53.3 (1958): 327–43.

Barton, Anne. *Ben Jonson, Dramatist*. Cambridge University Press, 1984.
Beard, Thomas. *The Theatre of Gods Iudgements: Or, a Collection of Histories out of Sacred, Ecclesiasticall, and Prophane Authours*, translated by Jean de Chassanion. London: Printed by Adam Islip, 1597.
Belsey, Catherine. *The Subject of Tragedy: Identity and Difference in Renaissance Drama*. London: Methuen, 1985.
Blissert, William. 'Lucan's Caesar and the Elizabethan Villain'. *Studies in Philology* 53 (1956).
Blits, Jan H. *The End of the Ancient Republic: Shakespeare's 'Julius Caesar'*. Durham: Carolina Academic Press, 1982; reprinted Lanham: Rowman and Littlefield, 1993.
Bloom, Allan, with Harry V. Jaffa. *Shakespeare's Politics*. New York: Basic Books, 1964; reprinted Chicago: University of Chicago Press, 1981.
Bloom, Harold. *Shakespeare: The Invention of the Human*. New York: Riverhead Books, 1998.
Bloom, Harold. *Bloom's Modern Critical Interpretations:* Julius Caesar. Chelsea House, 2009.
Bloomberg, Michael. 'The 2008 Time 100', *Time Magazine*, 12 May 2008. Available at http://content.time.com/time/specials/2007/article/0,28804,1733748_1733758_1736192,00.html (accessed 13 February, 2016).
Bonjour, Adrien. *The Structure of 'Julius Caesar'*. Liverpool: Liverpool University Press, 1958.
Bono, Barbara J. 'The Birth of Tragedy: Tragic Action in *Julius Caesar*'. *English Literary Renaissance* 24.2 (1994): 449–70.
Braden, Gordon. *Renaissance Tragedy and the Senecan Tradition: Anger's Privilege*. New Haven: Yale University Press, 1985.
Bradley, A. C. *Shakespearean Tragedy: Lectures on 'Hamlet', 'Othello', 'King Lear', 'Macbeth'*, 2nd edn. London: Macmillan, 1950.
Bullough, Geoffrey. *Narrative and Dramatic Sources of Shakespeare: Volume V, The Roman Plays*. London: Routledge and Kegan Paul, 1966.
Burnett, Andrew. 'The Augustan Revolution Seen from the Mints of the Provinces'. *Journal of Roman Studies* 101 (November 2011), 1–30.
Burns, Timothy. 'Julius Caesar: The Problem of Classical

Republicanism'. In *Shakespeare and the Body Politic*, eds Bernard J. Dobski and Dustin Gish. Lanham: Lexington, 2013.

Burt, Richard. '"A Dangerous Rome": Shakespeare's *Julius Caesar* and the Discursive Determinism of Cultural Politics'. In *Contending Kingdoms: Historical, Psychological, and Feminist Approaches to the Literature of Sixteenth Century England and France*, eds Marie-Rose Logan and Peter L. Rudnytsky, 109–27. Detroit: Wayne State University Press, 1991.

Burton, Robert. *The Anatomy of Melancholy/Robert Burton; Edited and with an Introduction by Holbrook Jackson; and with a New Introduction by William H. Gass*. New York: New York Review of Books, 2001.

Bushnell, Rebecca W. *Tragedies of Tyrants: Political Thought and Theater in the English Renaissance*. Ithaca: Cornell University Press, 1990.

Bynum, Caroline Walker. 'Violent Imagery in Late Medieval Piety', 15th Annual Lecture of the German Historical Institute, 8 November 2001, *Bulletin of the German Historical Institute* 30.3 (2002). Available at http://www.Ghi-Dc.org/publications/ghipubs/bu/030/3.pdf (accessed 13 February 2016).

Bynum, Caroline Walker. *Wonderful Blood: Theology and Practice in Late Medieval Northern Germany and Beyond*. Philadelphia: University of Pennsylvania Press, 2007.

Callon, Michel. 'What Does It Mean to Say Economics is Performative?' In *Do Economists Make Markets? On the Performativity of Economics*, eds. Donald MacKenzie, Fabian Muniesa, and Lucia Siu, 311–57. Princeton: Princeton University Press, 2008.

Candido, Joseph. '"Time ... Come Round": Plot Construction in *Julius Caesar*'. In Julius Caesar: *New Critical Essays*, ed. Horst Zander, 127–38. London: Routledge, 2005.

Carney, John. 'Sandy Weill: I Fired Jamie Dimon Because He Wanted To Be CEO,' *Business Insider*, 4 January 2010. Available at http://www.businessinsider.com/sandy-weil-i-fired-jamie-dimon-because-he-wanted-to-be-ceo-2010-1 (accessed 13 February 2016).

Carpi, Daniela. 'Law and Sedition in *Julius Caesar*'. In *Shakespeare and the Law*, ed. Daniela Carpi, 103–15. Ravenna: Longo, 2003.

Challis, Christopher Edgar. *The Tudor Coinage*. Manchester: Manchester University Press, 1978.

Chambers, E. K. *The Elizabethan Stage, volume 2* (4 vols.). Oxford: The Clarendon Press, 1923.

Chapman, Alison A. 'Whose Saint Crispin's Day Is It?: Shoemaking, Holiday Making, and the Politics of Memory in Early Modern England', *RQ* 54 (2001): 1467–94.

Chapman, George. *The Tragedy of Caesar and Pompey* in *The Plays of George Chapman: The Tragedies* Vol. 2, ed. Thomas Marc Parrott. New York: Russell & Russell, 1961.

Charlton, H. B. *Shakespearian Tragedy*. Cambridge: Cambridge University Press, 1948; reprinted 1961.

Charney, Maurice. *Shakespeare's Roman Plays: The Function of Imagery in the Drama*. Cambridge, MA: Harvard University Press, 1961; reprinted 1963.

Charney, Maurice. *Shakespeare's Villains* (Madison, NJ: Fairleigh Dickinson University Press, 2012).

Chernaik, Warren. *The Myth of Rome in Shakespeare and his Contemporaries*. Cambridge: Cambridge University Press, 2011.

Cicero, Marcus Tullius. *De Officiis*, trans. Walter Miller. London: Loeb Library, 1913.

Cicero, Marcus Tullius. *De Officiis (On Obligations)*, trans. P. G. Walsh. Oxford World's Classics, 2001.

Cicero, Marcus Tullius. *Letters of Cicero*, trans. L. P. Wilkinson. London: Godfrey Bles, 1959.

Cicero, Marcus Tullius. *Philippics*, trans. Walter Ker. London: Loeb Library, 1957.

Clare, Janet, ed. *Drama of the English Republic, 1649–60*. Manchester: Manchester University Press, 2002.

Colclough, David. 'Talking to the Animals: Persuasion, Counsel and their Discontents in *Julius Caesar*'. In *Shakespeare and Early Modern Political Thought*, eds David Armitage, Conal Condren and Andrew Fitzmaurice, 217–33. Cambridge: Cambridge University Press, 2009.

Cole, Nicholas. 'Nineteenth-Century Ciceros'. In *The Cambridge Companion to Cicero*, ed. Catherine Steel. Cambridge University Press, 2013.

Coleridge, Samuel Taylor. *The Literary Remains of Samuel Taylor Coleridge*, ed. Henry Nelson Coleridge, 4 vols. London: William Pickering, 1836.

Corti, Claudia. '"The three-fold world divided": *Julius Caesar* in the Light of *Theologia Platonica*'. In *Shakespeare, Italy, and*

Intertextuality, ed. Michele Marrapodi, 176–93. Manchester: Manchester University Press, 2004.

Cox, Tony. 'What Shakespeare Can Teach Us About Money', *Marketplace.org* (28 December 2012). Available at http://www.marketplace.org/topics/life/what-shakespeare-can-teach-us-about-money

Davis, Lloyd B. 'Embodied Masculinity in Shakespeare's *Julius Caesar*', *EnterText* 3 (2003): 161–82.

Dean, Leonard F., ed. *Twentieth-Century Interpretations of* Julius Caesar. Prentice Hall, 1968.

Deleuze, Gilles. *Nietzsche and Philosophy*, translated by Hugh Tomlinson. New York: Columbia University Press, 1983.

Desan, Christine. 'Christine Desan's "Making Money"', November 2014. Available at https://www.youtube.com/watch?v=bCdKI5dGn9c (accessed 13 February 2016).

Desan, Christine. 'Creation Stories: Myths About the Origins of Money,' *Harvard Public Law Working Paper* 13–20 (30 July 2013).

Desan, Christine. 'Booms and Busts: The Legal Dynamics of Modern Money', *OpenCulture.com*. 12 December 2011. Available at www.openculture.com/2011/12/eight_lectures_from_the_occupy_harvard_teach-in_watch_online.html (accessed 13 February 2016).

Desan, Christine. *Making Money: Coin, Currency, and the Coming of Capitalism*. Oxford: Oxford University Press, 2015.

Digges, Leonard. *Upon Master William Shakespeare, the Deceased Author, and his poems*. Gale Research, 1988.

Dodd, Nigel. *The Social Life of Money*. Princeton: Princeton University Press, 2014.

Donaldson, Ian. '"Misconstruing Everything": *Julius Caesar* and *Sejanus*'. In *Shakespeare Performed: Essays in Honor of R. A. Foakes*, ed. Grace Ioppolo, 88–107. Newark: University of Delaware Press, 2000.

Dowden, Edward. *Shakspere: A Critical Study of his Mind and Art*. 1875; reprinted London: Kegan Paul, 1909.

Drakakis, John. '"Fashion it thus": *Julius Caesar* and the Politics of Theatrical Representation'. *Shakespeare Survey* 44 (1992): 65–73.

Feather, Jennifer. 'To "Tempt the Rheumy and Unpurged Air": Contagion and Agency in *Julius Caesar*'. In *Shakespeare and*

Moral Agency, edited by Michael D. Bristol, 86–98. London: Continuum, 2010.

Flecknoe, Richard. *Love's Kingdom: A Pastoral Trage-comedy: Not As it Was Acted at the Theatre Near Lincolns-inn, but as it Was Written, and Since Corrected* [electronic resource]. London: Printed by R. Wood for the author, 1664.

Fulbecke, William. *An Historicall Collection of the Continuall Factions, Tumults, and Massacres of the Romans and Italians During the Space of One Hundred and Twentie Yeares Next Before the Peaceable Empire of Augustus.* London: Printed by R. Field for VVilliam Ponsonby, 1601.

Gainsford, Thomas. *The Rich Cabinet*, trans. Giovanni Della Casa. London: Printed by Iohn Bealefor Roger Iackson and are to be sold at his shop neere Fleete Conduit, 1664.

Garnier, Robert. *Cornélie*. Paris, 1574.

Gayton, Edmund. *Pleasant Notes Upon Don Quixot* [electronic resource]. London: Printed by William Hunt, 1654.

Geneva Bible, The, a facsimile of the 1560 edition. n.p. Madison, University of Wisconsin Press, 1969.

Geoffrey of Monmouth. *The History of the Kings of Britain*, ed. by Michael D. Reeve. Woodbridge: Boydell, 2007.

Giddens, Eugene. 'Honourable Men: Militancy and Masculinity in *Julius Caesar*', *Renaissance Forum* 5 (2001): 1–34.

Goldberg, Jonathan. *James I and the Politics of Literature: Jonson, Shakespeare, Donne, and their Contemporaries.* Baltimore: Johns Hopkins University Press, 1983; reprinted Stanford: Stanford University Press, 1989.

Gosson, Stephen. *Plays Confuted in Fiue Actions.* London: Imprinted for Thomas Gosson dwelling in Pater noster row at the signe of the Sunne, 1582.

Gosson, Stephen. *The Schoole of Abuse.* Printed at London: for Thomas VVoodcocke, 1579.

Grady, Hugh. 'Moral Agency and Its Problems in *Julius Caesar*: Political Power, Choice, and History'. In *Shakespeare and Moral Agency*, ed. Michael D. Bristol, 15–28. London: Continuum, 2010.

Grady, Hugh. 'The End of Shakespeare's Machiavellian Moment: *Julius Caesar*, Shakespeare's Historiography, and Dramatic Form'. In *Shakespeare and Renaissance Literary Theories: Anglo-Italian Transactions*, ed. Michele Marrapodi, 119–36. Farnham: Ashgate, 2011.

Graeber, David. *Debt: The First 5000 Years*. Brooklyn: Melville House, 2011.
Grafton, Anthony. 'Cicero and Ciceronianism'. In *The Classical Tradition*, eds Anthony Grafton, Glenn W. Most and Salvatore Settis. Cambridge, MA: Belknap, 2010.
Green, Jeffrey Edward. *The Eyes of the People: Democracy in an Age of Spectatorship*. Oxford: Oxford University Press, 2010.
Griffin, Julia. 'Shakespeare's *Julius Caesar* and the Dramatic Tradition'. In *A Companion to Julius Caesar*, ed. Miriam Tamara Griffin, 371–98. Hoboken: Wiley, 2009.
Hadfield, Andrew. *Shakespeare and Republicanism*. Cambridge University Press, 2008.
Hamer, Mary. *Writers and their Work: William Shakespeare, 'Julius Caesar'*. Plymouth: Northcote House, 1998.
Hardin, Richard F. *Civil Idolatry: Desacralizing and Monarchy in Spenser, Shakespeare, and Milton*. Newark: University of Delaware Press, 1992.
Harrington, James. *The Commonwealth of Oceana*, ed. J. G. A. Pocock. Cambridge: Cambridge University Press, 1992.
Harris, Robert. *Imperium*. London: Hutchinson, 2006.
Harris, Robert. Interview with Claire Armitstead, Guardian Books Podcast, 16 October 2009.
Harris, Robert. *Lustrum*. London: Hutchinson, 2009.
Harris, W. V. 'A Revisionist View of Roman Money'. *The Journal of Roman Studies* 96 (2006): 1–24.
Hartley, Andrew James. *Shakespeare in Performance:* Julius Caesar. Manchester: Manchester University Press, 2014.
Hartsoe, Steve. 'Of Shakespeare and Financial Decisions,' *Duke Today*, 14 September 2012. Available at http://today.duke.edu/2012/09/forlinesclass (accessed 13 February 2016).
Hawkes, David. 'Shakespeare's *Julius Caesar*: Marxist and Post-Marxist Approaches'. In Julius Caesar: *New Critical Essays*, ed. Horst Zander, 199–212. London: Routledge, 2005.
Hazlitt, William. *Characters of Shakspeare's Plays*. Boston: Wells and Lilly, 1818.
Heller, Jack. '"Your Statue Spouting Blood": *Julius Caesar*, the Sacraments, and the Fountain of Life'. In Word and Rite: The Bible and Ceremony in Selected Shakespearean Works, eds Beatrice Batson and Jill Peleaz Baumgaertner, 77–93. Newcastle: Cambridge Scholars, 2010.

Heywood, Thomas, and I.G. *An Apology for Actors* and *A Refutation of the* Apology for Actors. 1612. New York and London: Garland, 1973
Higgins, Charlotte. Review of Harris, *Lustrum*, *Guardian*, 17 October 2009.
Holmes, Christopher. 'Time for the Plebs in *Julius Caesar*'. *EMLS* 7 (2001): 1–32.
Honigmann, E. A. J. *Shakespeare: Seven Tragedies, The Dramatist's Manipulation of Response*. London: Macmillan, 1976.
Hopkins, Lisa. *The Cultural Uses of the Caesars on the English Renaissance Stage*. Aldershot: Ashgate, 2008.
Hutchins, Christine E. '"Who is here so rude that would not be a Roman?": England as Anti-Type of Rome in Elizabethan Print and *Julius Caesar*'. *BJJ* 8 (2001): 207–27.
Ingham, Geoffrey. *The Nature of Money*. Cambridge: Polity Press, 2004.
James, Heather. 'Shakespeare's Juliet and Ovid's Myths of Girlhood', *Shakespeare Association of America Annual Meeting*. 1–4 April 2015. Vancouver, British Columbia.
Jones, Ernest. 'A Psycho-Analytic Study of Hamlet'. In *Essays on Applied Psycho-Analysis*, ed. Ernest Jones, 1–98. London: The International Psycho-Analytical Press, 1923.
Jonson, Ben. *Ben Jonson*, ed. C. H. Herford, Evelyn Simpson and Percy Simpson, 11 vols. Oxford: Clarendon Press, 1925–52.
Jonson, Ben. *The Complete Poems*, ed. George Parfitt. London: Penguin, 1975; reprinted 1988.
Jonson, Ben. *Catiline His Conspiracy*. In *The Cambridge Edition of the Works of Ben Jonson*, eds David Bevington, Martin Butler and Ian Donaldson, 7 vols. Cambridge: Cambridge University Press, 2012.
Kahn, Coppélia. *Roman Shakespeare: Warriors, Wounds, and Women*. London: Routledge, 1997.
Kahn, Coppélia. '"Passion of some difference": Friendship and Emulation in *Julius Caesar*'. In Julius Caesar: *New Critical Essays*, ed. Horst Zander, 271–83. London: Routledge, 2005.
Kaula, David. '"Let Us Be Sacrificers": Religious Motifs in *Julius Caesar*', *Shakespeare Studies* 14 (1981) 01: 197–214
Kerrigan, John, *Revenge Tragedy: Aeschylus to Armageddon*. Oxford: Oxford University Press, 1996.
Kewes, Paulina. 'Julius Caesar in Jacobean England', *The Seventeenth Century* 17 (2002): 155–86.

Kezar, Dennis. '*Julius Caesar*'s Analogue Clock and the Accents of History'. In Julius Caesar: *New Critical Essays*, ed. Horst Zander, 241–55. London: Routledge, 2005.

Knight, Charles. *Studies in Shakespere*. London: George Routledge and Sons, 1868.

Knight, G. Wilson. *The Imperial Theme: Further Interpretations of Shakespeare's Tragedies Including the Roman Plays*. Oxford: Oxford University Press, 1931; reprinted London: Methuen, 1965.

Knight, G. Wilson. *The Wheel of Fire: Interpretations of Shakespearian Tragedy*. Oxford: Oxford University Press, 1930; reprinted London: Methuen, 1965.

Kyd, Thomas. *Cornelia*. London, 1594.

Langbaine, Gerard. *The Lives and Characters of the English Dramatick Poets*. London: Thomas Leigh, 1698.

Leggatt, Alexander. *Shakespeare's Political Drama: The History Plays and the Roman Plays*. London: Routledge, 1988.

Lemon, Rebecca. *Treason by Words*. Ithaca and London: Cornell University Press, 2006.

Liebler, Naomi Conn. 'Buying and Selling So(u)les: Marketing Strategies and the Politics of Performance in *Julius Caesar*'. In Julius Caesar: *New Critical Essays*, ed. Horst Zander, 165–79. London: Routledge, 2005.

Liebler, Naomi Conn. *Shakespeare's Festive Tragedy: The Ritual Foundations of Genre*. London: Routledge, 1995.

Liebler, Naomi Conn. '"Thou Bleeding Piece of Earth": The Ritual Ground of *Julius Caesar*', *Shakespeare Studies* 14.1 (1981): 175–96

Lloyd, Richard. *A brief discourse of the most renowned actes and right valiant conquests of those puisant Princes, called the Nine Worthies*. London, 1584.

Logan, Marie-Rose and Peter L. Rudnytsky, eds. *Contending Kingdoms: Historical, Psychological, and Feminist Approaches to the Literature of Sixteenth Century England and France*. Detroit: Wayne State University Press, 1991.

Lovascio, Domenico. 'Jonson's *Catiline* and Machiavelli's *Istorie Fiorentine*', *Notes & Queries* 57 (2010): 411–13.

Lucking, David. *The Shakespearean Name: Essays on* Romeo and Juliet, The Tempest *and Other Plays*. Bern: Peter Lang, 2007.

Lüdeke, Roger, and Andreas Mahler. 'Stating the Sovereign Self: Polity, Policy, and Politics on the Early Modern Stage'. In *Solo*

Performances: Staging the Early Modern Self in England, ed. Ute Berns, 209–27. Amsterdam: Rodopi, 2010.
Lupton, Julia Reinhard. *Afterlives Of the Saints: Hagiography, Typology, and Renaissance Literature*. Stanford, CA: Stanford University Press, 1996.
MacCallum, M. W. *Shakespeare's Roman Plays and their Background*. London: Macmillan, 1910; reprinted 1967.
McCanles, Michael. *Dialectical Criticism in Renaissance Literature*. Berkeley: University of California Press, 1975.
McCutcheon, Robert. 'The Call of Vocation in *Julius Caesar* and *Coriolanus*'. ELR 41 (2011): 332–74.
Machiavelli, Niccolò. *Discourses*, ed. Bernard Crick. Harmondsworth: Penguin, 1970.
Mahler, Andreas. '"There is Restitution, no End of Restitution, only not for us": Experimental Tragedy and the Early Modern Subject in *Julius Caesar*'. In Julius Caesar: *New Critical Essays*, ed. Horst Zander, 181–95. London: Routledge, 2005.
Mahon, John W. 'Providence in *Julius Caesar*'. In *Shakespeare's Christianity: The Protestant and Catholic Poetics of* Julius Caesar, Macbeth, *and* Hamlet, ed. Beatrice Batson, 91–110. Waco: Baylor University Press, 2006.
Malamud, Margaret. 'Manifest Destiny and the Eclipse of Julius Caesar'. In *Julius Caesar in Western Culture*, ed. Maria Wyke. Oxford: Blackwell, 2006.
Marlowe, Christopher, *Lucans First Booke* in *The Complete Works of Christopher Marlowe* Vol. 1, ed. Roma Gill. Oxford: Clarendon Press, 1987.
Marshall, Cynthia. 'Portia's Wound, Calphurnia's Dream: Reading Character in *Julius Caesar*'. *English Literary Renaissance* 24.2 (1994): 471–98.
Maurer, Margaret. 'Again, Poets and *Julius Caesar*'. *Upstart Crow: A Shakespeare Journal* 28 (2008): 5–16.
Menzer, Paul. *The Actor's Inhibition: Early Modern Acting and the Rhetoric of Restraint*. Northwestern University Press, 2006.
Menzer, Paul. 'That Old Saw: Early Modern Acting and the Infinite Regress'. *Shakespeare Bulletin* 2 (2004): 27.
Meres, Francis, and N. L. *Palladis Tamia*. [electronic resource] (London: Printed by P. Short, for Cuthbert Burbie, and are to be solde at his shop at the Royall Exchange, 1598).

Miles, Geoffrey. *Shakespeare and the Constant Romans*. Oxford: Oxford University Press, 1996.
Miller, Anthony. *Roman Triumphs and Early Modern English Culture*. Basingstoke: Palgrave, 2001.
Miola, Robert S. '*Julius Caesar* and the Tyrannicide Debate', *Renaissance Quarterly* 38.2 (1985): 271–89.
Miola, Robert S. *Shakespeare's Rome*. Cambridge: Cambridge University Press, 1983.
Mommsen, Theodor. *The History of Rome*, trans. W. P. Dickson, 5 vols. London: Macmillan, 1913.
Muldrew, Craig. 'Interpreting the Market: The Ethics of Credit and Community Relations in Early Modern England'. *Social History* 18.2 (May 1993): 163–83.
Muldrew, Craig, *The Economy of Obligation: The Culture of Credit and Social Relations in Early Modern England*. London: Palgrave Macmillan UK, 1998.
Munday, Anthony. *A Second and Third Blast of Retrait From Plaies and Theaters*, trans. Salvian, of Marseilles. [electronic resource] (Imprinted at London: By Henrie Denham, dwelling in Pater noster Row, at the signe of the Starre, being the assigne of William Seres. Allowed by aucthoritie, 1580).
Nashe, Thomas. *Works of Thomas Nashe*, ed. R. B. McKerrow. Sidgwick & Jackson, 1910.
Nietzsche, Friedrich. *On the Genealogy of Morals*, trans. R. J. Hollingdale and Walter Kaufmann edited by Walter Kaufmann. New York: Vintage, 1989.
Nietzsche, Friedrich. 'On Truth and Lies in a Nonmoral Sense', *Philosophy and Truth: Selections from Nietzsche's Notebooks of the early 1870s*, edited and trans. Daniel Breazeale, 79–97. New York: Humanity Books, 1993.
Nietzsche, Friedrich. *Twilight of the Idols*, trans. R. J. Hollingdale. London: Penguin, 1968.
Norland, Howard. *Neoclassical Tragedy in Elizabethan England*. Cranbury: Associated University Presses, 2009.
Osmond, Patricia, and Robert Ulery. 'Constantius Felicius Durantinus and the Renaissance Origins of Anti-Sallustian Criticism'. *International Journal of the Classical Tradition* 1 (1995): 29–56.
Ovid, P. *Ovid's Metamorphoses: The Arthur Golding Translation, 1567*, 1st edn, eds John Frederick Nims and Jonathan Bate. United States of America: Paul Dry Books, 2000.

Ovid, P. *Fasti*, ed. G. P. Goold and James George Frazer. Harvard University Press; W. Heinemann, 1989.

Owens, Margaret E. *Stages of Dismemberment: The Fragmented Body in Late Medieval and Early Modern Drama*. Newark: University of Delaware Press; Cranbury, NJ: Associated University Presses, 2005.

Palmer, John. *Political and Comic Characters of Shakespeare*. London: Macmillan, 1962.

Park, Katharine. *Secrets of Women: Gender, Generation, and the Origins of Human Dissection*. New York: Zone Books, 2006.

Parker, Barbara L. 'From Monarchy to Tyranny: *Julius Caesar* among Shakespeare's Roman Works'. In Julius Caesar: *New Critical Essays*, ed. Horst Zander, 111–26 (London: Routledge, 2005).

Parker, Barbara. 'The Whore of Babylon and Shakespeare's *Julius Caesar*'. *Studies in English Literature 1500–1900* 35.2 (1995): 251–69.

Paster, Gail Kern. '"In the spirit of men there is no blood": Blood as Trope of Gender in *Julius Caesar*', *Shakespeare Quarterly* 40.3 (1989): 284–98.

Pennacchia, Maddalena. 'Antony's Ring: Remediating Ancient Rhetoric on the Elizabethan Stage'. In *Identity, Otherness and Empire in Shakespeare's Rome*, ed. Maria Del Sapio Garbero, 49–59. Farnham: Ashgate, 2009.

Pennacchia, Maddalena. 'The Stones of Rome: Early Earth Sciences in *Julius Caesar* and *Coriolanus*'. In *Questioning Bodies in Shakespeare's Rome*, eds Maria Del Sapio Garbero, Nancy Isenberg and Maddalena Pennacchia, 309–25. Göttingen: V&R Unipress, 2010.

Perry, Curtis. 'The Uneasy Republicanism of Thomas Kyd', *Criticism* 48 (2006): 535–55.

Phillips, James Emerson. *The State in Shakespeare's Greek and Roman Plays*. New York: Columbia University Press, 1940.

Phoon, Adrian. '"A vision fair and fortunate": Ideology, Politics and Selfhood in *Julius Caesar*', *Sydney Studies in English* 30 (2004): 21–41.

Platt, Michael. *Rome and Romans According to Shakespeare*. Salzburg: Institut für Englische Sprache und Literatur, 1976.

Platter, Thomas. *Thomas Platter's Travels in England, 1599*, ed. and trans. Clare Williams. London: Jonathan Cape, 1937.

Plutarch, *Plutarch's Lives, Vol. 2*, trans. John Dryden, ed. Arthur Hugh Clough. New York: Modern Library, 1992.
Plutarch, *The Liues of the Noble Grecians and Romaines*, translated by Thomas North. London, 1603.
Proser, Matthew N. *The Heroic Image in Five Shakespearean Tragedies*. Princeton: Princeton University Press, 1965.
Prynne, William. *Histrio-mastix* [electronic resource]. London: Printed by Edward Allde, Augustine Mathewes, Thomas Cotes and William Iones for Michael Sparke, and are to be sold at the Blue Bible, in Greene Arbour, in little Old Bayly, 1633.
Rabkin, Norman. 'Structure, Convention, and Meaning in *Julius Caesar*'. *The Journal of English and Germanic Philology* 63. 2 (1964): 240–54.
Randolph, Thomas. *The Jealous Lovers* [electronic resource]. Cambridge: Printed by Roger Daniel, printer to the Universitie of Cambridge: 1640. And are to be sold by Richard Ireland.
Rebhorn, Wayne A. 'The Crisis of the Aristocracy in *Julius Caesar*'. *Renaissance Quarterly* 43.1 (1990): 75–111.
Renker, Elizabeth. "Shakespeare in the College Curriculum, 1870–1920". In *Shakespearean Educations*, eds Coppélia Kahn et al. University of Delaware Press, 2011.
Ribner, Irving. 'Political Issues in *Julius Caesar*'. *Journal of English and Germanic Philology* 56 (1957): 10–22.
Ripley, John. *Julius Caesar on the Stage in England and America, 1599–1973*. Cambridge, 1980.
Roach, Joseph R. *The Player's Passion: Studies in the Science of Acting*. Ann Arbor: University of Michigan Press, 2008.
Robson, Mark. 'The Hour is Unknown: *Julius Caesar*, et cetera'. In *Shakespeare and the Urgency of Now: Criticism and Theory in the 21st Century*, eds Cary DiPietro and Hugh Grady, 188–209. Basingstoke: Palgrave Macmillan, 2013.
Roe, John. *Shakespeare and Machiavelli*. Cambridge: Brewer, 2002.
Rogers, Thomas. *A Philosophicall Discourse Entituled, The Anatomie of the Minde*. London, 1576.
Rose, Mark. 'Conjuring Caesar: Ceremony, History, and Authority in 1599'. *English Literary Renaissance* 19 (1989): 291–304.
Royle, Nicholas. 'The Poet: *Julius Caesar* and the Democracy to Come'. In *Julius Caesar in Western Culture*, ed. Maria Wyke, 205–27. Malden: Blackwell, 2006.

Rubin, Hariett. 'Lessons in Shakespeare, From Stage to Boardroom'. *New York Times*, 10 November 2007. Available at http://www.nytimes.com/2007/11/10/business/10shakespeare.html (accessed 13 February 2016).

Sallust (Gaius Sallustius Crispus). *The Conspiracie of Cateline*, trans. Thomas Heywood. London, 1609.

Schanzer, Ernest. 'The Problem of *Julius Caesar*'. *Shakespeare Quarterly* 6 (1955): 296–308.

Schanzer, Ernest. 'Thomas Platter's Observations on the Elizabethan Stage'. *Notes and Queries*, 3 (1956): 465–7.

Schanzer, Ernest. *The Problem Plays of Shakespeare*. London: Routledge and Kegan Paul, 1963.

Shackford, Martha Hale. '*Julius Caesar* and Ovid'. *Modern Language Notes*, 41.3 (1926): 172–4.

Shakespeare, William. *Cymbeline*, ed. J. M. Nosworthy. Cambridge, MA: Arden, 1960.

Shakespeare, William. *Julius Caesar*, ed. S. P. Cerasano. Norton, 2012.

Shakespeare, William. *Julius Caesar*, ed. David Daniell. London: Arden, 2003.

Shakespeare, William. *Julius Caesar*, ed. T. S. Dorsch. London: Arden, 1966.

Shakespeare, William. *Julius Caesar*, ed. John Dover Wilson. Cambridge: The New Cambridge Shakespeare, 1949.

Shakespeare, William. *The Pelican Complete Works*, ed.. A. R. Braunmuller and Stephen Orgel. Penguin 2002.

Shell, Marc, *Poetry, Language, and Thought: Literary and Philosophic Economies from the Medieval to the Modern Era*. Baltimore and London: Johns Hopkins University Press, 1982.

Siegel, Paul N. *Shakespeare's English and Roman History Plays: A Marxist Approach*. Cranbury: Associated University Presses, 1986.

Sims, Matthew. 'The Political Odyssey: Shakespeare's Exploration of Ethics in *Julius Caesar*'. In *The Hero's Journey*, ed. Harold Bloom, 95–105. New York: Bloom's Literary Criticism, 2009.

Skinner, Quentin. *Liberty before Liberalism*. Cambridge University Press, 1998.

Skinner, Quentin. *The Foundations of Modern Political Thought*, 2 vols. Cambridge University Press, 1978.

Sloterdijk, Peter. *Nietzsche's Apostle*, trans. Steven Corcoran. Frankfurt: Semiotext(e), 2013.

Smith, Gordon Ross. 'Brutus, Virtue, and Will'. *Shakespeare Quarterly* 10.3 (1959): 367–79.
Smith, Suzanne. 'Shakespeare and the Politics of Honor: Purpose and Performance in *Julius Caesar*'. *Interpretation: A Journal of Political Philosophy* 33 (2006): 243–80.
Spencer, T. J. B. 'Shakespeare and the Elizabethan Romans', *Shakespeare Survey* 10 (1957): 27–38.
Spenser, Edmund. *The Faerie Queene*, ed. A. C. Hamilton. London: Longman, 1977.
Spotswood, Jerald W. '"We are undone already": Disarming the Multitude in *Julius Caesar* and *Coriolanus*'. *TSLL* 42 (2000): 61–78.
Stapfer, Paul. *Shakespeare and Classical Antiquity*, trans. Emily J. Carey. London: C. Kegan Paul, 1880.
Starks-Estes, Lisa. *Violence, Trauma, and Virtus in Shakespeare's Roman Poems and Plays: Transforming Ovid*. Houndmills and New York: Palgrave Macmillan, 2014.
Steel, Catherine, ed. *The Cambridge Companion to Cicero*. Cambridge: Cambridge University Press, 2013.
Stirling, Brents. *The Populace in Shakespeare*. New York: Columbia University Press, 1949.
Stirling, Brents. *Unity in Shakespearian Tragedy: The Interplay of Theme and Character*. New York: Columbia University Press, 1956.
Suerbaum, Almut. 'The Middle Ages'. In *A Companion to Julius Caesar*, ed. Miriam Griffin. Chichester: Wiley-Blackwell, 2009.
Taylor, Gary. 'Bardicide'. In *Shakespeare & Cultural Traditions*, eds Tetsuo Kishi, Roger Pringle and Stanley Wells, 333–49. Newark: University of Delaware Press, 1994.
Test, Edward M. '"A dish fit for the gods": Mexica Sacrifice in De Bry, Las Casas and Shakespeare's *Julius Caesar*', *JMEMS* 41 (2011): 93–117.
Thomas, Vivian. *Shakespeare's Political and Economic Language: A Dictionary*. London: Bloomsbury Arden Shakespeare, 2015.
Thomas, Vivian. *Shakespeare's Roman Worlds*. London: Routledge, 1989.
Thomas, Vivian. *The Tragedie of Caesar and Pompey or Caesars Reuenge*. London, 1607.

Thomas, Vivian. *Twayne's New Critical Introduction to Shakespeare: Julius Caesar*. New York: Macmillan: 1982.
Traversi, Derek. *Shakespeare: The Roman Plays*. London: Hollis and Carter, 1963.
Trollope, Anthony. *The Life of Cicero*, 2 vols. London: Trollope Society, 1993.
Turner, Frank M. 'British Politics and the Roman Republic'. *The Historical Journal* 29 (1986): 557–99.
Ure, Peter, ed. *Julius Caesar: A Casebook*. London: Macmillan, 1979.
Vickers, Brian, ed. *William Shakespeare: The Critical Heritage*, 6 vols. London: Routledge and Kegan Paul, 1974–81.
Weever, John. *The Mirror of Martyrs, or the Life and Death of that Thrice Valiant Capitaine, and Most Godly Martyre Sir Iohn Old-castle Knight Lord Cobham* [electronic resource]. London: Printed by Valentine Simmes for William Wood, 1601.
Wells, Robin Headlam. '*Julius Caesar*, Machiavelli and the Uses of History', *SS* 55 (2002): 209–18.
Whitaker, Virgil K. *Shakespeare's Uses of Learning: An Inquiry into the Growth of his Mind and Art*. San Marino: Huntington Library, 1953.
Willbern, David. 'Constructing Caesar: A Psychoanalytic Reading'. In *Julius Caesar: New Critical Essays*, ed. Horst Zander, 213–26. London: Routledge, 2005.
Wilson, Richard. *Julius Caesar: New Casebooks*. Palgrave, 2002.
Wilson, Richard. 'Shakespeare's Roman Carnival'. In *New Historicism and Renaissance Drama*, eds Richard Wilson and Richard Dutton, 145–56. Harlow: Longman, 1992.
Wood, James O. "Intimations of Actaeon in Julius Caesar". *Shakespeare Quarterly* 24 (1973), 1: 86–8.
Woodbridge, Linda. *Money in the Age of Shakespeare*. New York: Palgrave Macmillan, 2003.
Worden, Blair. 'Politics in *Catiline*: Ben Jonson and his Sources'. In *Re-Presenting Ben Jonson*, ed. Martin Butler. Basingstoke: Macmillan, 1999.
Worthen, William B. *The Idea of the Actor: Drama and the Ethics of Performance*. Princeton, NJ: Princeton University Press, 1984.
Wyke, Maria. *Caesar: A Life in Western Culture*. London: Granta Books, 2007.

Wyke, Maria, ed. *Julius Caesar in Western Culture*. Oxford: Blackwell, 2006.

Zander, Horst, ed. *Julius Caesar: New Critical Essays*. Routledge, 2005.

INDEX

act of oblivion 151
Agnew, Jean-Christophe 130, 148
Alexander, Sir William 157, 182–4, 195
Anderson, Lindsay 65–6
Anne (Queen) 54

Barton, John 66–7
BBC 77–8
Belsey, Catharine 40
Benson, F. R. 57–8
Betterton, Thomas 54
Blair, Tony 73
Blits, Jan 38–9
Bloom, Harold 44
Bloomburg, Michael 127–8, 131
Bonjour, Adrien 29
Booth, Edwin 59–60
Booth, John Wilkes 59–60
Bradley, A. C. 25–6, 44
Bradley, David 76
Brando, Marlon 62, 64
Bridges-Adams, William 58–9
Burge, Stuart 76–8
Burt, Richard 44
Bush, George W. 73
Bushnell, Rebecca 40

Caesar Must Die 78
calendar (Julian and Gregorian) 2, 4

Catholicism 4–6, 116
Catiline see Jonson, Ben
Charles I 4, 51–2
Charlton, H. B. 28
Charney, Maurice 30–1
Chernaik, Warren 86, 157
Cicero 175–94 *passim*, 196, 202
Coriolanus 194–5
Cromwell, Oliver 53
Cymbeline 163

Daniels, David 70
Dante 4, 176
Davenant, William 55, 57
debt 146–51
DeMille, Cecil B. 64
Doran, Gregory 75–6
doubling 53–4
Dowden, Edward 24–5
Drakakis, John 43–4
Dryden, John 19, 55, 57

Edward VI 52, 143
Elizabeth I 3–6, 52

Farber, Yael 75
Forlines, John III 125–7, 131

Garnier, Robert 182
Geoffrey of Monmouth 162–3
George I 54
George III 55

Gielgud, John 62, 76
Globe Theatre 50–1, 72
Goldberg, Jonathan 41

Hall, Edward 72–3
Hamer, Mary 45–6
Hazlitt, William 23, 44
Henry VIII 4, 52, 143
Heston, Charlton 76–7
Hicks, Greg 72–3
Hollywood Black List 63
Honigmann, E. A. J. 30
Housemann, John 52–3

James I 4
Johnson, Samuel 22, 44
Jones, Ernest 26
Jonson, Ben 19, 176, 182, 185, 188–91, 194, 197
Julius Caesar (historical figure) 1–5, 138–9, 186–7
Julius Caesar (the play)
  Caesarism in 153–74 *passim*, 204–5
  comedy in 8, 45
  composition of 1
  criticism of 17–48 *passim*, 81–102 *passim*, 223–5
  economics and 125–51 *passim*
  forum scene 12–13, 55–7, 70–2
  hermeneutics in 83
  masculinity in 87–8
  murder of Cinna the Poet scene 53, 55, 60–1, 65
  oratory in 10
  performance of 45–79 *passim*, 112–3, 218–22
  philosophy in 96–8
  politics and 88–93
  populace in 93–6
  proscription scene 55
  religion in 99–100
  republicanism in 175–99
  structure of 8–10, 45, 82–3
  teaching 201–25 *passim*
  tent scene 55–6
  texts of 53, 57–8, 212–14, 217
  women in 45

Kahn, Coppelia 45, 91
Kemble, John Philip 55–6, 58
Kerrigan, John 136–8
Knight, Charles 23–4
Knight, G. Wilson 28–9, 31, 135–7
Kyd, Thomas 180–1, 194, 197
Kynaston, Edward 53

Leggatt, Alexander 39–40
Liebler, Naomi Conn 42–3, 94, 108

Macbeth 8–9
MacCallum, M. W. 27–8
McCarthy, Joseph 63
Machiavelli 85, 177
Macready, William Charles 55, 59
Mankiewicz, Joe 62–5, 76
Marcus Tullius Cicero, The Tragedy of 192–4
Martyrdom 113–18
Mary I 4, 52
Mason, James 62
Metadrama 118–24
Miles, Geoffrey 38
Miola, Robert S. 37, 40

Money, history of 131–4

Nietzsche, Friedrich 134–8, 141, 149
Nunn, Trevor 67–8

Ovid 104–13, 116, 118–19, 123–4, 202

Palmer, John 26–7
Paster, Gail Kern 46–7
Phillips, James Emerson 32–3
Pimlott, Stephen 70
Platt, Michael 36
Platter, Thomas 17, 50–1, 72
Plutarch 3, 18, 114, 138, 143, 145, 167, 204, 207–9, 211
Pompey 156, 187
Pope, Alexander 22
Protestantism 4, 116
Proteus 120–3

Rabkin, Norman 31–2
Ribner, Irving 34–5
Richter, Falk 73–4
Rymer, Thomas 19–21

Saxe-Meiningen 56
Schanzer, Ernest 29–30
Seneca 202
South African productions 74–5
Spenser, Edmund 165
Stirling, Brent 33–4

Thacker, David 70–1
Thatcher, Margaret 68–70
Thomas, Vivian 38
Tillyard, E. M. W. 32
Toneelgroep 74
Tree, Herbert Beerbohm 57
tyranny 6–7, 155–7, 177, 180, 184

Virgil 202

Warner, Deborah 73
Wells, Orson 59–62, 66, 67, 73
Whigs 54–5
Wilson, Dover 33
Wilson, Richard 42, 96
Wise, Herbert 77
Worthies, the 155–7, 162